A Life with Alan

The Diary of A. J. P. Taylor's Wife, Eva

BY THE SAME AUTHOR

Treaty breakers or "Realpolitiker". The Anglo-German Naval Agreement of 1935
Chartism
The Invaders. Hitler Occupies the Rhineland, 1936

PUBLISHED IN HUNGARIAN ONLY

British Foreign Policy versus the Hungarian War of Independence 1848–1849
Appeasers

A Life with Alan

The Diary of A. J. P. Taylor's Wife, Eva

from 1978 to 1985

"A wise old owl sat in an oak
The more he heard the less he spoke;
The less he spoke the more he heard.
Why aren't we all like that wise old bird?"

Eva Haraszti Taylor

HAMISH HAMILTON LONDON

ACKNOWLEDGMENTS

First of all I would like to thank my husband, A.J.P. Taylor, for providing me with such good material for my diary with his personality, wit and observations. I admire and appreciate his far-reaching radicalism and his great tolerance towards people and phenomena.

I would also like to thank Mary Seton-Watson (wife of Hugh Seton-Watson) for going through the first hundred pages of my diary and correcting my English and giving it the benefit of her historical knowledge and understanding. My main thanks are due to Hatty Sumption whose quick mind and fresh intelligent approach solved many problems in the text. Both of them, one of my generation and the other, three generations younger, showed great potential and a high level of professionalism, understanding, cooperation and humanity.

E.H.T.

First published in Great Britain 1987
by Hamish Hamilton Ltd
27 Wrights Lane London W8 5TZ

British Library Cataloguing in Publication Data

Taylor, Eva Haraszti
A life with Alan: Eva's diary.
1. Taylor, A.J.P.—Marriage 2. Taylor,
Eva Haraszti—Marriage 3. Historians—
England—Biography 4. Historians—
Hungary—Biography
I. Title
907'.2024 DA3.T39

ISBN 0-241-12118-3

Typeset by Input Typesetting Ltd
Wimbledon London
Printed by Butler and Tanner Ltd
Frome and London

To the memory of my parents

"One must get all the fruit one can
from every mood, for the mood will
soon pass and will never return."
Yeats

"Writing is a form of therapy; sometimes
I wonder how all those who do not write,
compose or paint can manage to escape
madness, the melancholia, the panic fear
which is inherent in the human situation."
Graham Greene

This diary is, in a way, a sterile one. I have left out all the wonderful details of our loving relationship and the sad impact on me of Alan's relationship with his first family.

The essence of my diary throughout these years is in what we did together, what we saw and experienced and discussed together. Perhaps what was important and new to me in Britain then, is not new to readers. All the same, it may be interesting to see what captured my attention amongst the many things which one of the most original and witty historians of the century offered me, as a native guide through past and present history.

Our married life coincided with the last active decade in the long and creative life of this extraordinary, tender and evasive character, Alan Taylor.

As for me, I had left behind a beloved country, two affectionate and much loved adult sons and a successful academic career. When I arrived in April 1978, already fifty-five years old, for months I felt I had only a half life. As time passed, as experiences both good and bad accumulated, I felt that my life had doubled in value.

My younger son used to say when he was five that I – his mother – and his granny were worth ten blackberries. And sometimes he said kindly to me with a little twinkle in his eyes: "There are still blackberries on the bushes."

Britain is my blackberry bush. Whenever I return to my homeland, to my sons, daughters-in-law and grandchildren, I take some blackberries with me.

This diary is dedicated to my loved ones. To Alan, Ferencz and Gabi, Pisti and Kriszti, to my grandchildren: Gergö, Andris, Andrea and Bálint who, sadly, was too young to have his picture on the jacket with the rest.

1978

19 April

The house is very homely. I like it very much. I think that creating a daily routine is much easier with Alan than with anybody else. He not only knows what he wants to do, but he does it immediately. If he does not know, he thinks a bit, looks quite worried and then finds the cleverest solution any man could think of. He is tidy himself, but does not mind when someone else is untidy. He fits into any society and gets on with everyone. He talks to everyone and is sweet with every woman. He tries to help his former wife in many ways. He is absolutely sweet with me.

Alan told me a fascinating thing yesterday when I said that the history of University College, London, was not at all interesting, Alan said that quite to the contrary, it was very interesting. It was founded in 1827 by the friends of Bentham who wanted to found a secular college with no chapel and no religious teaching. Bentham's criterion was: What is the use of it? On the other hand, at King's College, founded just after University College, there was a chapel and no lectures could begin until morning service was over.

Bentham wanted his body to be used for dissection but it was preserved and can now be seen in a glass case which is opened every Tuesday. The head is now a wax model, but the hat and body are genuine. When the Fellows of University College have their annual dinner, Bentham's cupboard is wheeled out and he joins them.

In the afternoon we had a long walk over the Heath, enjoying the good weather. We met a friendly lady who had been Alan's neighbour when he lived with his second wife in Croftdown Road. She and her husband were music teachers who later became public entertainers, singing music hall songs in clubs and on piers. She said that now their songs were old-fashioned and her husband had become melancholic, but she was still cheerful. In England people are not emotional. They have to be hard or, if they are emotional, they do not show it.

We went up the Heath to Kenwood House. I had seen the pictures before but loved to see them again and was glad to know that one of the painters from the eighteenth century was Angelica Kaufmann, the first woman to be elected to the Royal Academy. After her no woman was elected for two hundred years. Alan said it was a great pity that so many pictures by the same artist were hung together.

As we went along, a man came jogging past and said: "Hello, A.J.P." and ran on. Alan remarked: "What an extraordinary thing that a man should greet me while running."

We plan to go to St. Albans where there is a Roman Theatre, Roman walls and a cathedral to see.

20 April

Alan explained how he felt during the Second World War. He refused to send his children to America because he thought that after the war they would be needed to reconstruct this country. Now he feels there is no chance of making a worthwhile life here any more. It is all right for him; he does not want to change his life. But to anyone starting out who asked him what to do, he would say: "Get out of this country." Alan feels that the story of Britain after 1945 is a story of decay and he has no zest to write any more about this. In Hungary a new life began after the war, sweeping away the past. In Britain it was different.

I thought that even so, it would be worth writing the history of Britain up to 1975. I asked him to deal with his time more economically, as he used to do. When he goes to his little office, his time is divided. When he has two full days to work at home, I shall see to it that he can work undisturbed.

Last night an American journalist rang Alan to ask his views on the British monarchy. Before answering, Alan asked how much he would be paid. I think, in a capitalist society, that this is the right attitude to take.

Alan's behaviour to women is very sensitive. He gives each woman what she needs – care, love, understanding. Each woman feels a bit that she is the only one who really understands him and is closest to him in one way or another. Of course he has learnt from life; he never praises one woman to another, and he manages to keep all jealousies, or nearly all, out of his life.

21 April

Yesterday evening, at about ten o'clock, Alan returned from the Beefsteak Club. He was extremely pleased at having a warm and tidy home and a contented wife as well. He rushed in, rushed to the kitchen and then slowly calmed down, taking his pipe and settling down in his Oxford chair. I know this behaviour very well; I always did the same at home, coming back from my Institute and needing time to calm down. Alan's impatience to unpack and arrange things comes from the pleasure we shall have afterwards from being together and telling each other the day's news. Alan has finished his piece for the *Sunday Express* against metrication, which he thinks makes life too difficult for the housewife. Old family recipes, moreover, would be unusable. I do not agree, being used to the metric system.

I want to see all Alan's writings, but he does not want to show me his journalistic pieces.

Alan said that at the Beefsteak Club he had a good conversation with a diplomat just back from China, who said that the Chinese were a fine and cultured nation and much more relaxed after having got rid of the gang of four.

Yesterday evening I had a good telephone conversation with my eldest son, Ferencz. He is such a nice boy. He gave me some useful advice: I should work, and not talk too much on the telephone. I felt very close to Ferencz and he evidently felt the same. Budapest and London are not far away from each other at all. I can live here without ceasing to love my country, my home and the world I helped to build and which my sons continue to build after me.

22 April

We went to St. Albans and saw the only well preserved Roman theatre in England. The sun was shining and Alan took my hand.

Yesterday Alan made his weekly visit to his former wife, Margaret. He was quite nervous. I think he is always nervous before he leaves me for Margaret and also nervous when he comes back. It must be difficult to leave two women for quite different reasons.[1]

It is strange with Alan that, though he is not a nationalist at all, indeed the most internationally-minded man I know, he is a traditionalist and a believer in routine. He likes to preserve the old furniture and kitchen equipment he inherited from his parents. He likes to do things for the sake of routine.

25 April

Alan came home restless. I wonder what happened. In the evening we saw a short film about Chinese canals and I complained that they did not give such details about the Soviet way of life. He said the Chinese are a cultured people and the only ones who have a deep sense of duty towards their country. If they are told to have only two children in one family, they will agree to it. They will survive because of this extraordinary sense of duty and social awareness. "England is in decay," said Alan. Those who act decently will be the poorest; only disgraceful people survive in inflationary times. After twenty years or so, civilizations will end, oil will run out; only those countries which have coal will survive a little longer.

Alan has pains in the muscles of his back. He thinks it is serious. Tomorrow he will go to see his doctor.

26 April

We went to the Queen Elizabeth Hall to hear the Medici Quartet in the evening. They played Schubert and Janaçek. Perfect performances, tough young men. They did not give encores, but what they gave was very well done.

Relaxed evening talks. We spoke about English literature, Bennett, Priestley, Galsworthy. Alan admires Bennett very much, knew Priestley very well. He is fond of him, but more so of Bennett. Alan showed me the copy of *Il Principe*, by Machiavelli

1 Before Alan and Eva married they agreed that Alan would stay with his first, seventy-two-year-old wife at the weekends, to keep her company. They also agreed that Alan would visit his club – the Beefsteak – once a week. The third agreement was trivial: Eva would never use paper napkins.

which Lady Beaverbrook gave to Alan after Beaverbrook's death. This book had been given to Beaverbrook by Churchill in 1922.

Yesterday I saw William Blake's exhibition at the Tate Gallery. I loved the paintings of Voltaire and the illustrations for his books. Also, I liked the drawings of his wife. She was a great admirer of her husband.

I went to Alan's seminar. A young man spoke about the Left in the 'thirties. He spoke about economists and politicians on the Left. I thought he missed the point. There were two good brains present: Alan and Robert Skidelsky.[1] Alan said, rightly, that the trouble was that intellectuals at that time did not understand economic forces. Laski[2] was good only in politics. Cole[3] did not understand Keynes at all; Gaitskell grasped it a bit. Strachey's book on progress at the end of the 'thirties is highly interesting. Keynes' *On General Theory* (1936) made a great impact. The main issue in the second half of the 'thirties was: what are the beliefs of the Left and the moderates on foreign policy?

29 April

I spoke to Pisti[4] today. They are fine, though exhausted from managing on their own at home in Budapest. The house is being rebuilt. They have to work out their life, which is also exhausting. Ferencz is overworked at the moment, Pisti is dyspeptic and doesn't have much money, but enough. Everybody wants my letters. I just feel unable to write as usual.

Yesterday we had the Goldfingers[5] here. Ursula is my favourite. She gave up painting because she was no longer interested in it. She is too busy housekeeping for Ernő (nearly eighty) and for

1 Robert Skidelsky is Professor of International Studies at Warwick University. He is an expert on Mosley and Keynes.
2 Harold Joseph Laski (1893–1950) joined the staff of the London School of Economics in 1920 and became Professor of Political Science in 1926. He was chairman of the Labour Party 1945–46.
3 George Douglas Howard Cole (1889–1958) became reader in Economics at Oxford in 1925 and in 1944 Chichele professor of Social and Political theory. He was president of the Fabian Society from 1952 and wrote numerous books on Socialism. He also wrote detective stories.
4 Eva's younger son.
5 Ernő Goldfinger is a British architect (R.A. DPLG. FRIBA), born in Budapest in 1902. He has designed buildings all over the world from the Helena Rubinstein shop in London to monuments in Algiers.

Ernő's mother (nearly a hundred). They are going to Hungary and might stay in our flat. After they went, I watched Russell Harty on ITV. Alan went to bed – he is not egocentric, but likes a harmonious, quiet life. We are happiest together when alone and can speak freely about things which interest us both.

He spoke the other morning about how he deals with his money problems. He has three main sources of income: TV and radio, books and journalism. Each item has a separate heading in his account book and he writes everything down in it. Academic work is yet another source of income, but that does not count as freelance. I told him to give his grandchildren a regular sum each year. He said it was a good idea.

Off he went to spend the Saturday evening with Margaret. Alan is a lovely man, I have to care for him, to think about his needs. He is very sensitive, but his mind is so rational that one would not think so.

Bernard Levin wrote a very good review of Alan's *The War Lords*. He said something about Alan's "gamin-like attitude". Alan told me he would rather be mentioned for his serious historical writings. That is true. Nobody really knows how clever and cultivated and experienced a historian he is. A really good historian, but there are few historians who appreciate it.

1 May

Yesterday my sister and brother-in-law, Zsóka and István Borsody, visited us. Alan was enchanted by Zsóka, who is not only good hearted, but a warm person, very sensitive, understanding, a good listener and also well read and intelligent. Alan and István talked about Beneš, whom Alan knew and had gone to see during the war. Beneš then lived outside London, in a house where he was guarded. When Alan went to see him, Beneš asked his opinion about something. Alan replied: "Well, Mr. President, my views . . ." "First, before you say anything, I want to tell you" – said Beneš, and spoke for hours. When Alan left, he had scarcely had any opportunity to speak. In 1947, when Alan visited Czechoslovakia, he met Beneš in the Hradsin. There, in the course of the conversation, Beneš had looked out of the window and said, "This is the only city in Eastern Europe that was saved from Nazi destruction and all my doing." Beneš told Alan that he had had to accept the Munich agreement because he wanted to save his country. Later, after the Second World War, Beneš explained that if he had to choose between Russia and the Western Democracies, he would have to choose Russia. Alan said he paved the way for Communist Czechoslovakia.

István said that in 1938 the Czechoslovak army was not strong. At that time he was serving in the army. Morale was very low. Both of them, Alan and István, agreed that at the time of Munich, feeling in favour of appeasement was strong. Alan said that in Britain there were some who tried to oppose it, as he did when he spoke at several meetings. But the appeasers won. Alan told me that in 1940, after France collapsed, many people were happy in this country and thought that alone, with no allies, we could resist Hitler better. Alan and István did not agree over the question of Russia's strength during the Second World War. István said Russia had been disorganized and poorly equipped but the Americans sent them tanks etc. and so they succeeded. Alan took the view that Russia was strong enough and well equipped and that the spirit of the nation was excellent. I agreed with Alan, who said that quite a number of Russian officers were trained in Germany even after Hitler came to power.

On the subject of Trotskyism, István emphasized that under Trotsky the system might have been the same as under Stalin, but for the fact that he was a much more internationally-minded Communist than Stalin was. Stalin spent some days in England when he visited Lenin and a few weeks in Vienna, and that was all the time he spent abroad. Otherwise he did not know much about the world. Alan held that Stalin did not begin the Cold War and did not want to keep either Italy or Greece in his orbit.

István has had rather a tragic intellectual and political life, always in opposition to the mainstream intellectual view, first in Czechoslovakia, then in Horthyite Hungary and then in the States. He is, however, a great believer in Western democracy and in this he is in perfect understanding with Alan.

Alan said to Zsóka that his father had only one view when they got married. "Now, instead of tuppence you have to spend fourpence."

István thought Károlyi[1] had a confused mind and was not an intellectual at all and asked Alan why he liked him. Alan said he liked him because he was great fun, a witty man, an aristocrat who did not bother how he lived. He did so well when he represented Hungary in Paris as Ambassador. Alan liked him as a person.

1 Michael Károlyi (1906–1955) was a Hungarian Socialist Count who was President of the short-lived Hungarian Republic in 1918. He was a close friend of Alan Taylor.

Katinka, his wife was much more intellectual, but that was another story.

4 May

Local elections and the day of Alan's grand-daughter Alison's operation. Yesterday we had talked about this operation and Alan wept. "You will see," he said, "they will lose her." I said they would not, the doctors were not gamblers. "What else are they?" he said, "they always gamble with human lives." Today we spoke to Alison's father, Giles and he said this first day had not been good at all, but she was safely through it.

Alan is so tender, such a nice man. He reads *Diary of a Nobody* to me each night. We thoroughly enjoy it.

Yesterday I saw *The Old Country* (meaning England), a play by Alan Bennett at the Queen's Theatre. Alec Guinness is in it. It is a very good play about a British defector and his wife and it raises more than one question about one's homeland, about the English way of life, about class differences in this country, about changes in Moscow. A very good play, everybody enjoyed it. Good laughter. Zsóka and István could not quite understand the finer points, it was so English. I missed Alan very much, I had been without him all day long; my priorities were becoming so confused. I had met old friends from Hungary who talked about my sons, who have everything they need but who miss me so much. They have worked out how not to quarrel. On the whole I think we did well not to stay together, for later on, leaving them would have been even more difficult.

On Sunday, though it was very rainy, Zsóka, István and I had a cheerful time together with Alan. In the evening he showed us the reference book about the House of Lords Record Office where all the Beaverbrook papers are kept. This archive has the Herbert Samuel Papers. Alan told us about the Samuels, how Hilaire Belloc had written a funny poem about old Samuel, how Herbert Samuel, a Liberal, did not want to join Lloyd George's government, although he was invited to do so. The reason that he gave for this decision was that he did not see enough indications that the government would last long. Herbert Samuel was an anti-Zionist and later became the governor of Israel.

Another whom Lloyd George invited to join his government was Edward Montagu. He was a very wealthy man who had married the former girl-friend of Asquith, Venetia Stanley. Venetia had earlier revealed all the indiscreet letters that Asquith wrote to her, concerning confidential government decisions. She copied some of these letters and sent them to Beaverbrook. He appreciated Venetia very much, as he liked such vivid women and later put her on his "100 list", the list of women he liked to whom he gave £100 once or twice a year. Edward and Venetia died quite early, but Edward had a nephew, called Ivor Montagu, who was and still is a Communist.[1] Alan spent a week with Ivor in Wroclaw in 1948.

We spoke quite a lot about Dick Crossman whom Alan described as a dog following a scent, this way and that: he kept a diary during his ministership, but he did not really know what was going on.

5 May

We went to Oxford yesterday. Alan gave a lecture in the Library of All Souls in the afternoon at 5 o'clock. Pat Thompson[2] introduced him. There were about thirty to forty youngsters and some middle-aged fellows, including Kenneth O. Morgan[3] and John Clive[4], also some young historians. Alan spoke about the Soviet Union and the British Left, mainly in the inter-war years. I think it was a very good, clever and witty lecture and apparently everybody else did too.

Alan is invariably kind to everyone and does not make people feel inferior. His obvious cleverness makes one think that he is always right. As he gets older, he gets even better at pointing out the essential features of his argument. He began his lecture by telling the audience that Soviet policy was a determining factor in British policy in the inter-war years. Once Stanley Morrison told him – at that time he did not want to believe it – that the main question in British policy was whether to go with Germany or the Soviet Union. In 1914 it was possible to see that after the Great War, Russia would appear on the scene. From 1920 onwards, relations were icy cold. Not only was the Foreign Office

1 Now dead.
2 Pat Thompson is Fellow of Modern History at Wadham College, Oxford.
3 Kenneth Morgan is Fellow of Modern History and Politics at The Queen's College, Oxford. He is the author of several books on Lloyd George, on modern Britain and on Welsh history.
4 John Clive is a historian and a regular member of Alan's seminar.

hostile to the Soviet Union, but the Chiefs of Staff, who felt at that time that they understood foreign policy, were too. His story really ended with the German-Soviet Pact. His theme was mainly the changing attitude of the British between the wars. The intervention in 1918 was not supposed to help develop a democratic Russia, but to fight Bolshevism, to annihilate it. From 1918 onwards the British Left parted from the government. The amount of direct contact which the British Left had with the Soviet Union was on the increase. On the other hand, Lenin in Soviet Russia, in the midst of his revolutionary activities, had time to analyse the British Trade Union records and wrote one of his best books against Sylvia Pankhurst's[1] views. If ever there was a revolutionary period in Britain, it was then. A red flag flew over Glasgow's City Hall. In the 'twenties it was worthwhile to send correspondents to Moscow. They wrote about everything. They found the life very exciting. That was the time of the Third International. Until the end of the 'twenties the Third International was a genuine, effective working office, an alternative to official policy. This was also the first period of the British-Soviet relations. In 1924–25 the Anglo-Soviet Trade relations were created and worked. The British Left judged Soviet Russia on her own merit, not judging communism at home. Everybody could be a friend of the Soviet Union without being a member of the Communist Party, or considered a 'lefty'. In the 'twenties relaxation came in Britain, because inside Russia there was also relaxation. There was greater tolerance towards dissidents.

6 May

Friday: it was an awful afternoon and evening. First, I shopped at Selfridges. Later I went to join Alan at the National Film Theatre to see Chaplin's *A Woman from Paris*. First, in the pouring rain, I waited in vain for an hour for a No. 68 bus. At the last minute I caught a taxi, driven by a nice Scotsman. He drove me to the NFT negotiating the traffic congestion superbly. I asked him if women drivers caused the confusion, he answered: "No ma'am, women drivers are really fine, the trouble is the drivers who don't know where to go and who change lanes."

1 Sylvia Pankhurst (1882–1960), daughter of the suffragette, Emmeline Pankhurst, was active in Labour politics. She founded the Workers' Socialist Federation in London. Much of her work was devoted to Ethiopian affairs.

Alan was waiting for me patiently outside the NFT. He told me we would not get in – but we did. He is a worrier, inside impatient, but always behaves sweetly. I told him I was cold and he quite rightly answered, "Why did you not dress properly?" After the charming film we went home through the horrible Shell Centre. But the view above and behind the Thames was exceptionally beautiful, darkish grey and lit by lamps – like a watercolour painting. We wanted a drink at Waterloo Station but could not get one, because the elderly woman serving did not take any notice of us at all.

When we got home Alan criticised my shopping; he hoped that one day I would learn how to shop. I took the criticism very badly. He tried to show me that the scissors I bought were too expensive and useless, also the watering can too fancy, too expensive; I should take them back. I was astonished. Not because of what Alan said – which was true – but because when I looked at his face, I saw how worried he had become. Our approach to things is absolutely different and that was in his face. I later explained that it was not the scissors, but his face which frightened me. I asked, did he really think I could change in my mid-fifties? I begged him to take back the Selfridges card, I did not want to go on shopping. He replied, I must learn. I told him I did not want money, or to spend it, only to work.

7 May

The Tories won three seats in London from Labour on the 4th May. At Hillingdon, the new leader immediately ordered council officials to stop housing homeless immigrants who land at Heathrow Airport in the borough and to halt a multi-million pound housing and open space redevelopment.

Saturday evening: on BBC I Karajan said that the only thing which mattered was to work when you work, to eat when you eat, to do everything well and concentrate on bringing out the best in everything you do. He has 150 very different men to control and can make them do what he wants.

Alan and I agreed not to discuss financial things. He told me that he was a critical man and I must speak up for myself. My sons telephoned from Budapest on Mother's Day. They are fine and apparently get on well. We understand each other so well.

9 May

Yesterday we went to the Hungarian Embassy and ate and drank well. Lovely company. Alan was pleasant and spoke to some young Hungarians. One of them told him he had read all his books. Alan asked "How did you like my *Habsburg Monarchy*?" He did not know about it. "I caught him out," said Alan.

On the way to the Embassy, Alan showed me the pub, now called "The Russell", but until recently called "The Earl Russell". Alan was disgusted by the change of name. Evidently nobody any longer knew about Lord John Russell, Prime Minister (little John), actually the grandfather of Bertrand Russell. Passing through Gower Street, we saw the entrance to University College. The building was planned by the man who designed the National Gallery. The National Gallery's columns were brought from Carlton House. Alan said that the Foreign Ministry's building in Whitehall was far too big. Originally it was designed in Gothic style but in 1861 Palmerston said this was unsuitable; the plans for the building were changed to renaissance style and the original plans – Alan had been told – were adapted for St. Pancras Station.

We saw the old French Hospital in Shaftesbury Avenue; now it is a hospital and the Institute of Urology. Alan told me that on the top of one building near Shaftesbury Avenue there is an open air swimming pool. Businessmen and others used to go there at lunch time. "Always full," said Alan. Passing by the Beefsteak Club, I was astonished to see how small a building it was. Very nice and old from outside, there is one large room, thirty men can probably eat there at once, but usually there are four or six. Further on is the great Methodist Central Hall, the scene of the great gatherings of CND. Alan gave a speech there and got a large audience.

10 May

I did not go to Alan's seminar; the subject did not interest me. Alan said he thought people went to seminars to add to their knowledge.

Yesterday we had a pleasant evening with Sebastian, one of Alan's sons from his first marriage, and his wife Mary. She is witty, quick, understanding and a spendthrift. I think money means a lot in this society. Without money and education, you don't really count. I have just begun to read Graham Greene's *England Made Me*, a novel about the 'thirties; in this novel, someone says: "Honesty was a word which had never troubled him: a man was honest so long as his credit was good, and his credit stood high."

A fitness week starts now – "health and vitality week". The exercises lasted from 8 until 9 in Hyde Park. Mr. Sturges led the knees-bend programme to help participants attain physical fitness.

Mrs. Thatcher is very shrewd; she knows what she wants and how to get it. Her programme is to give another lease of life to British capitalism. Callaghan and the Labour leaders do not really know what they want. Thatcher will win the next election. I detest what she stands for and the means she would use to attain her aims. Parliamentary Question Time on Tuesdays and Thursdays in the Commons is most interesting. It is true, Thatcher gives straight answers; Callaghan mocks her. Housewives are shocked listening to the debates on the wireless. Alan said Thatcher is no danger as she has such an awful voice, and has become totally unsympathetic. This is not the case in my view, I'm sorry to say.

12 May

Alan went off quickly. He always runs to catch the bus before half past nine. He wants to be the first O.A.P. to get on the bus without paying anything. He is very proud of this.

He had a horrible session in the British Academy, lasting until four, arguing all the time in favour of this or that grant.

Then he went to the London Library, went through periodicals, then to the Beefsteak Club. He came home absolutely worn out. But he was very sweet, listening to me and asking for my news.

We were asked to a dinner, but Alan did not want to accept; it would be late in the evening and also he thought this invitation came with certain motives. The would-be host had just published a book and wanted a good review from Alan. That is why I like Alan so much. He is absolutely honest and clever, he sees through people's pretences. I have read his *Russian Picture Book*, which is absolutely marvellous. He showed such understanding towards the Russians, he despised the Cold War and tried to make people here understand the Russians. This is exactly how I felt, but I went through the Second World War in bombed Budapest and he did not. That makes him great, greater because he is cleverer than Macaulay.

This morning I got a sweet postcard from Ferencz, from Hajdúszoboszló, a lovely place, with hot springs. Ferencz's heart is always with me; what he experiences he wants to share with me. He is such an honest and clever young man.

13 May

Again a Saturday. Alan left at 11.30 as usual. We felt awful. For him it is worse. Yesterday we had a good walk on the Heath, windy, cold, but refreshing, had a beer and came home. After a wonderful dinner, Alan read *Diary of a Nobody* to me. During the evening meal we had a conversation about the likelihood and consequences of a Tory victory. He explained to me that Thatcher cannot undo what the Labour Party did. She cannot alter the system of comprehensive schools, she cannot alter the system of subsidising decaying industries, she can agree with the Trade Unions that only the skilled workers should get better pay but this would deepen the gap between the working classes i.e. deepen racial hatred, as the unskilled and underpaid are mostly coloured people. The latest the election will be held is next spring. I cannot vote this time as you have to have been resident in the country for six months after naturalisation to be eligible. Alan did not approve of subsidising the decaying industries. Why should the taxpayer pay for a badly run industrial firm? For instance, British Leyland, but nobody would dare to deny them the subsidy, not the Conservatives, nor Labour. That would mean a loss of at least twenty seats and a million unemployed. This is badly run capitalism.

I went to the PRO yesterday, a wonderful building in Kew, computerised. I shall take my typewriter with me next time and begin working on British-Hungarian relations 1945–55. I am still enchanted by Alan's book on the Russian War. He writes: "Thirty years afterwards we often forget how much the Soviet people did for Europe and for all of us. . . . As soon as the war ended all this was swept aside. Soviet policy was regarded with suspicion and the Cold War began – in my opinion the greatest disaster of our lifetime".

In the *TLS* today there is an interesting review by an intelligent man called Felix Gilbert about Meinecke's book, *The Age of German Liberation*, and Eckart Kehr's *Economic Interest, Militarism and Foreign Policy*. Alan read Kehr in his young days and rightly said that Kehr's great strength was that he was the first

German historian who placed a realistic emphasis on economic considerations.

We had grapefruit as hors d'oeuvre and Alan remembered how fashionable grapefruit for breakfast was in the 'twenties in Oxford. He and his friends took turns to go and buy them every morning early. Then after the grapefruit they ate porridge or ham and eggs. His second wife always gave cereal to their sons.

On my advice Alan gave the grandchildren a fixed small allowance to save or spend.

The Times yesterday had a good piece on divorces and another paper had an article on women who earn 18 pence per hour, the silent work force, the home workers, women who sew on buttons or make toys or fold advertising leaflets; there were 50,000 such workers in London, the paper said.

Two lovely letters from my sons. We feel closer now than we did when I left. Alan is worried about whether it was right to separate me from them.

14 May

Alan came home from Margaret and I became terribly depressed. I thought he was longing for his first marriage's best years. I told Alan. He answered that he was depressed when he was there. So I should not be depressed when he came back.

16 May

Yesterday we went to Southampton. The most curious thing happened. Alan was to be interviewed by Susan Barnes, the widow of Tony Crosland, the late former Foreign Secretary (who was Alan's brother-in-law by his second marriage to Eve Crosland). The programme was called "Face to Face". Anthony Howard was the producer. Before the show Susan had consulted Alan about what questions should be raised. She wanted personal questions as well, the question of his marriages. Alan told her that personal questions should be left out completely. Susan agreed. When the interview went on, Susan asked: Why is it, and how is it possible, that Britain's greatest historian has not got an honour? Alan said he did not want a knighthood, would even be offended were this to be offered. There was a pleasant question, the question of religion. Susan asked if it was true that when he was about ten, he heard a voice which said that there was no such thing as God. Alan said it was true and he was relieved. After that he didn't need to worry about religion any more. Susan became uncontrollable. She put the question of marriage. What did he think about marriage? He said when two people loved each other, they just wanted to live together. When they ceased to love, they parted. He never believed in marriage as a contract, nor ever believed it should be a matter of law. Susan asked, why did you marry then for the third time? Alan said: "No comment". He became terribly angry and sad. From this time on, he could hardly bear Susan's questions. He ended with the remark that the only thing he really liked in life was walking in the Lake District. It was interesting what he said about his books: he liked to finish them and to keep them brief. He was always aware of alternatives, and when he wrote about a subject, coming down on one side he knew there was always another side to the question as well.

It was a very good interview, in spite of Susan, because Alan is such a wise and clever much-married man. I never imagined it would be so difficult for him: he did not want to hurt his first wife. Though he does not love her, he feels pity for her and also their life is so mixed up with children and grandchildren and past memories and the trivia of day-to-day life. The routine of their past life made them close to each other. But still Alan is great: he made the decision to marry me at seventy-two. I should be more appreciative.

That evening we had a good chat about the French and Belgian resistance. In Alan's view, the Belgian resisters were the more pragmatic and realistic. Moreover, nobody suspected that these heavy, simple-looking men were part of the resistance.

The French were much more complex. Renouvin, the famous French historian, now dead, who lived in Paris during the 'forties said to Alan that he never saw a German. He went straight to the Sorbonne from his flat, went back and gave lectures on the Far East, evading Europe and the Nazis.

27 May

So many things have happened. I went to see Ursula and Ernő Goldfinger with Alan. Ernő does not like his mother, is not interested in his family at all. He knows that Ursula sacrificed her talents for him. Ernő thinks that the most beautiful city architecturally is Leningrad, then Paris, then London. He took me to Wheelers one evening for a fish meal. Posh and friendly place. Ursula is as sweet as she was thirty years ago. Ernő never lets her finish a sentence. She loved her mother, used to dream about her mother's wonderful soft, white skin, but she loved her nanny's rough hands as well.

Alan had a good seminar last week. He spoke about CND. His brilliant student, Kathy Burk[1], told me that Alan never showed his superiority, was never impatient with any less able students. Alan's *Accident Prone* – which I read today – is an excellent exposé of his views on his life and profession. His wisdom frightens me somehow. I feel much more interested in him intellectually when we are apart. Rilke was right saying that lovers should part.

Alan spoke about The Mill on the Isle of Wight, bought in 1954, when his second marriage was beginning to fail, to create a home for all the family. It really has been a home for them, they still love it; the grown-up children go there with their families and the grandchildren too. Alan told me they bought it for eight hundred pounds and the reconstruction was another three thousand. The Mill once belonged to an Admiral, who was Governor of the island. Admirals always used to be very rich men. When, in war-time they captured a merchant ship, the wealth which the ship contained was distributed so that each sailor got his share, but the officers got much more and the Admiral many times more.

Alan is simple and tidy, very understanding and very patient. He explains things to me many times and does not make me feel inadequate. We have not much imagination and I have not enough time to read.

29 May

This morning we went to see Anglo-Saxon and Roman churches, and Claydon House. We drove through Dunstable, Leighton Buzzard and arrived at Wing, where we found a wonderful, mainly eighth century Anglo-Saxon Church with Saxon arches and windows and the original roof. The next church we came to was Stewkley, called St. Michael's. It is Norman twelfth century, more ornamental, and has typical zig-zag ornaments on the main

1 Kathleen Burk is now Lecturer in History and Politics at Imperial College, London. In 1986 she contributed to a volume of essays in honour of A. J. P. Taylor.

door, with dragons and snakes. St. Michael's is Anglican High Church and so it is full of candles. Many Englishmen who began as High Churchmen have converted to catholicism. Cardinal Newman was such a one. Hillesden Church was next. A sixteenth century church, it stands in the middle of rural England. There is a market cross in the graveyard, bullet holes in the main door as it was stormed by parliamentary troops under Cromwell. The window glass is partly medieval. There are painted angels.

Today *The Times* had the obituary of William Strang[1]. Alan said he was one of the most ineffective Permanent Secretaries but he thought every Permanent Secretary was quite ineffective, including Vansittart.

Lord Chalfont in *The Times* reflects the fears of the British ruling classes, writing about how in Africa the spread of communism is totally due to a Cuban and Soviet conspiracy. How wrong he is. Next day in *The Times* it was shown, beyond a shadow of a doubt, that Mobutu of Zaire is one of the most corrupt leaders and the state suffers from seventy to eighty percent inflation; everything is corrupt there.

5 June

We discussed the personality of James Callaghan. Alan said he has developed, he has grown somewhat more shrewd, more astute and more informed. Once they had a talk on TV, on the programme "Free Speech". Callaghan took part, but he did not know what to say. Alan and he met and Alan told him everything he wanted to know or ought to have known before.

Alan does not very much like dogs. He prefers cats. He does not like dogs' eyes fixed upon him all the time, watching what to expect. When I told him that I had found a very good word for people who did not like to communicate – "non verbal" – he told me a story about Mme de Staël, who had a long and tormented relationship with Benjamin Constant. Constant wanted to escape and ultimately he married a sweet girl. However, Mme de Staël made such a fuss that he returned to her. She, however, soon became involved in an affair with an officer who looked beautiful,

1 Sir William Strang (1893–1978) was Eden's Permanent Under-Secretary of State to the Foreign Office and Head of the Central European Department of the Foreign Office under Chamberlain.

but spoke little. Benjamin Constant noticed this and told her. She answered: "Speech does not happen to be his language."

This morning we discussed the sleeping habits of the English. Although they are very individualistic, they sleep under the same sheet and covers. Continentals are more dependent on each other, but their eiderdowns are separate, separately covered, each with its own bedding. There is no family dispute over sheets and blankets.

7 June

The new TV series began yesterday. Eddie Mirzoeff is a very kind man; he is said to be the best director. We arrived at twelve for lunch, at three the performance began. Alan was grand. Speaking about the French Revolution, he finished by saying that this was the prototype for all future revolutions. From this time on, democracy, nationalism and socialism became three forces to be reckoned with, but at the same time they caused problems. He was very clever, saying that the French Revolution made it clear that property could belong to individuals, after Paine's *Rights of Man*. In the Middle Ages and later, castles and lands belonged to rich and powerful people. From this time on everyone could own a cottage, a house, a property and had the right to keep it. Only later when Socialist ideas began to flourish did the right to property become odious. He spoke about Robespierre as well: the only person in politics who had real integrity and could not be corrupted. But he liked power, nevertheless.

His next TV talk will be about Chartism. After that 1848, then 1870, then 1917. Good titles – tales of revolutions; and good music – Schubert.

Alan always says that the Russians are not hated because of their mistakes, but because they do not tolerate great landownership and industrialists.

12 June

Yesterday we went to hear the Beaux Arts Trio, an American ensemble. The pianist, a little fat man, was enjoying himself tremendously. They played Haydn and Schubert and the Schubert

(Trio, Opus 99) was wonderful: Alan said he would like to have this piece played on his death bed.

I told Alan I wanted to see the letter sent to him by Rear Admiral Scott inviting him for dinner as a guest of the American-English Friendship Society between Staffs. Alan answered saying that he would not go, because he was always in favour of detente and his views were different from theirs. If he addressed the guests, he would not conceal his views and this would cause embarrassment on both sides. In the evening we discussed this. I told Alan I wanted to keep all his letters because after our deaths, historians might distort his views. They might see him, in a way, as an establishment man, "Who cares, when I have gone," was the reply. "I do," said I, "because I believe in human progress and everybody has to add something – at least the truth as he sees it." When Alan dies, I would like to found a Taylor Centre. Not enough people read today in England and consequently they do not know Alan's merits. The Taylor Centre would help uneducated people in Britain to read about and understand their surroundings better than they do now.

Eva Figes, a writer who came to England from Fascist Germany when she was eight years old, still suffers from the past. She criticises the British, who are so different from the Continental people. They did not go through the atrocities and horrors that Europe did in the 'thirties and 'forties. Perhaps, this is why they are neither so sentimental, nor so sensitive. But who can blame them for this? The English people on the whole are the most unselfish and tolerant people in the world, with a ruling class whose power does not diminish, alas, because the class system is perpetuated by the public school system. But to be fair, as Alan said, the British ruling classes have been better than their French counterparts, for instance. Look at Peterloo – he said some ten people were killed then. Look at June 1848 in Paris or during the Commune, when thousands and thousands died.

18 June

Yesterday we went to Finchingfield in Essex. Enchanting little town with a church and almshouses, a windmill and a lake. I drove. We sat down near the little lake and Alan told me that he had come here with his second wife and his two little daughters from the first marriage some twenty-five years ago. On the way the girls laughed a lot and they were struck by an idea about a certain Miss Potter's bra. Alan's wife became angry, because in a school where she taught once, there was a Miss Potter. Her anger increased when Alan said perhaps Miss Potter had not got a bra.

I took some photographs, Alan was embarrassed and so the pose was unnatural. I notice most British people do not take portrait photographs, but prefer natural beauties and buildings. I am interested mainly in the expressions on people's faces.

I became very ill in the evening. I had bronchitis. I often feel that we two might not be enough for each other. Of course there are always "glass walls that surround a couple". I often feel that I confuse emotion and fact and also feel that men like to evade exclusive emotional relationships.

I asked Alan one evening "what is an intellectual?" He thought a bit, then said: "Intellectuals are those whose work or whose interests are centred around books or writings rather than around the actions of human beings."

Alan never passed a driving test. He has never had an accident apart from one in 1961. He drives very well. He taught me to slow down before going round a corner and speed up as soon as the road begins to straighten out again.

Once we spoke about Namier[1] again. Alan told me he was a bore in society, always spoke about history. British Oxford dons on the whole were hostile to him. When his appointment came, many asked how would he behave at dinner.

Alan likes to go to the Beefsteak Club. He says it is the habitat of good old Tory gentlemen. We discussed what he meant by gentlemen. He said it was a matter of character and behaviour, not of social class, left or right wing ideas or intellect.

Ceausescu, the Romanian President, came here for a visit. He was given a state reception and stayed at Buckingham Palace. He was well received because he took an independent line from Moscow and because they wanted to make a big bargain with him over the aeroplanes. It always bothered me that except during the Second World War, the British Government have always been so hostile to Soviet Russia. I think this dates back to Palmerston and to the Balance of Power idea of keeping the Habsburg Empire hostile to Russia. Now after the Second World War, the USSR

1 Sir Louis Bernstein Namier (1880–1960) was a British historian of Russian origin whose long and distinguished career was crowned with the professorship of Modern History at the University of Manchester from 1931 to 1952. His *Structure of Politics at the Accession of George III* and *England in the Age of the American Revolution*, Vol I compelled a re-thinking of British history.

did exactly what the British wanted: she created a cordon sanitaire around her borders as a safeguard. One should read the "Records on British-Yugoslav relations between 1945–55", about the role that was maintained for her.

Alan always thinks he is selfish. I think he is not. He usually tries to do things which are pleasant for others, always wants to cheer people up: he is a giver, not a taker. But he thinks that if he didn't do things for other people, then he would be able to go on undisturbed doing what he himself wanted to do.

Alan is very sweet. I am ill. He brings porridge up to me in the morning and tea with lemon or milk. He brings me up my lunch. Once he came up and asked whether I would like two slices of bread or one. He is a dear person.

19 June

Alan asked me whether I liked living with him. I said that I did, as nobody interfered. We shall soon have a stereo gramophone. Alan said he had had one gramophone at Holywell which he gave to his first wife when she came to live in London. He gave another to his second wife and that later went to his second son. Alan also had one in Oxford and that went to his younger daughter. His youngest son had the one which Alan bought for the family and used to play music for them in the sitting room. Alan's third son bought one for himself in order to be able to play music in his bedroom. He asked his brother to split the cost with him because his had been paid for by their father, and this the younger son agreed to do.

Alan could not say what would be the best way to eliminate the injustices in Britain. He could only describe the symptoms. Nowadays he says the inequalities between classes are disappearing because of the heavy taxes. But inequality in terms of property is not disappearing; in fact, it is growing. The property owners have more properties now than they had in the nineteenth century. Land distribution would lead nowhere. Nowadays in England land is cultivated mostly by farmers who both own their land, and rent huge parts of it from landowners and farm it on an industrial scale.

20 June

Alan said yesterday that the nationality issue between Romania and Hungary is again serious although it was thought that after the Second World War it had been buried for ever.

I asked Alan why he did not revive the "Free Speech" programme on the BBC. Alan said the only person with whom he could have revived it was Robert Blake[1]. But the BBC has to balance exactly the views of the main political parties. So they would ask the Conservatives whether Robert would be all right. He would be all right. And they would ask the Labour Party whether Alan was all right and the Labour Party might not agree because Alan had disagreed with the Labour Party over letting Great Britain join the EEC and they differ on various other issues. In a free country, "Free Speech" is not permitted.

When we came home, Alan was very depressed. He said his values are not appreciated any more. He asked me if even I knew what he believed in. I said I knew he was for humanity.

24 June

Alan sang revolutionary songs in bed. In the dark I watched his face, what a charming lovable man.

Oh! What a Lovely War was a great success. Joan Littlewood is now a sad and forgotten person. "I don't want to die, I want to go home for tea" – that is what the soldiers sang in the First World War.

We entertained two women from the BBC. They had a long talk with Alan about Randolph Churchill and Evelyn Waugh who, although they were very good friends, could not bear each other. Waugh belonged to two clubs in order to escape Randolph Churchill. Waugh was not a kind man and after his wife left him, he portrayed in all his novels a woman who made her husband's life a misery. They had a lot of children. Auberon Waugh is a fine critic.

Before Alan gave his TV lecture today, Eddie and his colleagues made him speak about his work and about his past. So he told

1 Rt. Hon. Lord Blake is Provost of The Queen's College, Oxford. He is an eminent historian of the Conservative Party and an expert on Disraeli.

them the story of Henrietta, an Austrian Social Democrat who came to England and stayed with the Taylors in Oxford after the Anschluss. Henrietta belongs to his Oxford war years. So in a way does Lord Longford who, Alan said, was twice hit on the head and after each blow he changed his religion. I told Alan he should write a book of anecdotes.

Graham Greene's *Human Factor* has become a world famous novel. Alan's book would attract great publicity; he is witty, compassionate, kind and clever and could tell all the stories about his contemporaries with an understanding that no one could better.

25 June

My younger son, Pisti, arrived on Sunday. He was astonished about my economising on small things. He said I ought not to give in to Alan so much. I should continue to be an independent woman. Pisti is very intelligent and looks upon things very wisely. Yesterday we left him alone in the house and went to the Bridge Hotel, Buttermere. Alan has become restless.

During the 'thirties many Cambridge dons stayed in Buttermere, including Pigou[1], who had a cottage here and the Trevelyans, who had one too. There are two lovely lakes where, in Alan's time, there had been many boats. In 1925 Alan stayed here for a short time at a nearby farm. In those days, of course, the farm had no hot water so they washed themselves in the kitchen where they heated the water on the stove.

1 July

Alan said that I don't know how much he loves me. After three months he asked: Is it better for me to live with him or not? I said, I thought much about what Rilke said: Lovers should part, but I thought Rilke was mad. "Love you Liza? I could chew your

1 Arthur Cecil Pigou (1877–1959) held the Chair in Political Economy at Cambridge from 1908–1944. He was the first to enunciate clearly the concept of the real balance effect, which as a consequence became known as the "Pigou effect".

blooming ear off," said a cockney lover – "That is how I feel," said Alan.

4 July

Alan feels guilty about going to the Isle of Wight to the family mill. Poor man, Alan. He goes on the hills with his blue waterproof trousers and coat, with his stick and with his grey hair and it looks as though he is going up to the sky. Oh, I love him so much; he is so human.

I asked him why is it that so many English writers write about Charlotte Street. Alan said it was because all the failed intellectuals liked to go there; it was like Montmartre in Paris. He used to share a flat with Douglas Jay in Percy Street. He went there when he had talks on TV or the BBC. "Where did the intellectuals who did not fail go?" I asked. "To the Ritz," he said.

5 July

In the early part of this century a lot of people still died from bronchitis. They suffered from colds and bronchitis and stayed in bed the whole winter. Alan's father died of bronchitis. He was getting better and went out one Friday to pay the greengrocer's and the butcher's bills as usual and his bronchitis got worse: he died on the Monday.

11 July

Pisti is wonderful. I poured out all my problems to him. Alan is gentle and evasive, whereas Pisti tells me what I ought to do. Can I make them happy?

12 July

Lovely evening. We have been playing gramophone records. Scott Joplin is on at this moment.

Alan has a heavy cold. I wish it would get better. Every morning he jumps into a bath of cold water for a minute, then jumps out. What a lovely disciplined, zestful man he is.

14 July

Callaghan said in the House that top people in nationalised industries should get top money. Alan said it was not fair. Everybody's income over £20,000 a year should be taxed 100 percent or 120 percent. I said that this was a tactical move before an election. Alan disapproves of such tactical moves as they are not a part of socialism at all.

At the Lakes or by the sea everybody can have his or her own private patch. Shelley's son owned a large part of the sea at Bournemouth. When Shelley died, his wife Mary consulted an aristocratic lady about where she should send her son to school. She was duly told where, with the comment: "In this school, your son will be taught to look after himself." Mary said: "Oh, I want him to go to a school where he could be like others."

Alan says he likes the Good Book because it is a wonderful read. He uses quite a lot of the phrases and expressions from the Old Testament (which he rates much higher than the New) in his own books. The Old Testament was composed by much more sophisticated men than the New.

17–21 July

International Graduate Summer School in Oxford. Three lectures from Alan. Wonderful. His thoughts and the structure of his thoughts work equally well. The three days were wonderful. Alan showed me Chenies Village with the surrounding land belonging to the Russells. There, in the Bedford Chapel of St. Michael's Church, lies "little John" Russell. On the way we went through Missenden where Attlee lived. Attlee never drove a car and his wife picked him up in the evenings when he returned from London. After his wife died he went to live in London.

In Buckinghamshire we saw the House of John Hampden. Buckinghamshire had been the home of many famous and wealthy landowners who in the Civil War fought against the King.

Another day we saw three houses designed by Ruskin. On Iffley

Road we went to see Iffley Church, one of the best preserved twelfth century village churches in England.

We saw Nuneham Courtenay and Chislehampton, where we visited St. Katherine's (1762), the best preserved Georgian Parish Church in Oxfordshire. Blue and white. In Dorchester Abbey there are lovely Jesse windows, c.1340. Langford Church has a figure of Christ on the porch. Two well-dressed ladies came out of the vicarage and said good afternoon to us. It is a very small, tidy town. William Morris's pet church is in a small place. As neglected as W. M. wanted it to be, because it escaped Victorian preservation. In Oxford, Alan showed me New College, and Christ Church, which was founded by Cardinal Wolsey, where Rowse, the first working class boy, had a scholarship. Alan showed me Rowse's and Lindemann's Room.

Alan's "old retainer" in Magdalen is Percy. Alan does not know anything about him, whether he is married or not. He works in the morning from seven to eleven and in the evening from six to nine. In between he does gardening for the president for an extra fee.

We had a wonderful dinner in Magdalen. Alan Raitt[1], who has a Portuguese wife, presided. We assembled in the smoking room. The butler came in to announce dinner, then we went in to dine. Three servants waited at table. After dinner we had sweets and madeira, port or claret. I got drunk from three madeiras and half a bottle of red wine. In the smoking room there is a book of photographs of fellows, presidents, and professors. There is a betting book and also a book of flowers and trees in Magdalen.

On the way home we drove through Cowley, industrial Oxford. Special buses pick up the workers from the neighbouring villages.

Dr. Johnson studied at Pembroke College.

25 July

Roger Louis[2] came for a drink straight from the PRO and we had a good chat about historians and about their works. He quite

1 Alan Raitt, MA, D. Phil, is reader in French Literature at the University of Oxford and a Fellow of Magdalen College.

2 William Roger Louis is Professor of History at the University of Texas at Austin. In 1979 he was awarded a D. Litt. by Oxford University in recognition of his many books on the British Empire and Commonwealth.

likes Raymond Carr[1] and agrees with Alan about Ted (E. H.) Carr. Louis is shy and shrewd, his views are balanced. He is at All Souls for a year as he has a scholarship as a visiting professor and will work in the PRO. He spoke about a Hungarian professor who was coming. In the evening we spoke about the Huns. Alan said in the First World War the Germans were called Huns, nasty Huns, but Alan said there were some nice Huns, like Dahrendorf. Churchill used to call the Nazis "nasties".

A good review one of Jung's books. Jung believed that marriage is the home. And in marriage, like in the nest, one is in and out all the time. I have to reconcile myself to the fact that Alan wants complete freedom. I should live free from worries.

28 July

We had a good conversation about Alan's article about the dissenters, on 16 July, in the *Sunday Express*. In this article he said, as he has all his life, that the Russian people are wonderful, only the leadership is bad. I think he is wrong. Communism as a principle and as a reality is better than capitalism, but these states inherited backward systems. All the corruption and snobbery cannot disappear immediately; it is bound to take time. Sixty to seventy years is not much. Alan thinks if there had been a Communist revolution in many countries at the same time, the situation would have been different.

30 July

Henry Moore is eighty. His main pre-occupation is with form, although he liked colour as well. His obsession is the reclining figure. Why, he cannot explain. He is realistic, a hard worker. He is interested in the triangular relationship of husband, wife and daughter. A simple man, clever and straightforward, extremely efficient and objective in looking upon the body, relationships, possibilities. He is like Alan, but life was kind to him, he was lucky with his wife. He, like Alan, loves women more than men.

1 Raymond Carr has been Warden of St Antony's College, Oxford, since 1968. Before then he was director of the Latin American Centre (1964–68) and Oxford Professor of History of Latin America (1967–68).

Alan said he liked Eastern European wives, because they are content when their husbands are content. I leave him alone to get on with his own work in his own way; meanwhile, I have my own work to do. I must trust him completely. I do trust him, but his softness towards aggressive and ambitious women makes his life more difficult and wastes his creative power on trivialities.

Beauty is in the eye of the beholder. You have to accept the fact that when something is not beautiful to you, it could still be beautiful to others. Beauty is everything, the whole thing, but for no two people is the whole thing the same.

5 August

Pisti has left. Alan is on holiday in the Isle of Wight. Alan asked me one night recently whether I prefer him to my children. But this is not relevant, all three of them are equally precious. To feel really alive I need any one of them. I have read Alan's autobiography and I feel I understand him better now that I live here in England. I no longer have the urgent desire to write down everything I feel, and notice; I can express myself in pictures, in photographs or in nothing. I am not interested in myself any more.

I had a wonderful day all alone. I went to Hyde Park and took photos of an extremely spoilt and fat dog who belonged to two women. I asked an elderly disabled man sitting eating chips near his specially fitted car the way to the Henry Moore Exhibition. When I came out of the exhibition I gave him a reproduction of one of Moore's statues – and I took his picture too. The little man confronted his situation with a perfect calmness and some sort of practicality and dignity. I took a photo of a lady with three wonderful dogs; she looked nervous and pale. She was very indignant because of a man who she said lived in Hyde Park in a public building which was getting very smelly because of his regular peeing there. I took a photo of this man as well and I asked him whether he really did live there. He said no and smiled and went on feeding the birds.

In the afternoon I went to the Richmond Theatre where I saw a comedy with Robert Morley acting in it. It was called *The Picture of Innocence*. I read in a Hungarian newspaper that Imre Varga, the famous sculptor had a statue in Salgótarján of a crippled warrior with a hat held in his outstretched hand. Passers-by put money in his hat. The artist was pleased; he felt he had communicated his meaning. It reminded me of what Henry Moore said on his eightieth birthday: he made his statues expressions of what he wanted to say and did not design them specifically for exhibitions. He said that exhibitions were not natural; statues should be in their natural surroundings.

20 August

Ferencz and Judi are here. I am very fond of them but I can't talk to them when they are together. Alan thinks that as a parent one should always keep in the background.

We went to the Isle of Dogs today to practise my driving. We drove near to St. Bartholomew's Hospital, founded in 1123, probably the earliest hospital in Europe. In the hall there is a wonderful Hogarth. Until the dissolution of the monasteries there was a priory as well and the priory chapel still survives.

We had a very good evening with Elaine and Stephen Koss[1].

27 August

Of course I shall never be, and do not want to be, British. I am constantly curious and appreciative about the British way of life and traditions, but everything about me belongs to dear Hungary. I realise the longer I stay in this country, the more I may change in my habits and outlook. My political and scientific outlook will not change, but now perhaps I look upon everyday life with more humour, wisdom and tolerance. Budapest will change, too; people who were close to me will die, things will happen in which I shall not be involved, my sons will marry and not want to share their feelings and thoughts with me any more. What else can I do? They have to live on their own. They have to have outlets for their own lives and they have to build up their own routines without my help. I have great confidence in them and in myself. If I cannot build up a permanent and good relationship with Alan, I have to learn to live by myself. And living in Britain has taught me how to live alone in Hungary. Alone does not mean lonely.

1 Stephen Koss was Professor of History at Columbia University until his tragic and early death in 1984. A distinguished academic, his works include *Nonconformity in Modern British Politics*, *The Rise and Fall of the Political Press in Britain* (2 Vols) and a biography of Asquith.

But still I feel, if I stay fit, I should be able to share a complete relationship with Alan who is very tolerant and understanding.

Yesterday we went to the Duke of York's Theatre to see the play *Half Life* by Julian Mitchell. The play was about Maurice Bowra, a well known historian of the ancient world, played by John Gielgud, a wonderful actor, superb elegance and style.

The play concerns a group of characters centred around the eminent Oxford don. One couple in the play, Francis and Helen Mallock are devoted to him. We were told by Stephen Koss that they personified our friends in Oxford. It was horrible, because the "Mallocks" really were like our friends and Alan and I both felt that our friends had been studied and mimicked.

In the evening we went to a pub and Alan spoke about Horrabin, the cartographer. I myself used Horrabin's atlases in my works and I was very interested to hear about the man. Alan said he was left-wing and a very charming man. He could draw his maps in such a way that they spoke for themselves. He drew the maps for Alan's *Habsburg Monarchy* and for *The Struggle for Mastery in Europe*. Horrabin liked Alan to explain the problems – i.e. the nationality problems – of the areas Horrabin was asked to draw maps of. He did very good economic geography maps in the 'fifties and made several appearances on TV in connection with this.

Alan spoke about his relationship with Rebecca West, whom he esteemed, but whose writings he did not like because she believed that the great Serbian dynasties had a place in history. Alan also disliked the settings of her novels. Still, they were friendly until one day, working on *Beaverbrook*, Alan found in an envelope a telegram sent by Rebecca to Beaverbrook. It read: "I shall go to your party, though it will be full of dull people. Amongst them, the dullest is H. G. Wells, whom I know personally, because I lived with him for fifteen years." Alan sent this telegram as a birthday present to Rebecca, thinking to amuse her, but she was offended and they never met again. I do so love to go to the pub with Alan; he always tells me such amusing stories.

29 August

Bank Holiday tomorrow. We are alone in the house. Alan is in a state of complete uncertainty. He is back from his holiday in the Isle of Wight, which must be a lovely place, still unspoilt and enchanting. Priestley admitted in his short contribution in the

Observer colour supplement that having lived there year after year, he was not completely convinced he did the right thing to abandon the island. He returned after seventeen years. He and his wife Jacquetta used to have a chamber concert in their house, each week, and Alan often went, probably with Margaret. Before Alan went to the island, he told me, I had no idea how much he detested Margaret. When he came back, he told me he did not detest her, nor did he love her. Alan is a fair man, though I now see him quite differently from how I had imagined he was. I still love him, and think he is a fine man and a good character.

21 September

Proust said a very clever thing: "Love is not shining and splendid but sordid and perverted. Love vanishes once it is obtained and can be kept alive only by incessant jealousy and suspicion." I think we are both jealous sometimes. Alan also gets very depressed occasionally and then I am inclined to believe that he is not happy with me. He is such a darling, and such a clever man. He knows himself so well. He told me the other night that his main faults are: vanity, evasiveness, egocentricity. I asked: dishonesty? No, he said, just evasiveness.

22 September

Alan told me about a Cabinet Minister who, being caught in bed with two women, had had to resign. He had intercourse with one, the other one was titillated by his hands. So he gave pleasure to both and they both inspired each other.

To hold a conversation is the most difficult art. When you have learnt this, you are really a master of life. How do you handle a woman? Love her. How do you handle a man? Develop in yourself those characteristics which he likes. How do you succeed in life? Take opportunities. Jessie Matthews said all these clever things. She was the star of stars in the 'thirties. Then she had twenty bad years. Now she is back again in her late seventies, looking lovely, gay and young.

When Alan had to give a lecture on the founder of Magdalen College, he told the audience – mainly youngsters – to be cynical, capricious and aggressive and then they would succeed in the world.

Yesterday Alan lectured in Hackney Hall on the end of the First World War. He said amongst other things that in capitalist countries taxpayers pay for the rich, in Socialist countries they pay for the bureaucrats. The capitalists, industrialists, bankers are said to gain by wars. But they gain in peace as well. They are a section of society which gains whatever the situation.

Lady Beaverbrook told Alan one day that once when Lord Beaverbrook was ill and wanted to have Alan to dinner, he asked Alan to tell his second wife not to come with him. So Alan did. And then Beaverbrook said of Alan: "That's a good boy."

25 September

I must be strong. Alan does not need an equal partner in life, what he needs is a woman who adores him, who surrounds him, who is intellectual and who amuses him at the same time. I did not know this before, because I was happy to entertain him for a fortnight. How can I go on? I have to concentrate on my own works. I am very weak, but I have to be strong.

27 September

Alan's son, Crispin is with us. He was sulky today because he was not pleased with the way he had shown us up to one of the hills. I like this boy. He is the eldest son from Alan's second marriage and in his mid-twenties. Tolerant, sensitive, very loyal to both of his parents. He does not like indecisiveness, he is a good teacher.

29 September

The whole week in Coniston was good. Crispin has a good scientific mind and has a great deal of commonsense and he knows how to stand up for himself. Sometimes you can see the child in him. He is very understanding with Alan; the relationship between the two is fine. This is partly because Alan is so tolerant and wise and Crispin is clever and sensitive . It was fascinating to see what happened when Crispin gave a boy a lift in the car. Both of them began to speak about the weather. The boy, poorly educated, said only yes or no. Alan and Crispin stopped talking so as not to embarrass him. But when the boy said something they encouraged him to go on. Both of them are the best types of liberal, socialist British intellectuals. Alan reminded Crispin when the boy left and thanked him that he should have said: "It was a pleasure." Crispin did not agree. "It is American." But he did agree that he should have thanked him back.

I have finished Liv Ullmann's charming book *Changing*. A very good and clever woman, though not a writer. But a writer enough to make it clear what she sees in her profession, which of course for her is the essential point. She understands America well enough, also herself, her roots in Norway and her inability to be solely wife or mother. She says: "A husband is a sort of alibi for a woman." (Not completely true but often.)

I have read Eliot's *Middlemarch*. Alan's second wife said Alan was like Casaubon. Crispin says Wilkie Collins' *The Woman in White* is excellent. "Everything is constantly in movement – including love – and therefore subject to the law of change."

2 October

The owner of the *Sun* newspaper wants to buy a whole section of Camden to build a large and modern printing area. The councillors in Camden have to decide whether they will let it be sold to him or not. The dilemma is to give this wealthy man a chance again, but the creation of new jobs would mean a lot for the working population in this area. The *Sun* has a circulation of over four million, its Sunday edition around five million.

3 October

Robert and Augusta came for dinner. They had a good summer near St Tropez, where the Káldors live during the summer. Káldor[1]

1 Nicholas Káldor, a Hungarian Economist, was professor of Economics at the University of Cambridge from 1966 to 1975, and in the course of his career was economic advisor to many governments throughout the world. He died in 1986.

was called Buddha and the other Hungarian economist, Balogh,[1] was called Pest. They told us that in France every village has a swimming pool, but no playground. In England quite the opposite is true.

Alan is thrilled with the paperback edition of his book *The War Lords*. Also he liked Chris Wrigley's[2] introduction to the huge bibliography of his work, but thought he did not write enough about Alan's historical works.

4 October

Alan is leaving his little office in Fleet Street. I am afraid he will miss the place.

In the evening we went to the local pub. Alan spoke about MacDonald. He saw him first in 1924; later he found him pathetic, vain, and full of self pity. After 1931 he was still ambitious, though he lost all his ability to concentrate. Alan thought he was a dreadful man. His biographer, David Marquand[3], found him exciting at first but later he felt the same way as Alan.

In the evening I watched *No Man's Land* by Pinter, starring Gielgud and Ralph Richardson. The acting and the play were magnificent. I also saw Thornton Wilder's *The Matchmaker*.

5 October

We were in Matlock. It is a wonderful place in Derbyshire, a spa, illuminations during the summer, a bit like Venice and the Lake District. Alan's grandfather withdrew here, as he thought for his last months and lived for another thirty years with a woman.

Alan gave a very good lecture about the origins of the First World War as the guest of the Historical Association. I understand

1 Thomas Balogh had a long and distinguished academic career and was Fellow Emeritus of Balliol College, Oxford, until his death in 1985.
2 Chris Wrigley is Reader in Economic History at Loughborough University. He edited a volume of essays in honour of A. J. P. Taylor in 1986.
3 David Marquand is a historian and journalist. He was made Professor of Contemporary History and Politics at Salford University in 1978. He has written for the *Guardian*, *New Statesman* and *Encounter*.

now why he likes to do it. It puts some variety into his life, to meet people and answer questions. How stimulating to see the wide-open eyes: they understand something and want to know more. Alan always destroys commonplaces. He stated there was nothing in *si vis pacem para bellum* and that it is not true that the great munition factories gained a lot by wars. They like to prepare for wars but when wars begin, sooner or later they lose out.

Alan spoke about a colleague of his in Magdalen, called Dixon, a mathematician whose French wife did not like the atmosphere in Oxford. She, therefore, lived at Folkstone nearer to France and her husband lived with her when his term ended. "Very good arrangement," said Alan. On the way he was anxious to get back in time for the lunchtime concert at the Bishopsgate Institute. He is the president of the City Hall Music Society which arranges these concerts.

Alan feels nostalgic about his little office, for his walks around Fleet Street, for the life with Margaret. This first wife was so much wiser than the second, who is still full of grievances and wrote to me an offensive letter and described how badly Alan behaved with her when their son was born. Alan said he had had to lead a double life and doing so, he had to cover things up. If he had not led a double life, he would have lost his children.

An Italian TV crew came. Alan spoke about Zionism. Palestine took the place of the Ottoman Empire and the British thought that, apart from making a home for Jews throughout the world, it would be a good thing to keep the British interests alive in that part of the world. They tried to do the same with Suez to keep the French out.

Alan is very good at maintaining people's interest in his works. He speaks about his books, and about his career on TV. He was not very much appreciated by the top BBC men during the period from 1948–60.

7 October

I had a good letter and, later, a friendly talk with Pisti on the phone. He said if I'm bored, I should watch TV. He is quite right. He gets up at six, does everything by himself, gives advice to friends (as somebody told me he is honest with everyone except himself). He invited only one friend to his diploma festival. I would like to see him more and be with him more. Ferencz is as nice as Pisti. I miss them terribly. Ferencz is now in Prague.

I am working on Tawney, who was a great and compassionate man. Still a student at eighty, his only complaint was that he slept too much.

I read the autobiography of Philby's wife. She wrote she was happy that Kim's father, John, did not see Kim's defection. Kim was anti-British only because Britain did not come up to his expectations. Alan is not anti-British, but critical. We spoke about Bismarck, who was autocratic, but also skilful in working with political parties. He wanted to make an end to the Reichstag, but never did. Gordon Craig in his German history does not mention Alan's book on Bismarck. Crazy. Of course he knows about it. Rowse wrote quite a friendly remark about Alan, called him "an ardent Mancunian" – something like that.

10 October

Alan has given up his work at the little office in Fleet Street. I think he is a bit upset about it. We came home through Paddington Road. He showed me the shops where he used to do his shopping and which he would not go to again. He has destroyed his archive. I thought it should have been saved. The letters which he got from all over the country expressed people's views: why they admired him, what they had learnt from him. I am biased, I am not admiring him, I just want to preserve what is precious or important. Cosima and Richard Wagner's life is preserved by Cosima's adoring diary. I do not want to do the same. For instance Wagner said to Cosima: "You would have better married a God." Cosima's answer: "But I did." Is that not awful? Alan, except for some years with his first, did not have good relationships with his two wives. Perhaps not because of his mistakes but because of theirs. If our relationship failed, he would never believe that they were always wrong. I am his last chance to prove that it is good and worthwhile to live with him.

14 October

Restless weekend. I felt lonely. Alan went to Margaret. When he came back, I told him how lonely I felt. He explained he never felt lonely. When he was in Oxford, he had his breakfast alone, then went for a walk alone, then for dinner, and sometimes he never spoke to anyone. He is quite happy by himself. I shall arrange the Saturdays somehow differently. Though I enjoy TV, reading, still sometimes I have doubts: what am I doing in this country, without my sons, whom I miss terribly? When I return to Hungary I miss Alan terribly.

We went to see Shaw's corner. Very common or garden living rooms, unaesthetic. It was very interesting to see how simple some great men are in their way of living and in their habits. Alan found an apple under the tree from which Shaw fell and ate it with good appetite.

16 October

Kafka once said: "A non-writing writer is a monster inviting madness." I am happy when I am writing my diary.

Alan came up with another clever comment: In the 'thirties it was possible to give voice to those who were anti-appeasement and they sometimes got very good reviews and articles in the newspapers, while for those who were anti Cold War, propaganda was really impossible, they could not get through to the media.

Also Alan said – which I did not know – that the publishers used to publish old time-tables for collectors. That was a great business for publishers.

People like to know much about the trains in this country. How to get there, when, where to change and so during the journeys very few people speak to one another because they think it rude. But in Germany everybody speaks to everybody, asking when they are due to arrive, where to get off and so on. An Englishman would be amazed, and wonder why they could not simply consult the time-table themselves.

17 October

There was a very good article in the *TLS* about heroines. The truth is, as it is expressed in many novels and short stories, that women are subservient to men; they seek the company of men and if they are emotionally and sexually involved, they become subdued somehow. A liberated woman: from what and from whom and why? Liberated means something different in various situations and times. A black woman in America who earns money helping to bring up other people's children, goes out every morning, although she would like to stay at home. To stay at home for her is liberation. For a rich or middle-class woman to get rid of the home is liberation. I told Alan that real equality in partnership occurs when both can offer each other what the other has not got or has got but cannot benefit from. I like Alan's approach to life, to problems – with him most things are easy. I feel he can solve many problems which I cannot because I make mountains out of mole hills. For instance when his children were young and at bedtime – when most children do not want to go to bed – he looked after them he used to say: "Now stay in bed, sleep or read – leaving the bed-side lights on – I want my time as well." They perfectly understood this, not because they had to sleep, but because he had a right to his privacy as well.

22 October

Yesterday I saw a Mercier play: *Cousin Vladimir*. The heroine came to the West, not for political reasons, but because she was a widow and felt lonely. After a while she decided to go back and so did her uncle, who had lived in the West for a long time. It is quite true what the TV critic wrote: dissidents are human as well. I probably expect too much from the West.

In England one does not speak much about death. Few people show their grievances, sorrows. This is well put in Graham Greene's novel *The Human Factor* – a very good but very sad book. He writes such things as: "Fear and love are indivisible."

Pisti phoned. He will soon have his dog. They are my loving sons. All the warmth, the real values are with them. My life here seems absolutely selfish: I do not contribute anything to shape this society. I do not contribute much to Alan's happiness and welfare either, because he is perfectly well able to look after himself and is not really inclined to share his intellectual interests with me. He has other outlets as well. Of course he does share his thoughts with me when I ask him to, but he never does it spontaneously. Also he does like people to speak about his works which I cannot do for any great length of time.

24 October

We listened to Hector Berlioz: *Grande Messe des Morts* which is an example of French musical romanticism; it is an immense funeral fresco designed to evoke the apocalypse. We went to the local pub tonight and had a good chat about Stephen Spender, whose book about the 'thirties has just appeared.

Then we chatted about the Foreign Office people. They always looked upon Hungary as a pet Eastern European country because they liked Horthy. They always preferred Horthy to Beneš, who was an obscure leader of peasant origins. Of course during the war Beneš was treated with much more respect than the Hungarians because he was never an enemy and Hungary became one. But still, after the war the Foreign Office had faith in Hungary's future until 1948. The Foreign Office always disliked Károlyi, largely because they preferred Horthy. Hubert Ripka was quite different from Beneš. Married to a French woman, during the war he was absolutely pro-Russian (as was Beneš) and made it clear that he believed that Czechoslovakia's future was and would always be connected with Russia, partly because of Slav brotherhood. Ripka was an intelligent, tall Slav, and unlike Beneš, he was not at all dull. He had been a journalist before and was also from a peasant background.

At dinner we had a conversation about Norman Gash,[1] who is a good historian himself and, like Peel, an enlightened Conservative. I told Alan it was easier to write about the same period for a life time; it is more difficult to change subjects as Alan and I have done.

Alan is like a conductor when he gives a lecture. At St Andrews he spoke about nationalism which, in his opinion, eventually creates hate and oppression.

25 October

At St Andrews Alan spoke for an hour. In the middle of his speech he thought he was going to sneeze. He stopped for a while and waited. Everybody was silent and thought that he had forgotten

1 Norman Gash has been Professor of History at St Salvator's College, University of St Andrews since 1955. He is the author of numerous books on Peel.

what he wanted to say. Then as it did not come, he said, "I stopped because I felt I was going to sneeze, but it did not come."

His views on *The Origins of the Second World War* are that the book is a joke book: a paraphrase of the book written about the origins of the First World War.

26 October

We went to Oxford. We saw a lovely little church, then arrived at Mary Thompson's house. Alan went to a restoration dinner. Being with Mary was like being at home. She is a very intelligent and easy-going woman, thinks before she speaks. She told me I was a giver, not a taker. So is Alan.

Pat and Mary said that Alan has been much happier since I have been with him. The main point about Alan is that he has to communicate.

Alan told me that history is the invention of historians. There are facts, but they are interpreted differently. I told him I would not always go and listen to his lectures and he could write them down afterwards. That he could not do, he said, because afterwards he forgets what he has said. I told him he was an improviser and he agreed.

29 October

Alan said he had noticed that he had begun to forget things, but nobody else would notice it yet. His mathematician colleagues in Magdalen used to forget words like table, but his logic was perfect. Beaverbrook was not forgetful to the day he died. He was very anxious not to forget things so, every morning at ten o'clock, he had a team around him who would check everything. Beaverbrook liked people who were clever and appreciative like Alan and Michael Foot. He liked to influence the whole British press. Once, when it became known that his friend's son was involved in homosexual affairs, the friend asked Beaverbrook not to let the news spread. It did not come out. "What is the good of being a magnate, if not to use one's influence in that way?" said Alan.

A good aphorism: "Such time as he can spare from the neglect of his duties he devotes to the adornment of his person."

30 October

Alan said that Greene was much more talented than Priestley. His wife converted him to catholicism, but later Greene said he was not a believer but a "practiser". By that he meant that he did not believe any more; he had once believed but then forgot the arguments which had made him a believer. He thought that when he practised his faith, the arguments which made him Catholic would return.

Priestley is a Yorkshireman, and was splendid in his involvement with CND. He used to say, "nobody asked me whether I wanted this weapon or not and I say I do not want this weapon." His first wife died, his second went off with a bird-watcher; when the third became his wife he said, "I can provide a woman with what she wants even when I am seventy."

I have received wonderful letters from my sons. They are my happiness in Budapest; they are clever, hard-working, loving and understanding. How happy I am with them and Alan.

4 November

We spent nearly a week in Scotland: Sterling, St Andrews, Edinburgh and Glasgow. In Sterling, Alan's lecture in the theatre was a great success, with some 500 people including teenagers and students. Sterling has a nice campus with an artificial loch. On the second day Alan's cousin, Ruth, picked us up and we went to see Dunblane Cathedral, in the town where Alan's great-grandfather lived. Ruth and her husband are a very kind couple but completely uninformed; they did not plan any sightseeing, though we went with them to St Andrews. Every year the International Golf Tournament is held here. For this week one might pay a thousand pounds for renting a house. The University's reputation is high, third after Cambridge and Oxford. We were staying in a house belonging to a fellow whose wife was a child psychiatrist and they lived in a Victorian house with their two small daughters. They bring up the children to be kind, independent and capable of making their own decisions. Of course they give them sensible things. The mother tells stories and the ones they like, they can listen to again on their own cassettes. They took the elder daughter to the London Museum where the child became interested in old London at the time of the great fire. It captured her imagination.

When they went to a bookshop later, the child asked for books which would tell her more about London and the fire. Thus, with her parents' guidance she collected a good deal of knowledge and a small library on the subject. The household duties were shared in this house; the husband laid the table in Victorian style.

Here in St Andrews, Alan's lecture was a great success again. About 150–200 people were present. He spoke about Lloyd George during and after the war. The applause was warm and genuine. Alan has not got special oratorical gifts, he goes on quietly explaining how things happened, how people reflected upon events, how these events developed and how he interpreted them. He has a strong will, but is gentle and means well. The structure of his lectures is very good in that first he explains why he chose this or that subject, then he starts from the beginning, referring to later developments, then again takes up the narrative and speaks about the protagonists' human traits and tells some funny, but true stories. He always ends in time, with a good and natural ending. What he does is extremely important for him. He makes history interesting for everyone and makes people think, and look upon events as they really happened from many different points of view. What is extremely important to him is the way he formulates his thoughts and gets newer and newer inspiration from his own thoughts. At the end, when great applause follows his lectures, his face becomes sweet and flushed with happiness and looks twenty years younger. I only knew one such man, and that was my beloved first husband, the father of my sons. It is a greaty pity that Alan's lectures are not recorded on cassettes.

Next day we went to Edinburgh, where his old pupil, Paul Addison[1], looked after us very well. Here the lecture was about the Bulgarian Horrors. The audience was warm and appreciative.

Then in Glasgow we were looked after by a historian and his young wife who was a doctor. They were extremely good people, believing in God and traditional values; they had simple tastes and much faith in mankind. They showed us the Glasgow National Gallery which has a wonderful collection of French Impressionist paintings, Mackintosh designs and furniture and paintings by Lowry. We had a wonderful dinner in a Venetian restaurant. Alan lectured about the Soviet image in Britain. Here

1 Paul Addison is a historian. He lives in Edinburgh and teaches at the University. His best work is *The Road to 1945*, published in 1975.

Alan wanted to show that the bias against the Soviet Union has always been present and that especially after the Second World War the suspicion was mutual. He told the joke about Kitchener, who was not drowned, but went to Russia and became Stalin. He made it clear that prejudice is not a thing which is worth harbouring, but he explained how and why it occurs. Whether or not the message reached the audience is impossible to say. The audience consisted mainly of undergraduates and fellows and there were at least four hundred people there and the applause was long and very warm. Alan looked so strong and young again.

I chatted with some sweet and good-hearted Scots and a girl told me how much less self-confident they are than the English. They speak very quickly and with a Scottish accent and so some English people do not understand them. We met a fellow who was Welsh and had a witty turn of phrase. He told me that when he became a fellow, he was reminded to behave well and comb his hair.

8 November

Alan said that he loves me so much, he really does not need to bother about me during his many activities, because he is so sure of his love. Alan is a good example of how flexible one can be in one's seventies.

I spoke to a West Indian warden in the PRO; he has lived here for twenty years, was educated in a Trinidad school and speaks only English. He makes a better living here than he would in Trinidad, but he does not earn enough to keep himself and his wife, so she went to the USA to earn more. He would never be in a position to have an English girlfriend, as he would be unlikely to meet any English girls. When he retires he will go back to where the sun shines, though the standard of living there is not as good for him as it is here. During the day he works, then goes to the pub, has his dinner at home and watches TV. His driving licence was taken away because one Sunday evening coming back from a party he drove too fast going round a roundabout. Policemen are on the alert for drunken drivers on Fridays, Saturdays and Sundays. He had been drinking so he was caught. He did not complain.

15 November

We met a nice couple the other day. They had been married for decades and had had their difficulties, but then they realised that each partner is an island and that they should not need to possess each other.

Alan said the other day that British men do not like the company of women. Ursula once had a very good housekeeper, who said to her, "Whenever you are told by your master or husband what to do, just answer 'yes Sir' and do what you think is best." I have a suspicion that this was probably the general attitude here in many circles.

We met Norman Davies. He excelled himself as a Polish expert. He came from a humble background, got a second-class degree, went to Poland and married a Polish girl who was very eager to come with him to England. Then she found she was homesick and longed for her mother all the time. He loved his son, but became fed up with his lamenting wife. Alan told him not to get a divorce unless he found someone else.

Alan liked his book on Polish history 1919–20. Alan always took the view that the Soviet Union only wanted to keep to the Riga Agreement and to the Curzon Line. And there was nothing wrong in the Molotov-Ribbentrop Agreement Clause on Poland. The Soviet Union would never have gone to war with Germany if Germany had not attacked her, as she was perfectly satisfied with her border with Poland.

We went to Gatton which was a famous rotten borough: on one occasion two Members of Parliament were elected by one voter. There is now a monument explaining this. Until 1887, during elections in Britain, a list was made of who voted for whom. These lists are of great use to present day historians. We also saw, near Gatton, a sixteenth century church built by a wealthy man who ordered that the building materials should be brought from Germany, Belgium and France.

Alan will soon give the TV talk on Liverpool, a city in a sad state of decay. The once famous port is closed. For miles the docks are closed. One can buy a house there for £600. Liverpool was more highly regarded than Manchester and so working men lived in Manchester, while gentlemen lived in Liverpool. Liverpool had many eminent American visitors, including Ralph Emerson, Herman Melville and Harriet Beecher Stowe. Cobbett came home from his second American tour with the bones of Tom Paine hidden in his luggage. I think Byron wrote a poem about this.

16 November

Alan made coffee for our guests. He sat in the kitchen and worked diligently. I watched him as I watched my father fifty years ago when he made his own cigarettes. Sometimes I felt sorry for him, as I sometimes feel sorry for Alan. He is so clever and so dutiful. Because of this he treats his women respectfully and wants to keep everyone in a good mood. I understand all this as how else could life be tolerable for him? He so hates sulkiness, scenes and fuss. He likes efficient action and interesting discussions about his works. Sometimes something that he says or writes seems shocking, but when one thinks about it, he is often right. And one can count on his compassion and moral sense. I think he prefers people who are down on their luck and not the successful ones and he has the courage to help them.

We had the Murphys and the secretary of the Academy for a drink. Mrs Murphy got to know the Germans and being a teacher she says they believe in group education, group movements. German husbands are still very feudal in their attitudes at home. She said that in Britain they believe that every child is an individual and should be treated as such, on his or her own merits. The Swedes are like the Germans; they are the nice Germans.

Sir Arthur Bryant[1] and Alan are working together. Bryant was an upper-middle class journalist, an appeaser, then he wrote many books and forgot that he was once an appeaser. He wrote about the similarity between the Napoleonic War and the Second World War, which Alan said was wrong. In the Second World War, Britain was on the right side and fought for survival.

I find the role of MPs very interesting. They fight for their constituency, surgery day is open to everyone, they represent mostly the interests of the local industrialists, bankers and firms, as they are able to express their grievances to greater effect.

18 November

Alan gave a good talk on appeasement in the Northern Polytechnic. When we came home our minds were on this topic. Alan

1 Sir Arthur Bryant was appointed to the Watson Chair in American History, London University, in 1935. He was a member of the Beefsteak Club.

said that Horace Wilson, the chief spirit behind Chamberlain, never left papers behind. When Alan's pupil, Martin Gilbert[1], went to see him one day when he was retired at Bournemouth and Martin spoke about Alan's *Origins of the Second World War*, Horace Wilson pointed out "this man is now sitting on the Isle of Wight" – meaning Alan. Even in retirement he seemed to know everything.

Alan's club, the Beefsteak, might close because of financial difficulties. I asked Alan why he does not join Whites. I think this was the club where Nye Bevan was knocked down from behind by an ultra-Conservative member. Such people belong to this club and I think it is time it changed. Alan prefers the Beefsteak because there is a big table in the middle. Nobody can sit anywhere else and thus it is easy to start a conversation. In some of the clubs there are separate tables, people sit alone at small tables with no one to speak to.

22 November

We spoke about ourselves as historians. We are emotionally still remote and Alan is completely uninterested in other people. We also spoke about Churchill, who was always jealous and always afraid that a rival would appear. He was absolutely self-centred, but Lloyd George even at the peak of his career, could be very sensitive about others, and was always a good listener.

26 November

My old friend is coming to see us from America. Then Alan can speak to her about Nixon. Alan thinks Nixon was no better or worse than any other President and a better statesman than many as he ended the war in Asia. Alan's views would create quite an upheaval, if ever John Junor were to publish them.

Alan's views on nationalism are very sound and he is now

1 Martin Gilbert is a Fellow of Merton College, Oxford. He is the official biographer of Winston Churchill and has been historical adviser to the BBC on several War documentaries. He has written a great many books, including one on the appeasers, which he wrote with Richard Gott (see page 183). In 1966, he edited a collection of essays presented to A. J. P. Taylor.

reading a book on Belgium and Holland which gives a lot of new information on the subject and strengthens his non-conformist views. The Flamands speak Dutch, they are Roman Catholics with generally enlightened and left-wing views. The wealthy Flamands, who, in the past, for the most part spoke French, now speak Flemish like the rest. The number of Flamands living in Brussels is ever increasing and now they want Brussels to be Flemish. The Flamands strive for total equality in Belgium and yet the High Civil Service and Army is dominated by the French.

29 November

It seems that *The Times* is closing down because of the dispute between the managers and the shop floor workers. In reality it is a debate between industrialism and backwardness. It is like the Industrial Revolution all over again: there was no longer any need to employ handloom workers. In computerising the publishing process, you dispense with the need for printers. I was told that the Letters column was a great contribution to the formation of democratic opinion in Britain.

Our personal life seems a bit dried up. Sometimes we can't communicate as well as we used to. It might be the consequences of being so close together. I read the other day in the *Observer* that Mme Kollontai[1], an emotional and independent woman, frequently fell in love and went through divorce after divorce. She could not be dependent on her lover or husband emotionally and intellectually: a very independent woman, she found it too much of a strain. I think she was right. I can only manage because I keep some parts of my life apart from my emotions. I mean, if it hurts, I do not think about it.

We had a nice American woman, Sue Myers, who is an old friend of mine, here for dinner. She is an expert on African history. I was friendly with her in 1948–49 when I worked on Palmerston here in London. She and Alan discussed many European problems which Sue did not understand. Alan explained to her that it is best for Germany to remain divided. I remarked that Western Germany is already the strongest power in Europe. Alan said a

1 Alexandra Mikhailovna Kollontai (1872–1952), a Russian revolutionary, was the first woman ever to hold the rank of Ambassador. She served in Norway, Mexico and Sweden. Apart from her diplomatic career, she was a novelist and a campaigner for the emancipation of women.

united Germany would emerge again as an aggressive power, as she had done twice before, with horrifying consequences. She would only get her way at the expense of Poland and Czechoslovakia. Eastern Europe is rightly under the Soviet yoke because it is so much better than under the Germans. Stalin understood well enough that it was not his business to encourage Italian and French Communists to take over power.

Sue asked about Mrs Simpson. She told us she knew a girl who was in the escort of the couple before the abdication crisis and there was no doubt that they lived together. They shared an apartment and were seen only after midday. Alan said that the Prince wanted love, Mrs Simpson wanted power, but neither of them got what they wanted and by the time Mrs Simpson realised she could not be even a morganatic Queen, she could not get out of the business. Her great love later on was an American homosexual – a great misfortune for her.

Randolph Churchill's wife became the wife of Harriman. She said Randolph suffered as a result of being the son of a great man, as did Roosevelt's son. Randolph once invited Alan to dinner and some of his research fellows were ordered to prepare the dinner for them.

Before Sue turned up we went to Alan's seminar at the Institute for Historical Research. Michael Holroyd[1] spoke about biographies, mainly in connection with Shaw. He said biographers are not liked. He quoted Flaubert who said that man is nothing, his writings are everything. The whole lecture was very elegant, but no more than a collection of literary reflections. Alan said that biographers deal with something which once existed, genuine connections with practical life. History on the other hand is pure fiction, a record of mankind. Namier said that the historian's task is to write short biographies and put them together. For instance, the history of Parliament would emerge as the biographies of all MPs put together. Public opinion is sheer imagination; you can speak only about tendencies. Nobody says, "I am one of the masses". "Poor imbeciles," said Alan, "the Greeks did not know they lived BC."

1 Michael Holroyd is the author of several biographies, notably those of Hugh Kingsmill, Lytton Strachey, Augustus John and George Bernard Shaw.

1979

8 January

I came back from Budapest with a heavy heart. My sons have problems with their health.

Alan charmingly waited for me at the airport. He is a typical Aries: he wants to do everything efficiently and quickly and has warm feelings. He says he always believes in simple solutions.

Len Deighton wrote a piece about the Kennedy murder. He did not believe in the report of the Warren Commission, and went through it again and again. He was uncertain about another man who was also shot at. Alan said he was not at all bothered. Somebody shot three times. The President was killed, that is the end of the story.

A woman interviewer came today to ask Alan's opinion for a Gallup poll. One of the questions was what did he lack in life. Alan thought for a bit and said: "Lack of exercise, lack of sex, lack of beer."

He considers himself upper-middle class. He has been a member of the Labour Party since 1929. He watches one programme on the TV, he reads the *Observer* and sometimes the *Sunday Express*.

Alan recently wrote a piece for John Junor about inflation. Of course it was not published. Alan said in it that inflation will continue to rise; people do not work efficiently, but they work long hours. In 1973 when, under Heath, there was a three-day week, we had the most efficient working week for a long time.

Yesterday we went to the Academy. The most interesting

woman there was Kathleen Tillotson[1]. She is very clever, knows much about her subject, and is very honest and democratic. She understands Alan and me too.

I told Alan I had a colleague in Budapest who wanted to marry me, but I only liked him as a friend. We wanted to publish a documentary volume about British views on Hungary during the 'thirties. Alan remembered the then British Minister in Budapest who, by Alan's judgement, was very pro-Horthy and a Catholic. He was Sir Owen O'Malley, who represented the revisionist or rather pro-revisionist British view expressed by the Foreign Office: if the French and the little Entente had been successful it would have been harder to appease Germany because she would not have been able to penetrate economically in the small Eastern European countries. Therefore it was more advisable to tolerate revisionist Hungary. Aylmer Macartney[2] had the same view. O'Malley was always very anti-Soviet, and expressed the view many times to Alan that a strong Germany and Horthyite Hungary would be a safeguard against Bolshevism. Alan said he believed O'Malley was corrupt and was convinced he had strong ties with Hungarian Revisionist financial circles.

16 January

I think it is better to keep a diary once a week, let's say on Saturdays, and look back on the whole week. My relationship with Alan is improving daily. It is wonderful that I can tell him everything: tell him about my worries, about my historical writings, about my new glasses, about getting older, about the tenseness when we look at each other. I am afraid he thinks I am stupid and old and he thinks about how old he is. All the same, we are sitting worrying in our little love-nest.

When I write a book about Alan, there will be many chapters. One about his character, one about his relations with women,

1 Kathleen Tillotson, an expert on Dickens, was Mildred Carlisle Professor of English in the University of London at Bedford College from 1958–71. She was made an honorary Fellow of Somerville College, Oxford, in 1965. She is a frequent contributor to literary periodicals and, as a well-known literary critic, has written introductions to re-issues of many 19th century classics.

2 Aylmer Macartney is a British Conservative historian and an expert on Medieval and Modern Hungary. He is the author of *October Fifteenth, A History of Modern Hungary.*

one about our relationship, one about how he worries about practical things, one about him as a father, one about him as a friend, another about him as a historian and a sensitive man.

The events of the last few days were many. Anthony Howard, once the editor of the *New Statesman*, interviewed Alan about Dick Crossman. The TV crew came to Twisden Road and Alan answered Tony's questions. Alan wrote a piece about Crossman in *The Bedside Guardian* (1959) in which he mentioned that Crossman was like Burke. Later Alan explained to me that Crossman began his career as a philosopher and he imagined he would be another Plato. Then he was sacked from New College, Oxford because of his divorce, became a freelance journalist and worked as the political commentator for the *Daily Mirror*. For a while he worked for the *New Statesman* and following Kingsley Martin, he wanted to be the editor. But Kingsley wanted John Freeman,[1] who did in due course become the editor and Crossman left the paper. When Wilson became PM in 1964, he invited Crossman to be his minister which he did until 1970. After that he became the editor of the *New Statesman*. He was bad in this job and nobody liked him. Anthony Howard worked under him. Crossman had an idea about the Third World. He wanted to create a Third World in Europe from Socialist Governments. When he published the first volume of his diaries, Alan reviewed it. Now the third volume has come out in Tony's edition and so there is a great deal of publicity. There is not only a thirty year rule in issuing documents in the Public Record Office, but a fifteen year rule for ministers who publish their memoirs: they cannot refer to confidential papers, but must rely on their own memories.

20 January

I think Alan is the gentlest man in the world. The other day we went to see the parish churches in London near to Fleet Street, through small back streets. His face was sad or so I imagined. The funny thing about his character is that he looks very determined, but is always full of worries about practical problems. He

1 John Freeman subsequently became British High Commissioner in India from 1965 to 1968 and was British Ambassador in Washington from 1969 to 1971. Since then he has returned to work in the media, being Chairman of ITN (1976–81) and Governor of the BFI.

has no psychological problems at all. He would not like to live for ever. He says he would not mind leaving this world.

I told him how interesting it was that when Beatrice Webb's mother saw her little son dying, she told him not to worry: either he would get better or the Lord would give him a better and healthier body and relieve him from his sufferings. Alan said he could never understand these things. Then we spoke about Beatrice Webb, who had a sort of mysticism about her which she might have inherited from her family background. Alan recalled a dinner in Manchester when Alan and his family, Namier and the Muggeridges were present. Namier told some rather unpleasant stories about Beatrice Webb. Kitty Muggeridge said how right he was because Aunt Bo was a dreadful creature. Namier asked who Aunt Bo was: Oh, Beatrice Webb – then Namier began to apologise and said all the same, Beatrice was a very intelligent and interesting person. Kitty began to laugh and laugh and told him to go on and stop apologising. There was always some arrogance in the Potters. I said there is a certain amount of arrogance in the Taylors as well. Alan reflected this for a while and agreed that it was true. All his children have inherited this, some without his kindness, tolerance and understanding.

In the Beefsteak Club now you can have a drink before dinner with your wife. Alan goes there every Thursday, and there are old and young men. They all speak about Eton and tell anecdotes like this: Thomas Hardy and Macmillan had both been at a great dinner party, and Hardy was asked about his heroine, Tess. Sitting quite far from Macmillan, Hardy shouted toward Macmillan: 'She was quite a good milkcow for us, eh, wasn't she?' That was all he said.

Macmillan's wife was the mistress of Robert Boothby and one of his children was Boothby's. Macmillan never remarked about the affair, never commented. That was the right thing to do, Alan added.

We had a long conversation about H.G. Wells. Rebecca West once told Alan that all the past mistresses of H.G. Wells formed a trade union and used to meet. Both Wells and Lloyd George still had, in their early eighties, a very active sex life. Alan is very worried about this; he is wonderful, though he is only in his early seventies.

When Alan lived at home or in Oxford, he was always looked after and served. When he married, the first thing he did was to buy a coffee grinder and a pair of scissors. He made up his mind that his contribution to the family would be to prepare the breakfast: he had bought the scissors to cut the rind off the bacon. Nobody had thought about this before.

I am now reading *Middlemarch*. Alan's second wife saw Alan as Casaubon, I see myself as the heroine, Dorothea. George Eliot had a very independent and interesting life; it would be a good idea to write her biography from a modern point of view. I prefer biographies to fiction.

Alan will never write a book again. He thinks things are going to be rotten in Britain, he sees no future in this country. He has lost interest in writing history. He is quite happy to do the reviews, which he does well and quickly. There are always interviews about him. He is asked several times to give his opinion about writing history, about Crossman, about Beaverbrook, about the present-day affairs in Britain. Since I have been with him, he has been interviewed by Thames, by Italian TV and by the Dutch TV. He spoke on the TV about his favourite movie: *The Mask of Dimitrios*.

21 January

At the Elizabeth Hall we met Eddie and his wife. He is one of the best TV directors, very fond of Alan and adores his techniques. Still, it might be the end of their co-operation because the top BBC men might not want Alan any more. I think the "Revolution and Revolutionaries" series might have been too much for them. Eddie could not and would not give a straight answer.

Again about *Middlemarch*. Alan is not Casaubon, but I am like Dodo. I am reading the whole partnership with great interest. The one wants to help the other, the other does not want her help.

I met Gizella Ringrose. We saw *The Wedding* together. Gizella told me that after living here for thirty years, her childhood memories come back from our homeland. She was struck by the kindness of the British after the war, when the war damages were great, and Selfridges had to be reconstructed and there was an inscription: "We apologise to our customers for the inconvenience, which is due to the repairing of war damages." The kindness, tolerance and co-operation are really great achievements in this country and due to the wonderful, patient and modest upbringing of many good families. Gizella said a clever thing as well: women are longing more and more for society, they mostly need to be appreciated by more than one man. That is the consequence of their status in society.

The Dutch TV people interviewed Alan today. Intelligent, quiet people, who wanted to know many things about the present political life in Britain, Thatcherism, the Common Market, the trades unions, etc. Alan rightly said that as a historian he was not a futurologist. What is wrong with Thatcher is her style and character; she is not handicapped because she is a woman. She is like a school mistress and that is not a sympathetic trait in this country.

The English people are soft and obstinate. Once they are in the Common Market, they won't march out. On the whole though they do not notice they are in, they do not think they are European. Europe is on the other side of the Channel.

Somebody told me today that Co-op shops have an inscription: Panic buyers are welcome.

Alan says now that Britain is not in decay. He lived through the 'twenties, 'thirties and there were always crises – the General Strike, Hitler, the Second World War – and they always survived. We spoke about the Nuremberg Trials. Alan did not agree that people should be hanged because of their policies and generals should not be either. Churchill said after the Nuremberg Trials: "That is a good lesson for me. Never lose a war."

23 January

Great snow. Alan told me that when he was young he used to toboggan in Buxton. The main road, the Manchester Road, was closed for this purpose. Twisden Road is absolutely quiet as in a fairytale.

I asked Alan why he said to the Dutchman conducting an interview about Britain that Britain is a good place, and that people are better off than during the 'thirties. I knew his opinion was different. He said: "I do not want to give the impression to a foreign journalist that my country is in decay."

We argued again about the War criminals. Alan said they should not have been hanged. Churchill, Liddell Hart, and Hankey were against hanging. Hankey wrote a good book about it.

Yesterday we had the Elliotts here. They were teachers. We all agree that education in England is not authoritarian. In progressive schools youngsters often do what they want to do. A forerunner to this sort of education was Neill's approach: he gathered together difficult children and enlightened teachers.

When a child wanted to run away, he went with him and they came back together after a while.

Asa Briggs's new volume on broadcasting has appeared. There are references to Alan in it. It turned out that he was the one who really fought for ITV, which was approved in 1953 and came into existence in 1955.

8 February

In conversation I discovered that Halifax was called "holy fox" and Chamberlain, "the coroner".

We went to see Wells Cathedral. Pevsner rates it the second best English gothic cathedral after Salisbury. I asked Alan how many pre-Henry VIII cathedrals there were in Britain. He promptly answered thirteen. Then it turned out that there were sixteen. I took photos of both the exterior and the interior of Wells Cathedral. Many schoolchildren visited the cathedral and were told what to look at. The priest explained to them the history of the famous clock and the new statue of Christ. He said Christ's hands were lively as the cathedral itself.

I felt sulky this morning. Alan likes to read to me from the morning paper, but I don't like it because I am not a good listener. He thinks I am stupid. I told him that I am not as stupid as he thinks. He said I was but disguised it well. I thought he might not go on loving me, but he said he does not change in certain things, like morning coffee and loving me.

His youngest son from the second marriage, Daniel, came to see us. We spoke about divorces and I said to him that divorces are common things nowadays, better to do this than living on together without love. We spoke about the Hungarian uprising in 1956. Alan explained to him why it was a reactionary thing: either Russian tanks or American money.

9 February

We had a short conversation about Churchill and Roosevelt. Alan said that Churchill realised in 1944 that Stalin did not want to extend communism and realised he was not dangerous to Britain. Nico Henderson, who at that time was at the Foreign Office, said that Churchill and Eden would rather have co-operated with the

USSR than the USA and hoped to co-operate after the War. Roosevelt had more sense of liberal statesmanship than Churchill, but personally he was a ruthless dictator, a wicked man. Somebody said that he had never seen such a wicked face; he was a sham benefactor (faux-bonhomme).

10 February

Alan told me in the evening we should always be happy because we are perfect together.

We had Maurice Oldfield[1] and the Kees to dinner. Robert[2] and Cynthia were extremely smart. I gave them my Chartist book with a fine inscription which they seemed to appreciate. Robert is working on a TV programme for ITV and is anxious about how to do it. He is often in the British Museum which he does not like very much.

Maurice was not smart at all, as usual. He is a round faced Graham Greene figure. Le Carré's book is going to be filmed and Alec Guinness will play him, so they met in Oxford and Guinness made a study of him. Guinness is now putting on weight and wears black framed glasses so as to look like Maurice. Maurice, once Chief of MI6, is now retired and works in a historical field connected with his former job: intelligence between the wars. He was one of Alan's pupils. He said that the main sources of information during the 'thirties were Christie Ball for the Conservatives and Churchill's man. This man gave Churchill all the information about the German Air Force and rearmament with the consent of MacDonald and possibly with the knowledge of Baldwin. Samuel Hoare did not know about it. Maurice said they possibly let Churchill be well informed so that he could use it in his opposition speeches. Robert put very good questions to Maurice: how does he feel now after retirement and how did he feel when he was in service? Maurice opened up a bit and told us frankly that when he was in service, he felt that it was the most important thing in the nation's business. Now he sees that this was not the case. His most embarrassing moment was when

1 For an account of Maurice Oldfield's career, see page 174.
2 Robert Kee is the author of several books about the Second World War including *1939, The World We Left behind* and *1945, The World We Fought For*. He was literary editor of the *Spectator* in 1957 and took part in current affairs programmes and documentaries for both the BBC and ITV.

Sir Keith Feiling, discovering who he was, asked him straight out: "How many spies have we got now in the Soviet Union?"

12 February

I had a good chat at the Institute for Historical Research with Dickens, former Director of the Institute and academician. He welcomed me and spoke freely about himself from the very beginning. He spoke about the death of his lovely wife, about his well-to-do Yorkshire background (he came from a business family) and about his home in Highgate. He wants to move to Primrose Hill, into a large flat, where he can hang his numerous pictures. He thinks it is a good thing to have a hobby outside his interest in 16th century Britain. His views are broad and enlightened. They had a large committee from the Soviet Union last year and they were very frank in their opinions. They thought that the Russian view about the outbreak of the Second World War was not correct. He himself remembers, as do quite a lot of British people, that the British did not go to war against Hitler because they wanted to preserve the Empire, but because they felt he was dangerous for Europe, for every nation, including Britain. Of course, apart from the humanitarian reasons they wanted to survive, but at that time they knew that they would have to give up India for instance.

When I came home and told Alan about our conversation, he told me that it was true. But there were hardly any other nations in the world who moved as slowly against a threat as Britain and looked back in such fear. And Alan saying this trembled and looked back and the whole scene was so funny and so true; so really true!

15 February

Alan wants to destroy his autobiography because he feels he was not fair to his second wife. But otherwise, he said, he could not have kept his children. If he left this out, the whole autobiography would be dishonest. He also feels he involved me unfairly.

16 February

We went to see an exhibition on Biedermayer, Vienna. It was closed, so we came back on this windy, damp February afternoon. On the way back we had a very good chat about Connie Zilliacus. He was Finnish by birth, a lovely character. He was one of those Labour MPs who were expelled from the party when there was a debate on Nenni and on Italian communism. About twenty were expelled, and none of them went back. Zilliacus used to write to the *New Statesman* under pseudonyms like Vigilantes or Covenanter. In 1932 he was secretary to Arthur Henderson during the Disarmament Conference. Someone should write a biography of Zilliacus.

17 February

Scafell is the highest point in England. Why do people go hill-walking? Exercise, joy, solitude, love of nature. Coming down is absolute torture.

When Disraeli came home each evening, his wife offered him a cup of beef tea. In those days people still gave it to tired or ageing people to make them stronger.

We went through British history to find out who had mistresses. The Kings usually had. Nell Gwynne was the mistress of Charles II. When the mob wanted to hinder her travel, she used to bend out from the coach and say to the mob: "I am the Protestant whore."

PMs usually had mistresses too, except Baldwin, Chamberlain, Balfour and Peel. When Rebecca West was young and sat between Lloyd George and Asquith at a dinner party, she was blue and red below from being pinched by Asquith. On the other side of her, Lloyd George tried to stir her by putting his hands up her skirt, but as he was not encouraged, he did not go any further.

21 February

I have become – I hope for good – very independent minded. I did not want to weigh on Alan and did not want to be like a chicken who forgets everything when the cock arrives. I want to be independent from his mind, though I go on loving him dearly. We discussed how he suffered from being too intelligent, though he tries not to suffer. Unlike Lord Birkenhead who said he would sooner keep a live coal in his mouth, than a witty remark.

We had a conversation about the *Guardian* correspondents in Europe before and during the war. Voigt was as anti-Nazi as he was anti-Communist. Dalma was the *Standard* correspondent in Paris before then, after him came John Waine. Dalma was educated in Germany during the First World War, then he became a correspondent in Berlin. In 1932 when Hitler made his election tour by aeroplane, he went with him. He was the only British journalist who was at the Reichstag fire. He enjoyed the company of Göbbels and Putzi Hofstaengel, because he got to know a lot about them and from them. For this reason, in Britain he was thought to be pro-Nazi. But during the war he made speeches in German for German Radio and made it clear he was not a Nazi. He wrote his autobiography – Alan said it was very interesting.

Wodehouse also became nasty in the eyes of many British, when he was asked to write about his experiences in a Nazi camp. He revealed quite frankly, that though he was elderly, he could adapt himself quite quickly, well and adequately to the hardships of the concentration camp. He could even write two good books there. Because of his statement – that some Germans could be humane as well – he was shunned by the English. Malcolm Muggeridge went to Paris and helped him escape to the house of Rothschild, then over the border to Switzerland, from where Wodehouse went to America and never returned to Britain. He aimed to write 100 books. He died before that. (He might have finished ninety.) Before his serious books, he wrote musicals.

22 February

We had a heavy discussion after Alan returned from his seminar. I said I did not accept the view that Hitler was pacifistic and orderly in 1936. I thought he could have been stopped at the Rhineland Crisis. Alan did not think this; he felt I judged history by morality. I do not. I was frightened when he, believing in contracts as he does, did not see that the Versailles Treaty was broken mainly and first by Britain. It was a mistake to make a bargain with Hitler. We could not agree. I felt he twisted my arguments; he felt I did not know enough.

Reading the second chapter of his autobiography I felt (and I said so) that I could understand him better, his fears, his audacity, his behaviour towards women. I said I was afraid he was a prey to flatterers. The difficulty is that Alan's flatterers flatter the right person. Alan said, why not be with people who like you, rather than those who dislike you and want to change your character? He said he was not a missionary, but a spectator. Me too – I said – but I am a missionary as well; I want to change people. He just wants to understand the other person's views, which might be intellectually stimulating.

23 February

I restore my spirits by writing my autobiography. Loving means giving up a bit of ourselves. It is difficult to find a happy medium between loving and preserving myself. I feel I am closer to finding it. To live completely alone is not good. To live with a loved one is to find a way to live alone and let your partner live alone in a routine, in a framework, a partnership. I think Alan is happier when I am having breakfast in bed. He looks after me and enjoys his morning independence. So it also gives me a little time to think about the past and the days ahead and also time to read more.

Yesterday Alan gave a very good interview, in which he said that the facts and dates provide him with the framework when he lectures and then it is easy for him to provide the narrative.

Maurice Oldfield wrote a very warm letter thanking us for the dinner. Alan said he was a cold-warrior and anti-Communist and he would sacrifice his friends and human feelings for his political conviction.

27 February

Alan was very distressed yesterday. He gave a contribution to the "Start the Week" discussion on Monday on BBC 4. He was not given enough opportunity to speak and he had companions whom he detested, like Nicolai Tolstoy, a tall, gaunt figure, a monarchist and a confused one, and Oswald Mosley from Paris, by telephone, who tried to show himself to be a good patriot who, when needed, would fly straight back to Britain.

We spoke about pornography. Alan said that *Fanny Hill* is still not available in the British Library except when you produce a letter of introduction. *The Rainbow* by D.H. Lawrence was banned for ten years in 1916, *Lady Chatterley's Lover* was published in Italy in 1960 and smuggled into Britain by individuals. *Ulysses* was banned until the end of the war. The catalogue sign 'ϕ' in the British Library means the work is pornographic and should not be given to readers.

Speaking about Churchill's V sign, Alan told me that it was understood by ordinary British people to mean "Serve you right . . . " Churchill did not know life at all, did not understand why his sign became so popular. Stalin understood.

Today a Brazilian man came and interviewed Alan. When I said something, as Alan always encourages me to do, he looked at me, amazed that I had spoken. The role of women in his country is probably entirely different.

28 February

We went to the local pub where we can chat so well. Alan said no one can judge history, we can only observe. For instance Voigt said before Hitler came to power that the Poles behaved very badly against the minorities in the Ukraine. When Hitler came to power the same Voigt said that the poor Poles should be defended against the nasty Nazi behaviour. He said that aggressive wars are very bad, but wars were always aggressive. At Nuremberg people were not on trial because Hitler was against the Jews, but because he was against Russia and the USA.

2 March

Alan is reviewing a book about anti-semitism in Britain. He thinks that the most attractive targets in Britain are still the Jews, because they have been given peerages and leading positions which the Pakistanis have not. Wilson did not give a peerage to a single Pakistani. The head of ICI is a Jew; Great Universal Stores is owned by Jews (Burton shops, Horne shops); Marks and Spencer is totally Jewish and they are Zionist, ardent Jews who participate in charitable activities for the benefit of other Jews; Unilever is Jewish-run. All the top schools do not like to take Jews. Highgate takes only ten percent. Westminster does not take anybody unless they go to Abbey which means Jews have to attend services. There is a social and latent anti-semitism.

Alan has kept a reading list ever since 1927. It shows that in his best years he read 300 books per year; now he is down to under 100. (Of course the 300 books included poetry and thrillers.)

Alan borrowed one of Lord Berners' books for me from the London Library. What lovely books he wrote! I liked best his *Far from the Madding War*. Frivolous without being cynical, sad and gay, clever and simple. Some examples: "It has been said that humanity may be roughly divided into hosts and guests. A psychologist has explained the types as representing two kinds of will, the will to power and the will to subjection". "Birth is a shock that very sensitive people never get over. American women have womb-chambers constructed in their houses so that they can shut themselves up in them whenever the complex gets bad. I remember in the Stuyvesant-Kruger divorce case, one of the principal grounds for divorce was that the wife always found her husband sitting in the womb-chamber when she wanted to go there herself". In nine cases out of ten, people commit suicide for completely different reasons from what one might imagine. It may be that one is suddenly overwhelmed by a sense of discouragement. Or perhaps one is merely tired of having to dress every day, like the suicide of Mark Twain, who left a note which read: "Tired of buttoning and unbuttoning". "If you are irritated by some characteristic, it often means you have got it yourself". "I am a mental coward and I can't face theories".

3 March

We went to the American School with Alan's son and daughter-in-law and grand-daughter. Here they teach small children from the age of two up to twelve with the famous Suzuki method. In a great gymnasium about eighty children played the violin with four violin teachers. They played Bach, Vivaldi and Schubert beautifully. The children cannot read the scores, they play by ear. This is the essence of the Suzuki teaching. This method has been very popular for two decades.

Alan has to write the obituary of Rudolph Hess who is now eighty-five years old. He used to write to his wife to tell her how to bring up their son who became an architect and used to visit Alan in order to persuade him to back a campaign to release his father. Hess always maintained that Hitler was right and it was the duty of Britain and Germany to fight together against Russia. Alan spoke about the Jews again. He said that the great anti-Jewish pamphlet, "The Elders of Zion" was written originally against Napoleon III. When many Jews came from Germany to England, people talked about "refujews" instead of refugees.

5 March

We invited Antonia and Harold Pinter and Joanna and Terry Kilmartin[1] for dinner. When I spoke on the phone to Joanna, Alan said I should say that the love-birds will be here as well (meaning Antonia and Harold). Joanna said she knew only one pair of love-birds in London and they are Alan and Eva. Alan wanted to invite Kathleen Tillotson and thought about inviting Stephen Spender with his wife Natasha, but changed his mind and said they were not on the same wave-length as Stephen. I said I was not on the same wave-length as Pinter. But Alan's answer was, "Nobody is on the same wave-length as Harold."

I went to the Public Record Office. I am preparing a book on British-Hungarian Relations after the Second World War. Tremendous material. They called the year 1948–9 the decisive year and the People's Democracies sometimes "transcurtainian" countries.

I met a girl from Venezuela, and she said there are only two progressive nations in South America, Venezuela and Columbia.

In the evening Alan read *Gulliver's Travels* to me. He said it was meant to be a satire, not written for children.

9 March

We are in Sheffield. On the way here we saw the wonderful cathedrals at Newark and Lincoln. The Lincoln one is nearly as famous as York Minster. It has a spectacular view; people say that from Lincoln Cathedral you can see as far as the Russian mountains. We were lodged in Sheffield in the house of a history

1 Terry Kilmartin has been the literary editor of the *Observer* since 1952. A French scholar, he has translated works by André Malraux, Henry de Montherlant and Proust.

professor who is going blind. He is already learning the Braille alphabet, and is very serene, no fuss, no complaints. Alan gave a lecture to the Sheffield Historical Association about "Economic Appeasement", about the relations between the Bank of England and Nazi Germany during the 'thirties and about the opposition of the private factories to British rearmament. About 500 people were present and the president thanked Alan for coming such a long way and for sharing his enormous knowledge with his listeners for no reward.

Alan gives a lecture in the same way as he speaks. He explains how things happened in such a way that it becomes clear to everyone. For instance he explained so simply why there are food shortages in wars. The peasantry are called up first of all, because the industrial workers have to stay in factories as long as possible. Alan thinks that journalism taught him to speak in a precise, dense and clear way. He is the historian, A.J.P. Taylor – Alan Taylor is the TV star. Poor Alan, sometimes he is very tired and very eager to get love and success. He has had great success.

After Sheffield we went to Leeds and on the way we saw one of the most famous Cistercian monasteries of England: Fountains Abbey. We not only saw how the monks lived, but also the way in which they became more and more worldly. In Leeds Alan spoke about Lloyd George. This was also a success.

Then came York which is, I think, one of the most beautiful towns in England. We walked on the walls, we visited Bootham School, the Quaker school which formed Alan's character in many ways. The school is 150 years old, untidy and smells of oil, as my old school did in Eastern Hungary, in my native town of Miskolc. It was very interesting to watch Alan as he walked about the town as he would have done at home. In York we settled down in the same hotel that Alan's parents used to stay in when they visited Alan. This hotel was built in the middle of the last century with an entrance from the train station. The corridors were wide in order that the ladies in their rich skirts could stroll easily with all their luggage and servants. From our room we could see the wonderfully illuminated Minster.

14 March

Today is my younger son Pisti's birthday. In my thoughts I went through my life with my children.

Yesterday we went to Simpson's in the Strand. It is an old and out of date place – at least that's what we felt. In the old days it was a place where gentlemen ate in the evening. Now second-rate businessmen and people from the countryside come here, and it's quite a good place to show to visitors. We had a lovely rare beefsteak there.

I am now reading the story of Victor Gollancz. I would like to collect all the LBC books. Alan talked about John Strachey and his family a great deal. His uncle was Lytton Strachey and his sister is Julia, a good writer. One of his sisters married an architect, called Ellis. They all kept up their left-wing views except for John who tended to the right. He wrote an angry letter to the *New Statesman* when Alan was fighting against nuclear warfare. Strachey said in his letter that such a man as Alan, who wants to leave his motherland without defence, should not be a fellow of Magdalen. Alan answered that he might well not be good enough to be fellow of Magdalen, but that should be decided by historians, not by politicians. One thing he could say was that he had never fought with Mosley or been directed by the Marxists. His widow told Alan that this letter killed John Strachey.

There was a good article in the *Guardian* about lavatories. In the early nineteenth century there were coaches which collected the night soil in London and took it away to Western Gardens. In the middle of the nineteenth century wells were still polluted – for instance the one at Windsor which caused the Prince Consort to die of typhoid fever.

22 March

Yesterday we had Antonia Fraser and the Kilmartins to dinner. Antonia looked very smart and serene. Her good, controlled behaviour is probably the consequence of her Catholic education. Pinter could not come because of the National Theatre strike. Twenty-seven people are on strike and Harold is on the committee dealing with the problem. Antonia said actors are not well paid; Gielgud might get £300 a week, but none of the ordinary actors get more than £150. None of our guests sympathised though with the strikers; they said they had money and wages enough, they just wanted more.

Later we spoke about Michael Károlyi with Alan and he remembered how few followers he had as the leader of the Democratic Club in London. He hired a flat for the club and took teapots and teaspoons with him in a bag and the members were mainly waiters and Michael Polányi[1]. And Károlyi said, "Here are my followers, waiters, all of them work in cheap restaurants." Alan remembered that amongst the Czech emigrés, Osusky[2] and Beneš always quarrelled. That is why Osusky went to France where he died much later, after the war.

This will be the first time that I vote. Choosing candidates is an expensive affair. It costs about £150 to put up a candidate and on top of that there is the cost of distributing the election leaflets about him. Sometimes Conservatives take the electors to the polling station. It is a common joke by Labour voters, that they let themselves be carried by Conservative cars, then vote for the Labour candidate. Alan's first son, a staunch Labour man, said the main thing is to make the people go to vote.

26 March

Dinner with the Kees. Peter Jenkins[3] and his wife and John Grigg[4] and his wife were there. There were champagne and servants to wait at table. Cynthia and Robert's children were present as well. Cynthia, talking about Antonia, said I should read a book written by Antonia's sister about her: *The Beautiful*. She also said what a good friend Joanna Kilmartin was to her. Robert collected us at Kew Station. We discussed our works during the dinner. Robert said it was not a good idea that I was allowed to make Xerox copies in PRO instead of copying. John Grigg disagreed and said he thought it was much quicker and more efficient. It is just a question of money. Peter Jenkins insulted Alan, and so he wanted

1 Michael Polányi (1891–1976) was a Hungarian physical chemist who did notable work on reaction kinetics and crystal structure. He was elected a Fellow of the Royal Society in 1946 and awarded the American le Comte du Nouy award in 1959 for his books on the compatibility of science and religion.

2 Stefan Osusky (1889–1973) was a founder of the Republic of Czechoslovakia and a leader of the resistance against both Nazi and Communist domination. He was Ambassador to Britain and France and a Representative at the League of Nations.

3 Peter Jenkins became Political Commentator and Policy Editor on the *Guardian* in 1974. Before then, he was Labour Correspondent and Washington Correspondent for the same paper. He was also Theatre Critic on the *Spectator* from 1978 to 1981.

4 John Grigg was a columnist for the *Guardian* from 1960 to 1970 and was active in Conservative politics until 1982 when he joined the SDP. He has written several biographies, among them, one of Nancy Astor.

to leave. (He said nasty things about Beaverbrook.) John's godmother and godfather were Nancy Astor and Philip Kerr[1]. He said their relationship was not at all platonic.

I got a letter from my son Ferencz. We are very close to each other.

28 March

I asked Alan whether he had ever hated anyone in his life. He never has. He disliked some, but did not seek the company of those he disliked. He dislikes aggressive, conceited people, who think that what they say is right, who always seem to know best. Of course, Alan said, he himself knows best, but he does not show off about it. He does not want to convince others.

Alan said *Alice in Wonderland* is the most wonderful book he has ever read.

I am now reading Lord Berners' *First Childhood*. He describes life in a public school. He thought it was terrible in many ways. Games were the key to a strong character and unless you happened to excel in them there was little likelihood of you ever being good at anything in later life.

30 March

Yesterday we had Bob Boothby, his wife Wanda (and her dog Fufu), Alan's daughter-in-law Janet and his son Giles to dinner. Bob is dying. But even so, he could still be charming and polite and contribute something to the conversation. Of course it was easy to see that he was a society man. Always had something to tell; when there was a silence in the conversation, he asked Alan where he would go for a holiday, what would he most prefer? Then I recognised the public school education in him. He said about himself: "This is what old age does." He is eighty. He does not eat. He drinks a lot of wine and coffee and smokes cigarettes. He loves his wife Wanda and Wanda loves him. Wanda is a bit vulgar, but has picked up a cut glass accent and a frivolous

1 Philip Henry Kerr, Marquess of Lothian (1882–1940) was a journalist and statesman. His last appointment was as Ambassador to the United States in 1939.

way of speaking. For instance, when the conversation turned to Baldwin and his lover, Mrs Davidson, Wanda asked abruptly: "And was there any good fuck between them?" Janet was shocked. Bob said there was, which was something Alan did not know. Alan was funny, kindly criticising Bob all the time for publishing his memoirs five times. Bob retorted saying what an extremely readable book it was. They agreed on Baldwin, whom they liked. Once Baldwin said to Bob that he had never been interested in foreign affairs and never really interfered. Boothby very much disliked Chamberlain; he said he had never known a more horrid man. But it might be the aristocrat in him against the Birmingham businessman. Boothby was the first and best Keynesian. He was also the lover of Lady Dorothy Macmillan for some thirty years. Lady Dorothy was a very strong-willed woman, as Wanda is. Bob could not marry Wanda as long as Dorothy was alive. Macmillan took his revenge on Bob when he made him a life peer instead of First Lord of the Admiralty, which he wanted so much to be, so that he could have the yacht which goes with this position and take his friends sailing.

1 April

Malta has become independent and the last British Navy ships have withdrawn from the island. Alan told me a lot about this historic event, explaining that it had been prepared for a long time and the day, this day, was fixed far in advance. Even the Labour Party wanted to keep the island; the last plan was that they should ask the USA to keep the island and allow the British Navy to stay there, but the Americans did not want to be involved. Alan said that with no Navy in the Mediterranean, there was no need to keep Malta. Malta had been a good place for repairing ships during the Second World War. The Maltese order, the Order of St. John, had two places: one in Prague and one in Rome. Many retired British people wanted to settle down in Malta as it has a good coast, uses sterling and the cost of living is lower, but many came back when it became clear that independence was inevitable.

Alan spoke about the Red Cross. Henri Dunant, the Swiss philanthropist, went to see the battlefield of Solferino in 1859 and was upset by the cruelty going on. In Geneva, he set up the centre for the Red Cross and appealed for money to sovereigns in Europe. The Czar Alexander was most generous. Under Stalin the Soviets did not want to belong to the Red Cross and so in the Second World War the Red Cross could not interfere with the Germans' treatment of Soviet prisoners.

Alan was furious that he had to answer questions for the coming election about his race, the date he came to Britain and so on. He decided to answer: race: Human; date of arrival in England: In 1906; place of birth: Womb – and so on. Speaking about the elections, it is clear that everywhere elections were thoroughly corrupt. Until the time of Baldwin it was not stated how much a Conservative could give to the party to be a candidate. Later the Conservative Party made a rule that candidates could not give more than a certain sum, otherwise the wealthiest man would always be the successful candidate. It was really the secret ballot at the end of the nineteenth century which put an end to the corruption. Until then the people did not dare to vote for the candidate they preferred. In about 1912 there was a pit owner who found out that the miners had not voted for the Conservative and he turned them all out of their cottages as a result.

3 April

Yesterday we visited Snigs End, which was a Chartist settlement, before going to Lowbands a few miles away. That was a grim experience. From outside, the Chartist houses all looked the same. When we went into the pub, which was the school for the Chartist children, it was raining heavily. The pub was dark and cold. One deaf old man sat in the corner, contentedly sucking his pipe. I asked the man who ran the pub if he had heard about O'Connor, about the Chartists. None of them had. The deaf man probably could not hear what I asked, the others just reflected on "those allotments". There were no carpets and the pub had oiled walls, like an old, cold unpleasant school-hall. We saw about a dozen houses of the old Chartist settlements with a small patch of land in front or behind them, in very good condition.

Lowbands looked more cheerful. The sun came out for a while and the houses looked brighter as well, surrounded by low hills.

It seemed to me that Chartism had no effect at all in this Island. It does not belong to the so called national and traditional history of this nation. Feargus' weather-beaten workers are still here, but they have never heard about Chartism. The young generation is looking forward to buying houses, cars, going to the East or to America, having colour televisions and so on.

I told Alan that I should go away for a while because I miss the devoted letters which he wrote to me in Budapest. He said that was a bad idea and that we should not waste time as we do not have much left.

8 April

Coming back from Wales. Alan spoke with a wisdom and compassion which is rare in human beings. There is a hopeless nationalistic feeling amongst the Welsh. They want to preserve their national identity. They try to do so in a way which will make them stand apart from England, but the influence of the whole British system has already made them completely attached to England.

Swansea is the place where Dylan Thomas was born. Alan, who knew and disliked him, said he did not speak Welsh at all. South Wales is very industrial and not regarded as properly Welsh by the North. Quite a lot of people have never heard of or visited Lampeter, where we were. There are five universities in Wales; most of them have more English students than Welsh as Welsh students usually prefer to go to English universities. The land in Wales belongs mainly to the universities and some to English landlords.

I asked Alan to write a book about historical figures, he knows so many funny things about them. Also I asked him to write about how famous people died. He knows quite a lot about this as well. Alan said that when Hume died, he said: "I am off." Boswell asked Johnson how he felt. He said he would like to bargain with Charon, but Charon said, "go on, hurry up there are lots of people waiting for me". Voltaire said: "I am going to meet the great beyond." Alan wants to ask the doctor what the symptoms are and before he answers, he will die.

12 April

We ate at the Gay Hussar. Everything was pleasant, everybody greeted Alan with great reverence: "Mr Taylor, oh . . ." The Hungarian meal, stuffed cabbage and everything was very good, but tasted unhungarian, fake. Never mind, we were looked after very well. Alan said Soho is a place which could be found in every great city, with pseudo Italian, Chinese and French restaurants. Tottenham Court Road is different: vulgar, rather seedy English.

14 April

We went for a walk on the Heath on this wonderful Easter afternoon. We had guests, among them Christopher Faulkus from Weidenfeld. One guest said that Churchill's family did not provide Martin Gilbert with the letters Churchill had written. There may be many personal documents waiting for future historians.

15 April

A new book came out about the death of Hitler. Alan believes that nothing new can be said on the subject after Trevor-Roper's classic account. Witnesses, the survivors might add something, but witnesses are usually unreliable.

Sebastian, Alan's journalist son, told us that North Sea oil will make England richer for the next ten years. Already ninety-one percent of oil used in Britain comes from the North Sea. Also there will be a new phenomenon: three million unemployed. There might be negative inflation, which means that prices will go down.

Walking in Highgate Cemetery. Wonderful view. Volunteers have been asked to help clear the cemetery, to plant new seeds and trees. Henry Hunt[1] lies here, Walter Neurath[2] and many others.

18 April

We went to see Heronsgate or O'Connorville (another name for it), the first of the Chartist allotments, 103 acres altogether. The Chartist allotments are still the same: two, three and four acres

1 Henry Hunt (1773–1832) sometimes called "Orator Hunt", was a radical agitator whose speech on the occasion of the Peterloo massacre cost him three years imprisonment. He was an active campaigner for the repeal of the Corn Laws and MP for Preston 1831–33.

2 Walter Neurath founded Thames and Hudson Ltd, the art publishers.

each. I met a woman called Dorothy Haig who still lives in the old Chartist house and is very proud of having the original four acres. She drew the map for Miss Hadfield's work on the Chartist allotments. Dorothy, the daughter of an architect, is now an elderly lady with a cat. She is a perfectionist. The whole community is still a community, middle-class conventional people. The Chartist houses now have every comfort, even swimming pools. The owners like to ride and everyone has a car; the houses are now worth £70,000 – £80,000. The whole area around Heronsgate (near Watford, twenty miles from London) is a stock-broker area.

Later we went to see Hughenden Manor, the home of Disraeli – not a big house, but a nice place to work. Disraeli spent more than thirty years here; his wife died here in 1872 and he remained here until his death in 1881. The Berlin Congress room is very interesting, as are his study and the library, and the staircase where all the portraits of men whom he liked were hung.

Alan and I discussed which historians were also journalists and we found: Friedjung, Szekfü, Macaulay, Carlyle – not a bad company.

21 April

We had Alan's granddaughter, Claire, for the day. Alan read her funny rhymes and told her about television and televisioff – a good joke. Alan is fed up with life. He sometimes quotes Wells who said on his death bed: "Damn you all." Gulliver considered the human race to be a bad race, and that is why he rather loved horses. I do not share these views.

23 April

We spoke about the House of Lords. At least 100 Lords do not turn up; Alan said some might be insane, some hereditary ones might live in Canada or in the States or even not be British subjects. He thinks that democracy works in such a way that the majority does decide things but so slowly the delays can be damaging.

25 April

Alan spoke about his second wife who was very jealous of the first family, of "the others". She imagined that love is as big as that – Alan showed a loaf-length – and then if you love somebody else, there would remain less for her. Alan said love was immeasurable, could be infinite.

Yesterday a man came to the door and said "Hello Mr. Taylor, I'm from the Conservative party". Alan simply answered "No thank you" and shut the door.

26 April

My days in Venice with Alan. This was the first time that I had been to Venice, not from Budapest, but from London. It is interesting to watch British behaviour at the airport; they are always so well-informed and confident on the plane and abroad. In Venice everything is European again. Women are not as kind as in Britain, the clothes they wear are more monotonous. Venice airport is very small and not as well organized as Heathrow. The British are very practical and independent.

Visiting Venice is like coming home. Our Hotel, "La Calcina" is where Ruskin used to stay in 1877. He hated the view; he could not bear to look at Palladio's church. I find the view tremendous. I am now reading Elizabeth Bowen's *The House in Paris*. The girl, Henrietta, is very English and looks upon the French woman as a foreigner whose mind and way of thinking are also foreign. It is true. The English girl was taught not to disturb people if they were deep in thought, but this would not have occurred to the French girl.

In Ravenna. The town lost more people during the Second World War than any other Italian town. Resistance was strong here, because the main railway line to Germany went through the city.

27 April

We went again to see the best small building in the world: Santa Maria di Miracoli. In the evening, Alan fell asleep in my arms; I did not want to move. It was complete harmony. He said later his former wives did not find him lovable as I did. I said they did not know how to love. The first was unhappy, the second spoilt. I have had so much love from my parents, sisters, husband, children and friends that I have some to give.

We went to see the Modern Art gallery. Two Matisses, one Arp, and an early Henry Moore were excellent. Across the Rialto we found a good little German place to eat. Then we went to see more churches; amongst them was the most beautiful one, Scuola S. Giorgio with the Carpaccios. Alan said he came to Venice in 1964 specially to see the Carpaccio exhibition and Beaverbrook paid his travel expenses.

I loved the Tiepolos in the Chiesa della Pieta.

29 April

A day in Padua which reminded me of Miskolc. It is a rather neglected small Italian town. I did not like the way people behaved. They are not kind to their children. The northern inhabitants in each country are ruder. The university is interesting enough from the outside, but not as much as one would have thought. I took photos of the Statue of Gattamelatta, the Venetian Condottiere, a masterpiece by Donatello and the first great Renaissance bronze cast in Italy. The best thing in Padua is Cappella Scrovegni. The interior is decorated with Giotto's famous frescoes, painted at the height of his fame.

Returning home: Venice. I commented to Alan that we have many homes. One at Twisden Road, one in Venice, one in Budapest (for me), one in Oxford (for him) and one in the Lake District.

Alan said in the evening that all his life he has been an international Socialist. He does not bother about the Labour Party or any others, but is a Socialist nevertheless. I said that he not only is a Socialist, but always acts as one.

3 May

Today is election day in Britain. I hope Thatcher doesn't win, although Sebastian said every change is good and economically it would not make much difference. I doubt that.

I hear the morning noises: Alan jumping into a cold bath and out again quickly. It means to me his efficiency, gaiety and self-assurance. I suddenly thought how kind he was when I came back from Budapest; he had kept all my post carefully, and we sat down together and read everything. Love is so precious, we have to keep it, guard it, feed it and preserve it.

4 May

Thatcher is in. Alan said we shall now see the blessings of the Conservative Government.

Yesterday we went to Grado and Aquileia. Grado is wonderful. The church, the basilica and the whole atmosphere of the little seaport is lovely. My parents came here quite often. It belonged to Austria-Hungary until 1918. I did not like Aquileia as much; it is a show place. The Basilica's mosaic is unique. The people, the sounds, the flowers, were all very like those of Tapolca, my childhood holiday resort.

I am now reading Jane Austen's *Persuasion*. She is rather liked by aristocratic Tories, like Cecil and Macmillan. Though she is very critical towards them, the milieu which she evokes and criticises is very familiar to them.

6 May

A day in the cemetery at St Michele. We visited again the graves of Stravinsky, Diaghilev and Ezra Pound. The cemetery is cheerful, everything is white marble. On the stones there are the photos of dead people, young and healthy looking children. Only the Greek and Evangelical parts of the cemetery are neglected. When we came back a woman told us she could not afford to be buried in St. Michele.

We then went and sat in "our" garden, where we usually go when in Venice. Girls were skating and cycling, boys played with balls, everything was noisy and cheerful in that typically Italian way. I found the Italians very polite, but felt that they do not bother about how they look.

8 May

Coming back from Ravenna, I found in my hotel room in Venice twenty lovely roses from my sons. Mother's day, but it was more. They understood me and loved me.

9 May

As I am reading Tom Sharpe's *Porterhouse Blue* Alan told me that it is based on Magdalene College, Cambridge, which is smaller than Oxford's Magdalen and much more sociable. It is run like a social club and fellows from Oxford's Magdalen are courteously received by the President.

16 May

When one does not yet feel at home living in a foreign country, one has to make the best use of each day. I met Alan in the bus station by chance; he looked different: a little old man with a sweet face. When I saw a picture of him taken in 1962 by Tom Blau, I saw a man of strong character with a wonderful, forceful profile. He has become much softer in his seventies and probably a bit more inclined to follow other people's advice though not too much. He has a way of pushing his lower lip forward, which means he still has a very strong will.

I saw a wonderful film called *Wifemistress*, about a woman who, after the death of her husband, becomes thoroughly independent. She does not belong to anyone any more. I have often seen this happen with widows.

We often speak about historians. Alan told me a lot about the background of Cole and Carr. Cole was much closer to the working classes; he was adviser to the Trade Unions, and politically active until the end of the 'twenties when he discovered that he was diabetic and felt he had to preserve his strength. He was a man of great passions. Carr's background was probably not high middle class, but civil servant. He was in the Foreign Office. He felt unhappy in Riga. Though he calls himself Marxist, it is difficult for him to build up close relations with the workers.

We spoke about Chaucer. Perhaps these days Chaucer is not

much read by the working classes, but he was. Some miners and railwaymen in the last century went to evening classes in order to be able to read Chaucer and Shakespeare.

I am often asked what the secret of Alan's productivity is. Apart from his quick mind, his main advantage is his ability to concentrate on everything he does and the fact that he crams all sorts of different activities into his days: reading, crosswords, letter-writing, working, lunch, sleeping, walking, tea, reading, dinner, reading, music.

I am now reading C.M. Vines's *A Little Nut-Brown Man. My three years with Beaverbrook*. Alan said Vines was so stupid that he really entertained Beaverbrook through his stupidity. Neither Beaverbrook's wife, Christophor, nor Vines had a sense of humour. Vines believed everything that Beaverbrook said.

20 May

Alan said about Christophor Beaverbrook that she was the secretary of James Dunn, the aluminium king in Canada, the great friend of Beaverbrook. Christophor nursed Dunn when he was old and ill. She said to his wife, please will you nurse him or I shall do so. She did and then she married him. Then she nursed Beaverbrook and when he died, she wanted to nurse Lord Roseberry, but he was very cautious and said: "You must have a hobby." And so horse racing became her hobby. Now she spends at least £300,000 a year on her hobby.

22 May

When Beaverbrook wrote an introduction to Alan's sixtieth birthday volume, he was already going to die. He told Martin Gilbert, the editor, that there were three versions of the end and the choice would depend on whether he was dead or alive. He was dead, and this version was kept. Beaverbrook's book *Courage* was written about his wife's first husband, James Dunn. In this book Dunn was a caricature of himself and so after publication Lady Dunn went and bought every available copy of it. Now the book is very rare and very expensive.

When Alan was a boy, his friend's mother said of him: "This boy is satanic." So he is. I am glad to hear this. In a way it is flattering as it shows that he was remarkable at such an early age. I went to see the portrait of Alan painted by June Mendoza. Frightfully good, except the nose and mouth, which she promised to correct. Mendoza is a sensitive, attractive woman, emotionally free and open. She lives in a pathetic, sombre house, at least so it seemed to me; her husband and children are all busy. She is Australian by birth. Her difficult mother brought her to the brink of a nervous breakdown.

We spent the other evening with Robert Skidelsky and David Marquand. Both are lively, nice scholars. Robert is arrogant but in a nice way; he said that every nation did better without Keynes. Britain, whose leaders tried to follow his advice, is the worst off and the most muddled in her economic thinking. David Marquand spoke about Brussels and the EEC. The top men are worthless, he said; those who do the job and understand what goes on cannot be followed; there are many bureaucrats and well chosen appointees from every country.

A hostess told me that whenever a guest is not welcome, the drink is kept back for a while. That is called "freezing out a guest".

26 May

A holiday in Buttermere: Bridge Hotel. It is mainly Conservative businessmen who come here from the north. Labour people cannot afford it and Labour intellectuals do not regard it as smart enough. The conversation revolves around, "Where do you come from? By which route?" "What fells did you do? Which fells are you going to do?"

Alan is not really intellectual in a Continental sense. I doubt whether a British historian is ever intellectual. Their upbringing is so different, they do not analyse, they do not comment on personal things and feelings. They play sports, they walk, they travel, they always do and plan things, they know how to live in a capitalist society: You have to be competitive, you have to be economical. No time for sulkiness, for sentiments. In a pub I read: "When the floor is full, please use the ash tray". Yes, and above everything, humour.

28 May

I have read the last part of a biography of Brendan Bracken.[1] He was a man who deliberately wanted to strengthen, in a funny, reactionary way, the establishment. He was elitist, anti-Keynesian, anti-appeaser, in favour of private ownership. Clemmie, Churchill's wife, had no sense of humour at all. She detested the three Bs: Birkenhead, Beaverbrook and Bracken. She thought they were a bad influence on Churchill – as indeed they were. Mary, Churchill's younger daughter, told Alan in the British Library that none of the children liked Clemmie, but preferred their father. Brendan was considered the son of Churchill. Brendan died a very painful death but he faced it bravely. Churchill only asked, when he heard the news of Brendan's death: "Did he die well?" Churchill had many strokes. The first was in 1951 and his doctor was faced with a dilemma: he was not fit to be PM but, on the other hand, it would have done him good to work.

30 May

Churchill became mentally ill in his last years; he did not speak at all. Before that he had often had depressed days, which he called black dogs.

Alan spoke about George Lansbury. He was a good friend of Alan's father, a staunch Labour man, and a good businessman. He started the *Daily Herald* and was a fine editor. He became a pacifist after the Abyssinian crisis when sanctions failed. His grand-daughter, Angela Lansbury, is a leading film actress now. Alan said that George Lansbury told him many things about Lenin; in fact it was he who took Lenin to meet English workers. Lenin immediately enrolled himself in the local branches of Socialist workers. Lansbury helped Lenin to find a place for the meeting to take place in London in 1902. They really wanted it in Brussels or in Germany, but the police were after them. Lenin borrowed money from a rich soap manufacturer called Fell who

1 Brendan Bracken (1901–1958) was an Irish journalist and Conservative politician. He was managing director of the *Economist* from 1928 to 1945, Minister of Information 1941–45 and First Lord of the Admiralty in 1945. In 1951 he founded the magazine, *History Today*. He became a Viscount in 1952.

gave him enough to hire a hall for the meeting. Lenin promised to pay back the money to Fell and he did so immediately after 1917. Fell got a cheque from Zurich and Lenin sent a message saying that though he would not pay back the debts of the Czar, he would pay back his own.

31 May

We went to Preston and Alan showed me his parents' Preston house, where he lived from 1919 to 1929. He really spent only the Christmas month there and some parts of the summer holiday. It was 17 Rose Terrace. They had a big garage which had been a stable for a pony and trap. Behind the garage there was a wash-house with a boiler; the kitchen had a big open fire. Alan's parents had a daily routine. The mother was not seen until eleven in the morning, she had her breakfast in bed, then they went shopping with the father. The fishmonger came every week with freshly caught shrimps and fish and also the potato woman came every week. The chimney sweep arrived once a quarter. They kept the soot because the gardener wanted it to keep the slugs at bay. Alan said that Garstang was the best place for Lancashire cheese.

4 June

His first TV lecture began on the history of the period between the wars. He pointed out something I had never thought of: how much less statesmen travelled in the 'thirties than after the Second World War.

Alan mentioned the hunger marchers in the 'thirties. He said the hunger marchers were a happy lot, supplied during their march with tea, food, beds and money to return. This was mainly done by local authorities.

Speaking about the 'twenties and 'thirties, Alan mentioned that when Sidney Webb was a minister and made a speech in the House, the Tories all made nanny goat noises because that's what he looked like.

7 June

The last time we were in the TV studio, a new foreman told Alan what to do, then he forgot about him. Alan stood there and stood and stood. Finally he remarked: "I am quite used to sitting and waiting quietly, but am I of any use now?"

Alan explained to his youngest son that all his life he had been waiting for something final to happen: the collapse of capitalism, the great depression, nuclear war, the collapse of oil sources.

11 June

Alan reviewed Mary Soames's book on Clementine Churchill. Alan quoted Clementine who, returning from Churchill's funeral said, "It was not a funeral, it was a triumph." And Alan's eyes were filled with tears.

I heard on the radio that students will get cheap tickets in the front rows of theatres as they are poorer than the middle-aged members of the audience; their enthusiasm is good for the actors.

20 June

Today we went to Soho where Alan showed me the shops where he used to buy chicory and coffee (Grain No. 5 – since 1931 he has always bought the same grain). This street, Old Compton Street, used to have very good butchers and vegetable shops. Then he showed me the place where he lived when he was married and living in Oxford and used to come down to London to give TV or BBC talks. This is 33 Percy Street, north Soho. This and the other parts of Soho were much frequented by Dylan Thomas and his friends.

In the local pub where Alan ordered a half of bitter and a Campari for me, suddenly I felt as though I was in a film. Everything was half-dark, soft and Fellini-like.

We always have fascinating conversations in the pub. We often speak about historical problems and personalities. This time Alan recalled Louis Namier again. He told me that Namier had chosen between snobbery and him. He had chosen the former.

30 June

We spent the afternoon at Waterlow Park. We again spoke about historians. Isaac Deutscher, who came from Poland in the 'thirties, was a Trotskyite and wrote Trotsky's biography and later that of Stalin, praising him after the war. Isaiah Berlin is different, he arrived from Petrograd in 1917 and settled down in Britain; his interest in Russia is like an Englishman's interest. He went to the Soviet Union to see Tolstoy's house and he met Akhmatova. He wrote an apolitical biography of Marx. Alan told him, "Do you not think that Marx had an influence on the revolutions in 1848? And did you not write a word about it?" "I am not interested in the political sphere," he said, "only in theory."

3 July

Eddie and his wife and Amelia and Bob (Alan's daughter and her boyfriend) came for dinner. Eddie was at Queen's College, Cambridge. His secretary told me that when Eddie was chosen for the BBC job there were 300 applicants. Among those, fifteen were taken on; from those fifteen, ten came from Oxford or Cambridge.

10 July

Alan met Kreisky in Vienna, when Nico Henderson was there as press attaché. The *Arbeiter Zeitung*, the organ of the Social Democrats in Vienna, was financed by the Labour Party in London. Other newspapers were financed by the French and others. In Vienna Alan of course met Pribram[1] and Srbik[2], the historians. Srbik became a Nazi after the Anschluss. After the Second World War he wrote letters to British historians – amongst them Charles Webster[3] – explaining that it was a sheer necessity

1 P.A.F. Pribram was an authority on Cromwell and on European diplomacy.
2 Heinrich von Srbik was an able historian of the Habsburg Monarchy.
3 Sir Charles Webster was an eminent diplomatic historian and professor at the London School of Economics.

for him to enter the Nazi Party. Webster told Alan, "I was not going to reply to such a man."

14 July

The top people from India or from elsewhere who were educated at British public schools were called the brown Britons (like Nehru for instance).

When Alan was in Vienna, his passport was taken away and the consul cancelled his permission for overseas journeys. Alan's uncle complained about this to Hugh Dalton who was then the Under-Secretary at the Foreign Office and the Viennese consul made a correction in Alan's passport and apologised. Alan accepted the apology and thereafter they met at the Viennese Beefsteak Club. The British create clubs wherever they go.

15 July

I am getting like Boswell with Johnson: scribbling, scribbling every time I hear something interesting. We always have our best chats at tea time and in the pub. Today at tea time my husband spoke about Johnson, whom he rates very highly. I asked him who else he put as high as Johnson. He said, "Cromwell, Dickens, Darwin, nearly Cobden, William Morris, Bertrand Russell." "And yourself," I added. He said: "Nonsense."

The other day I heard the dustman saying when he collected the bin: "This is the house of Taylor – the historian, you know!"

17 July

We saw Hatfield House, the House of the Cecils. This house was always regarded as a suburban historical house. Queen Victoria's Prime Minister did not like staying in London and so he came home every evening and the house is opposite the station. In the garden we saw one of the Cecils, a woman in a great straw hat collecting some herbs. Nearly the same straw hat was shown inside the house worn by Queen Elizabeth. The library was beautiful and there was a reading chair, my favourite piece of furniture. The Cecils were always good business people; they charge a pound for visiting the house and the garden.

At Oxford in the dining room I sat next to a Dutchman and Roger Hood, an old friend of Alan's son. He is one of the best crime writers in the country and a reader at All Souls. He is going to write a book called *Chartists, Fenians and Suffragettes in Prison*. We had a good conversation about capital punishment; he said nobody has a right to extinguish a life. The evening was very pleasant; Alan's old butler was around and chatted with Alan. What a nice man he was. A Canadian sat next to Alan and told him that *The Origins of the Second World War* was always his best reading and he kept it on his bed-side table. The Canadian did not like the English class society; he said the Canadians were more open and richer.

Alan gave a lecture on Britain from 1870–1914. What was good about it, apart from the jokes and wise statements, was the opinion he expressed about the British view of Europe and the lack of commitment to Europe. I told him he should make a TV series about the European view in British eyes and what Europe means to British people historically and culturally.

After the lecture we went to Stratford-upon-Avon, a commercialised town, but the Church where Shakespeare lies is very nice and quiet. Ben Jonson had a dinner with Shakespeare and they drank so much that a week later Shakespeare died at the age of fifty-two. On St. George's Day, all the Ambassadors come here by car, flags flying and commemorate Shakespeare in the town hall. At the end of the 'thirties, Ivan Maisky the Soviet Ambassador gave the speech.

24 July

We had a chat about Arthur Koestler who visited Alan at Holywell Ford. Koestler came in the afternoon and said: "I want wine and women." Alan answered "You can't have wine in the afternoon, but if you bring them yourself, you can have as many women as you like in this house."

I saw *The White Guard* by Bulgakov. Excellent play. He was admired even by Stalin. The woman who was taking the tickets said, "Go ahead, the seats at the front are not sold and you will see better there." The ordinary English people always want to help.

14 August

Alan came back from the Isle of Wight. He told me he did not want to write cleverly any more. Johnson gave him the following advice: If you write something, read it over and leave out what you admire the most. "In the past I wanted to show how clever I was. Now I don't anymore, I just want to say what is in the book and make comments. I do not want to entertain people any more," Alan said. He wanted to put on his pullover; I was going up anyhow, so I brought it down for him. Alan said I should not have done this. "Why not?" I asked. "Are we not equal?" "No," he said, "women are more delicate." "They were in the nineteenth century," I answered, "not now."

15 August

When Alan decided to write a biography of Bismarck he did it because his American publisher asked him to. He liked the subject and he had previously written a lot about Bismarck in *The Course of German History* and in *The Struggle for Mastery in Europe*. Bismarck said that the English Tories were more radical than the Liberals. Alan commented now: "It is still valid in a way: they have chosen the first woman PM."

3 – 9 September

In Amsterdam. We took our post with us. One letter was from the Pedestrian Society. Britain is a country of Societies. One can join the Ramblers' Society, Heath Society, Pedestrian Society and so on.

Wonderful day. People are noisier than in England and the toilets smell. Amsterdam is like Miskolc, my native town in East Hungary. Yellow trams. In the King Hotel everything is very expensive and there is no bathroom, only a shower. I saw a wonderful gay couple at Rembrandtplatz. The elder looked seedy, the younger much more in love and slender. We went to see *The Night Watch* by Rembrandt at the Rijksmuseum. Amsterdam is dirty, nobody cares about anyone else, about money or clothes. But they have a sophisticated culture. It was the best in Europe in the seventeenth century. We went to see John Six's famous house, a seventeenth century luxury home, which was turned into a museum in 1922. Only foreigners can go and see it and then only if they have a permit. A wealthy bourgeois family have always lived there and the last member of the family, a famous surgeon, lives there still. They survived Napoleon and Hitler and kept everything they had: a wonderful Rembrandt, many seventeenth century pieces of furniture and pictures. We saw another patrician house, a canal house at Herengracht; it is called Museum Willet-Holthuysen. Of course we also visited the house in which Rembrandt lived from 1639 to 1658. Saskia lived here in 1642. It did not impress me much. Alan wrote in the visitors' book: "AJPT. London-Oxford". I wrote: "EH. Hungary". He loves to write "Oxford" in guest books. Then we went to the Red Light district. Saw the women in the windows. I thought they should have been more sophisticated. They were just wretched creatures.

We spent a day with Louis de Jongh. He is the official historian of Nazi-Occupied Holland and the Fifth Columns in Europe. He last met Alan in 1947, in Monte Carlo, where Unesco organized a conference on Nazism. They got wonderful fees, but Alan and Baumont, the French historian, spent only a little part of their fee in cheap restaurants while Jongh spent all his money on gambling. Jongh found out that there was no fifth column and Alan, speaking about the rise of Hitler, came to the conclusion that Hitler was pushed to take power by von Papen. Both views created uneasiness. Both men, Alan and Jongh, are historians who want to tell things as they happened. They both see Hitler as a man who took advantage of situations as they arose. They did not diminish Hitler's responsibility for the Second World War and killing the Jews, they just wanted to show how history developed at that time. Alan said this was the case with Tobias's book on the Reichstag Fire. Von Lubbe started it – actually he did three at that time and the Nazis made use of this, but it was not the Nazis who caused it. Mommsen was asked in the Zeitgeschichte Institute to tell the truth. He could not find anything other than what Tobias found. Jongh left his country on the day the Germans entered Holland (early May 1940). He and his wife had just got married. They lived in Hampstead and went back to Holland in 1945. They had four children. Now his wife is seriously ill with cancer of the liver and she was told eight months ago that she only had eighteen months to live. Jongh worked for the BBC during the war. When he came back, he began to work on Nazi Holland. Socialists wanted resistance in Holland during the war, but nobody dared and the Socialists were listed. There were no mountains in which they could hide. There were, however, many forged identity cards, particularly for Jews. Now he is working on his ninth volume (there will be twelve altogether) under the aegis of the Ministry of Education. He was the only historian who had access to everything. He even saw the Queen's papers. Wilhelmina, the old queen, wanted to recreate Holland; she had a strong personality, like de Gaulle. She did not succeed, she passed on the Crown to Juliana, whose husband was crooked. Their daughter, Beatrix, will be a good Queen. They will have difficulties finding royal highnesses to marry their children.

Monarchy in Holland does not matter. There are at least four big parties and several tiny ones. Elections are at least every four years. People are politically conscious. Eighty-five percent go to vote. There are no major differences in the aims of the parties.

We saw the Western part of Holland, full of wonderful windmills. There used to be 1,000 of them but now there are only about 500. There are wonderful farmhouses. People are rich here. The countryside is beautiful, though flat and dull. The town halls are very impressive, mainly mid-seventeenth century. Alan said at the end of our tour that it was worth coming to Amsterdam to see Jongh again. He is a great friend of Wiesenthal from Vienna. He was also impressed with Budapest and by the Hungarian historians at the Second World War Conference.

11 September

We went to Salisbury rather unwillingly. We knew the interview would be held late at night, that meant 10 o'clock, which is nearly bed-time for Alan. Alan promised himself, "Never again". Then, arriving on a sunny afternoon, walking on the grass around the cathedral, somehow I felt it would have been a mistake not to take part in the Salisbury Festival. After all, we can't sit at home all the time, however wonderful the working days are, however much, when we move out, we long to come back to our Victorian working-class terrace house. At the playhouse, which is a modern building, our interviewer showed Alan the scene of the interview, where David Cecil was interviewed the night before.

The interview began some minutes past ten. They sat down and the friendly talk began. It was very much a conversation between a very wise, mature man, who is *the* historian of the country, and a well combed, business-like, restrained and experienced journalist. The latter was very good in his limited capacity; he put good realistic short questions and let AJP speak. It was obvious from the very beginning that Alan caught the sympathy and attention of the public. He was sitting calmly and spoke gently and without any reservation. He answered every question with the greatest co-operation and honesty. Everybody could see that though he derived his views from different sources these views were well thought out. His wit and charm were apparent to all. About his professional life, he said that he was a posthumous professor. He writes history because he likes it. He is a narrative historian. Nearly every character in history is invented by historians. Of course historians draw their characters from the available sources and data. The problem is really how to be selective about information. Is it possible to write true history? Every history is a statement about what happened at a certain time, but it is only the historian's version of events. A precise statement is impossible. What is possible is an attempt at the most likely version: a history of conscience. Alan said he wrote history to satisfy his own conscience, a reasonably fair account of past events and he wrote because of the money. Every historian should write an autobiography because it is possible in this way to see how unreliable you are. Every autobiographer puts himself in the middle of things, which he is not. The more your book is attacked, the more it sells. He did not like David Irving's books, because some of them were wrong-headed and not only that, but calculatedly wrong-headed. As to himself, answering a question, he said he was a lonely child. Even now, he feels that he would prefer his own company to anybody else's.

After the interview many questions were raised. Why does he not like Lawrence? Pretentious. He does not like to be told things, to be taught. Novels should tell stories, like Arnold Bennett, H.G. Wells. Nowadays, he says, he cannot understand the stories, they have double meanings. History, on the other hand, can provide much more entertaining material than fiction; like any good novel, it entertains as much as it instructs. Historical institutions are inevitable. Can we learn from the past? We learn from old mistakes only how to make new ones. Every situation is unique. There are only vague similarities. History gives a wider understanding of human nature. The lesson of history is that everything is different, but people derive whatever lessons suit them best. The only things you really know are that all men die and everything is temporary. On the whole men's hopes are not fulfilled, but some things turn out as badly as expected. New problems will always arise. In the end the deterrents will not deter. Has he faith in politicians? No, but he used to have great faith in Tito; Russia?

There is a misplaced belief that Russia wants to conquer Western Europe. This mistaken impression began at the time of the Bolshevik Revolution and has caused great harm since.

14 September

On the way back from Salisbury, we talked a lot in the car. Alan told me that Beaverbrook's son said that his father's main interest was charity. He went one day to St. Mary's Hospital, to the outpatients where a woman offered him tea for a penny. She looked at him and must have thought that he was very poor because she said, you don't have to pay the one penny. Later Beaverbrook said to the director: "This woman got you the money which you wanted for the hospital."

18 September

Alan thinks that after a while things always go wrong. I asked if he thought I was stronger. Yes, he did. I asked if he thought there were such things as strong women. Yes, but he could not find one.

He had begun to write his autobiography again and is contemplating a review of Stalin and Trotsky. We do not agree on democracy and dictatorship. He believes that social justice can come about through toleration and persuasion. I don't think that very rich and powerful people could be persuaded to give up some of what they have.

20 September

I wrote my article on Beesly. I saw *Pretty Baby*, a film on child prostitution. I thought is was perfect. The moral and ethic of the film is unquestionable.

We went to Yorkshire for three days from the West Riding to Lasthingham, to a family hotel. We usually had our lunch and pre-dinner drink in the local pub, which is a well kept Victorian place full of real and pseudo Victorian bric-a-brac. I told Alan that for me it was a research holiday: I got to know how people behave in such a hotel, what they eat, what conversations they have. My favourite new dessert is pineapple slices with pear brandy. The after-dinner conversations were very formal, the views expressed were cautious and narrow. This country is still the place of gentryfolk. In the time of Alan's mother, these people found even the habit of reading *The Manchester Guardian* outrageous.

As we approached the hotel we visited the house of Sterne in Coxwold where he wrote *Tristram Shandy*. The outstanding feature of the trip, which made it all worthwhile, was looking around the twelfth century Cistercian abbeys: Byland Abbey, Easby Abbey, Rievaulx Abbey. In the last of these 140 monks and 500 worldly monks lived as in a bee hive – or so it seemed to me. One can see their bedrooms, chapel, hospital, kitchen, mainly in ruins. All these abbeys were built in wonderful places; the scenery is beautiful and, of course, they were built near rivers. We also looked at many castles, amongst others, the famous Richmond Castle, which Turner loved so much. We saw two wonderful folk museums in Ryedale and in Pickering. Private individuals collected these mainly nineteenth century items. It should be done in every country before they are lost. We were at Whitby, near the sea and saw the church which was the favourite church of both Pevsner and Betjeman. It is peculiar and charming: the people sit in private little boxes in the church.

30 September

We saw a programme on Hugh Gaitskell produced by Anthony Howard,[1] who is a restless man with talent and great intelligence. He asked Alan to write The Langham Diary in the *Listener*. Gaitskell, who died in 1963, was an arrogant and conceited man, according to Alan, who disliked him intensely. Alan said: "There was not a man whom I disliked more."

5 October

"Travel is glamorous in retrospect" – it's a good phrase, but I mostly enjoy our travels in the present. We came to Bristol

1 Anthony Howard has been deputy editor of the *Observer* since 1981. Before then, he worked on the *New Statesman* and was editor of the *Listener*. In 1979 he edited the *Crossman Diaries*. See also pp. 15, 52.

through Newbury, Hungerford, Speen and Bradford on Avon. Alan drove and explained things to me. There was a great battle in Newbury centuries ago. Speen had the Speenhamland system and Marlborough has a public school. Betjeman went there and hated it.

We spent two nights with the Averys. Roy is the headmaster of Bristol Grammar School and he is in charge of about eighty teachers and more than 1,000 children. He is campaigning for co-education and there are already some girls in the sixth form. He also invites interesting people to give lectures for the sixth formers. He showed us the great Victorian Hall in the school. As a seven-year-old boy in Bristol he never imagined he would become the headmaster of this huge school. Headmasters get nearly as high a salary as professors. The social life of his wife can be important. Roy has a talented, sweet and sensitive wife who is mainly sensitive about women's cattiness. Alan said that men could be catty as well, particularly in Oxford colleges.

Alan gave a lecture to the Bath Historical Association about British succession. Alan told me how he began his Historical Association lectures in Manchester in 1930. His first lecture was on Metternich.

10 October

Dinner with Suzanne and Keith Kyle.[1] Keith spoke about Alan. He first saw Alan in his Magdalen flat with Colette the cat in his lap and his pipe in his hand. Alan would sometimes scratch his devil's horn (which he got rid of after the 1948 Wroclaw Conference when Kingsley Martin mentioned it in the *New Statesman*). Keith spoke about Thomas Balogh, the economist of Hungarian origin. He does not have good command of the language. Kissinger's brother, who spoke very good English, was asked how this could be, when Kissinger did not. He answered: "I always listened, he never did." Balogh did not listen; Kingsley Martin hated him. Once he threw Balogh out of his office because he was looking through the letters on his desk.

Paul Johnson, who was present at the dinner with his wife, said that Alan was always very business-like with his students. The

1 Keith Kyle was one of A.J.P. Taylor's pupils. He is now a distinguished economist and journalist.

moment they left, he began to type, and he typed until the last minute before they came. He was not emotional, but impressed them tremendously.

16 November

Alan told funny stories about bishops and deans. Davidson's was a famous case. Preaching on Sundays in Cambridge, coming back to London for the week, he spent his week days with courtesans and actresses to study them. He was unfrocked, he regretted this, went on hunger strike, and put himself in a circus ring with a lion. In the end the lion ate him.

At the turn of the century, in Magdalen, the Dean realised that he had lost his faith. He went on being Dean but seven years later they did not elect him again and he became a history professor, and wrote excellent books on the French Revolution. His name was Thompson; they used to call him Tombi. His widow is still alive in Oxford.

Yesterday we went to the Pedestrian Association's reception. The Bishop who is the president of the Association was a Jew, then became a member of the Church of England and is now a bishop.

21 November

We spoke about loyalties. The Blunt affair is in the news. Alan told me he knew Harold Nicolson well; they met often at the BBC; he was a nice old man, not cynical, but frivolous. At the time when Burgess defected, Nicolson said what a nice man Burgess was. Alan did not like Burgess because he was always dirty and smelt. Alan has no loyalties apart from radicalism. No loyalties to the Establishment. I asked, "What about Oxford?" When lots of dons and their wives went to America in 1940, Alan stayed at home with his family. His eldest son Giles came home from the Dragon School and said this and that child is going to America. Alan said, "Son, you will not go" – and as he recalled it, he wept. Alan said they did not fear that the Germans would come. They felt they would never leave the country in danger. Actually they did not believe Britain could be in danger.

We had the seminar meeting this afternoon. I gave a talk on

Britain and Hungary in 1948 and 1949. Alan introduced me kindly and at the end he thanked me kindly. About twenty people were there and some four questions were raised. I answered satisfactorily and Alan was quite content. Later he confessed he felt like coming to my rescue and saying what I meant to express. But there was no need for this. Alan said also that he had feared I might be out of my depth in the seminar, but it all worked out well. After the seminar I had a long talk with Robert Skidelsky, mainly about Alan and about my work and about Russia and China. I said I was a détente woman. He said he agreed, there was no other alternative. But he thought problems would arise outside of Europe. I asked why the British criticise China less than they do the Soviet Union. Robert said China was never really Marxist. Mao was an alien phenomenon there. And once he had gone, everybody felt here they could again step into the area. He said also that the Chinese, Japanese and others, apart from being under Capitalist or Communist governments, have something in common.

Alan said in the evening that we suffer from too much love. I felt I concentrated on him too much. He said, "Nonsense." Then he remembered a picture of Matthew Arnold and his niece, who was admiring him. Arnold, with his long hair, stood gravely and his little niece, admiring him, said "The only thing I cannot understand with you uncle, is why on earth can you not be serious once?" That is our relationship too. Alan is not serious at all; nothing is too important for him, everything is understandable. Alan has no faith, I have a lot (not religious though). He is not optimistic, he is practical and not nervous at all. He learnt early not to be. When he was young and at Bootham on the last day of term, the younger ones felt excited about going and left their pork pies. Alan quickly took them and not only ate more than one, but took some home as well.

22 November

Len Deighton and his wife Isabel were here for dinner. He is a nice, clean chap, very practical, loves technical details. Both of them love cooking, children, living in Ireland and going to Irish funerals because in Ireland they are very merry affairs. They live very simply. Len works a lot and does nothing else really: working, bringing up children. Isabel is a good wife for him. She is Dutch, but rather cosmopolitan; she left Holland with her parents at the age of four. Len used to be an anarchist.

24 November – 6 January

I went back to Budapest for six weeks. My eldest son has got married. When I got back I felt extremely happy. Both my sons were fine and I liked the women in their lives. I spent a wonderful time there, content and busy. Also I have changed in a way. I have become more tolerant and understanding towards everyone. The main reason for this, I am sure, is that I was so happy to speak Hungarian and express myself easily. Some people had aged, but on the whole everybody lives quite well and happily. Every third day I got a letter from Alan, full of love and tenderness and wit. When I came back to London and saw Alan at Heathrow, saying "Eva", I felt terribly touched. He was elderly, tender and warm. He is a wonderful man. All our misunderstandings arise from our different upbringings and traditions. For instance, he does not like it when I ask a question he cannot answer and then he says it is a silly question. Of course the British do not put personal questions and so they do not know a lot of things about each other.

1980

9 January

Yesterday we went to the annual meeting of the British Academy. Met Hugh Trevor-Roper, Freddie Ayer, Michael Howard,[1] Kathleen Tillotson and others. Michael Howard is very good looking and entertaining. Fred Ayer did not put his label on, declaring that anyone who did not know him should not know him. I confessed I did not know who he was. He said he was Ayer, but now he had grown much fatter and so I did not recognize him. He had a pretty girl with him who did not say a word. Trevor-Roper looks younger than he is and his face is not intellectual at all. Kathleen Tillotson said she was still working on Dickens' letters. There are 13,000 and still some might be discovered. She does not write monographs any more and her last, rather successful book will not be republished. We met the Hobsbawms[2] as well. Marlene is very lively. We invited them for dinner with Alan's daughter, Sophia, (who is a history teacher) and her husband.

Today we met Sophia and Rob by chance at the Queen Elizabeth Hall. Sophia said she hoped that the 'eighties will be the decade of revolution in Britain.

1 Michael Howard, CBE, was made Chichele Professor of the History of War in the University of Oxford in 1977. He is the author of many works on historical themes, including a history of the Franco-Prussian war which won the Duff Cooper Memorial Prize in 1962.

2 Eric Hobsbawm is Professor Emeritus of Economic History at Birkbeck College, London University. In 1986 he contributed to a volume of essays in honour of A.J.P. Taylor. He has written many outstanding books on Britain and International Social History.

10 January

We went to the Heath after lunch and spoke about our relationships with our children and step-children. I said I liked his family but I like other people as well. I recalled that an old girlfriend had once told me that a mother-in-law should do three "Ss": *Schweigen*, *schlucken* and *schenken*. Whereupon Alan said there was an English saying: Sons you lose when they marry, while daughters always stay with you. I do not believe it is true. Sons are nearly always close to their mothers. Mine are.

In the afternoon a Canadian chap called Karl Samuelson came for tea. We had a good conversation about Hitler. He liked Schramm's book on Hitler best. Alan told him about Schramm's background. He was a German medievalist. Speaking about the Holocaust and immigration, Alan said the immigrants to the States did not state whether they were Jews or not, they simply had to declare their nationalities. France was better about letting in Jews than Britain. Britain let in Jews if they could make use of them: good scientists, industrialists and so on. Before the Battle of Britain all German immigrants in Britain were put on the Isle of Man. They lived there for six months and had the best scientists, who ran the German University of the Isle of Man for them.

14 January

Alan told me how happy he is. Having said in his autobiography what a miserable personal life he has had, he now sees that this is not so; not now, nor in his early life.

Yesterday afternoon we visited the back parts of the Tower which are hardly visited by tourists. It was here that the first dock in the Thames, called St Katherine's Dock, was built.

19 January

The situation in the world gets worse and worse. Tito is nearly dead; already the Croats in England are beginning to organize themselves. Afghanistan is used by the Americans to create anti-Soviet feeling everywhere. And all these manipulated opinions about the Olympic games are ridiculous. Thatcher wants to move the games from Moscow. She behaves like the leader of a great Empire, but Britain is not that any more. But the people are lovely. Sir George Schuster once wrote: "We are great as a nation as long as we can get our individuals to work independently. But we are damned bad at planning. We now seem to be doomed to mediocrity because everything has passed out of the hands of individuals to the bureaucracy."

Yesterday I saw the Shah of Iran interviewed by David Frost. The Shah was feeble but calm. He said he was responsible for Iran as a ruler, but what he said was totally irresponsible. But he is a shrewd and wealthy man. He won't last long. His eyes were feverish.

I am longing to be with my sons.

20 January

I am afraid I am very ill, bronchitis or pneumonia. I might die here. What a pity to leave life.

I am reading *The Old Wives' Tale* by Arnold Bennett. It is lovely reading about how they behaved towards servants who lived in the cellar of a philanthropic family. Also one of these creatures did not marry a Chartist man whom she loved because the family did not approve of his views.

Yesterday Marlene and Eric Hobsbawm and Sophia and Rob were here for dinner. Marlene and Eric are very compassionate. Eric is giving a seminar talk on why shoe-makers were radicals. Alan told me after the dinner: "You see now that your husband is nothing else than an old-fashioned radical." So he is. But he stands by his principles. He might resign from his membership of the Academy over its condemnation of Blunt.

23 January

Alan gave an interesting interview about the Battle of Britain to the German TV man. Alan recalled that in Oxford they all thought that the Germans would destroy Oxford because that was where the best brains in Britain lived.

25 January

Yesterday we had guests for dinner, the "Feet" (that means Michael and Jill Foot) and Alan's eldest son Giles and his wife Janet. Michael looked fantastic, good looking, fit. Alan told me he was not like this at all. He has had asthma and bad skin problems on his face so that he could hardly shave. Jill is a feminist, a kind person, clever, but uncertain without him, slightly wary. She has ideas of her own about politics, but she can't influence her husband. I think they are very close to each other and her constant striving to convert him to her views, which are coherent, makes a strong base for their love. She thinks as I do, that England has a male-orientated society. I asked what made her think that. She cited the Pill as an example. Men should have pills as well and put up with all the side-effects. The problem is that scientists do not do research on pills for men. Michael definitely did not want to speak about politics. He made Alan speak all the time. The whole evening showed me how different men in England are in the way they regard women. In Hungary, in our intellectual circle we women would have the right and the opportunity to speak in society. Of course in principle in England they have the same rights and the opportunities, but in fact in society in Britain women either listen to men or make them speak or stick to small talk. When I begin to speak about my experiences here or in life or about my research, they listen with open eyes; they don't comment and when I have finished, they go on with what they were saying as if I hadn't uttered a word. Mike was the same. It was impossible to involve him in a conversation about British politics or the British role in world affairs. He thinks he knows it better. Before he came I thought he knew it better. As a matter of fact, he did not. He is a very charming man but he does not reveal his political ideas enough. He believes in British values, which is right. Jill said that the referendum to decide whether or not Britain should join the Common Market was a cheat, a manipulation of the votes.

2 February

I know I should not worry but I am concerned about my eldest son, who got married last Christmas. I wrote them several letters. No answer. Perhaps they are busy.

Alan is fine. He looked after me very well when I came near to catching pneumonia. He said I would die of this illness. Might well be the case. He also liked my first review in England, printed in the *Observer* about Arnold Bennett's *The Old Wives' Tale*. I love it and it has been translated into Hungarian.

We went to the Heath this afternoon. Watery sun, trees, children in red jumpers. Extraordinary sights on both sides. Alan told me during our walk about his friends who used to collect train tickets from all over the world. He observed that on the continent they never did that. In England it is an old tradition. Alan is going to speak on Granada about the first great railway line 150 years ago: the Liverpool-Manchester line. He said people did not realise that railways revolutionised the world much more than anything else since the alphabet, reading and writing.

At home we had ham with spring onions as an hors d'oeuvre. That reminded Alan that in old English hotels there was always a nice big ham and cold beef at the end of the dining room in case somebody wanted cold lunch.

We saw Peter Ustinov on TV. He has never played Shakespeare. Now he will play King Lear. He felt it was a dreadful thing to be senile and a very difficult part to play. About the Russians he said that he saw that they had their difficulties. It is no good putting politics into sport. Art and sport should not be mixed up with politics. Alan said that Ustinov once imitated him in the Free Speech programme.

Yesterday we went to see *Wise Blood* (John Huston) with Alan's youngest son, Daniel, and with Margeret, his first wife. A nice little group. Famous film. A mad film about mad Americans. Alan waited for us. Margaret does not want Alan back; she can't cope with having somebody in the house.

We went yesterday with Shirley Hadi, my old friend, to see the exhibition of Moholy-Nagy, the great radical Bauhaus artist at the ICA. Her ex-husband came to visit her and their son. He stayed for six weeks. Now her son Rashid could see why his mother loved his father and also what was not so lovable about him.

Yesterday we went to see a play by Priestley called *When We are Married*. It had a good moral: make the best of it. And it turns out how differently they felt when they were not married. Priestley portrays the limits of country life, village life, bourgeois life very well. One of his best aphorisms is: "There is only one thing better than a story, and that is a character."

11 February

Alan said tonight that Churchill's funeral took place just as he finished the proofs of his *English History*. He was moved and he added to the note on Churchill: "The saviour of the country". "That's what he was," Alan said. And I said to Alan: "You are also a saviour of this country." "Saviour from what?" Alan asked. I hesitated, I wanted to say saviour from snobbery, saviour from the establishment. Alan laughed and simply said, "Saviour from boredom."

14 February

Yesterday: a good evening with the Goldfingers. Ursula is as well as ever. The photographer, Kertész, was there; he is eighty-six. He left Budapest in 1925, left Paris for New York in 1936. He hates New York and yet he has spent most of his life there. The problem is that people are snobbish about this; they love to think how great it is to live in Paris or in New York and then they don't want to leave their richer life there. And they cannot be happy again at home. Jim Richards, the former editor of the *Architectural Review* was there. They spent some time in Wroclaw when Alan was there in 1948. He was then against Alan, now he says Alan was wonderful.

19 February

Seminar about the Cold War by Thomas Brian. Very interesting topic, well done. Alan says the reason he lost interest in history is this: he could not understand why and how British Socialist statesmen initiated the Cold War. Bevin, Attlee and Nye Bevan hardly put up any opposition to it.

21 February

The problem with Margaret is that she "treats" people. I do not need her treatment and Alan is adult enough not to go back to her every second day for this "treatment". I think it is a catch 22 situation but Alan denies it. I do not like his visits to Margaret as Margaret treats him as though he were still her husband. If Alan does not go, he gets very depressed. If he goes, I am very dejected and it spoils our relationship. I am interested in what is going on between real people, not between fake ones, fake relationships. That is a silly game that these two elderly friends play, pretending they do not need each other and it is dangerous for me and for my relationship with Alan. If they do, let them stay together, if they do not, let them make it less often or leave me alone. There is really nothing to be done. I have to work, that is all.

23 February

We went to Waterlow Park yesterday to see Charlie, the talking bird. Lonely elderly ladies go there, sometimes with their elderly sisters, to speak to Charlie: "Charlie darling, how are you? Say something. I came to see you, I am off now; it is chilly you know."

Sometimes we have not much to tell each other. We have not got imaginative minds.

I went to the City Lit. and agreed with a nice literary woman teacher that I would speak on "A woman historian". Gizella wants to correct my English, because sometimes it is difficult to understand what I am saying.

My children are fine, they have got that lovely family (their in-laws) behind them.

I had a chat with my friend, Elizabeth Barker. The good thing about ageing is that you get more integrated. She spoke about Elizabeth Wiskeman, whom she described as often rigid and intractible, and George Buday, who was very easy to work with in the Second World War.

2 March

A good article on Auden. I asked Alan why he had not included his impressions of Auden in Oxford in his autobiography. As they were both survivors, Auden began to talk to Alan as a friend when he became Professor of Poetry at Oxford for a year. He was like a Buddha sitting and nodding. He loved gossip, but there was nobody left to gossip with: they had all died. At that time Auden already had a terrible American accent. He was interested in psychology. An amateur psychiatrist.

Yesterday my old friend Laci Ujházy[1] was here. He and Alan spoke about being elderly. Neither of them feels his age. They are quicker than youngsters, more experienced, but they are shrewd enough to show their cleverness to the youngsters. Laci's mother, Nanóka, is in her eighty-seventh year, half lame, still enjoys life and feels young inside. Laci said they both liked to perform, meaning Alan and himself. It is essential to them. Suddenly I felt how much I missed my sons. They are my friends, or rather brothers. Laci and Alan feel that they had got everything wrong in their lives.

4 March

Alan does not want to live without me. If we were to separate because of Margaret – for her lifetime only – we could never come together again. I am very depressed and do not like being alone in Twisden Road. I think the whole Margaret affair is connected with my stay in England, especially as, being far away from my sons and work and settling down quite late in life in a different country, is not an easy thing in itself. It is not easy for me to live here. I, who worked in my own style and expressed myself in my own way and to whom tradition means a lot. Another problem is that my English is sometimes very bad and I am not interested enough to make it better. Sometimes people do not understand me. Alan told me from the very beginning that I would not improve much because I had got used to bad English.

When I am not depressed, I am quite all right. I enjoy reading English novelists. I have just finished Bennett's *Riceyman Steps*, a lovely book, one of my favourites.

A great event has taken place: Mugabe has become Zimbabwe's leader. It was terribly funny to watch the whole proceedings. This time the British really tried hard for more than ten years to represent their interests in Rhodesia; the minute they had to give it up they became democratic and broad minded. Even Alan said what a wonderful thing it was to give it up in this generous way,

1 László Ujházy was Commercial Councillor in London in the 1960s.

without bloodshed. Now they want to preserve their economic interests there.

17 March

Alan said: "My mid old age health has come to an end."

We had Elizabeth Tomalin here. Alan recalled when speaking about the Tomalins that one of the brothers-in-law's sons, the journalist Michael Tomalin died in Vietnam. Alan wrote to his father who wrote back: "He should not have died." Alan said that the British ways of solving problems by compromises would have been a good, perhaps the best, idea as every problem has two sides, but the whole thing is interwoven with personal interests.

My Chartist book is used by reporters and investigators who make reports on the claims of the Chartist settlement people.

18 March

Alan said that the Academy once had the Queen Mother as a guest. When the academicians left at the end of the dinner, somebody asked Alan to come back as the Queen Mother wanted to speak to him. He went back and the Queen Mother said: "You see, I only know you, and so I wanted to speak to you." And they had a hearty conversation.

Yesterday I heard Brendel play. He was like a surgeon. He began to play immediately, no fuss, just simplicity and grandeur as though he did not want anything but to play his music.

I went to a reception in the Hungarian Embassy. There I found Clara Hatvani, who introduced me to Mr. Cushing, who was a Lecturer in the Eötvös College in Budapest, now in SSEES. His pronunciation is excellent, his knowledge of Hungary and Budapest's streets is accurate. I asked who his professors were. He said Dezső Keresztury and János Horváth. He said when he went to see Horváth, his grandchild was sitting in his lap and he was reading him (or her) the poems of János Arany, the great nineteenth century Hungarian poet. I answered that that is what grandparents do in England. He likes the work of Ágnes Nemes Nagy very much.

Alan explained to me about old Kentish Town. Gillian Tindall wrote a book with a title *The Fields Beneath*, explaining every building in Kentish Town.

20 March

I gave a talk on "History and myself" at the City Lit. I spoke about preconceptions, about Chartism, methodology, my interest in literature and added how much I liked to read novels. Alan quoted a story for me from *The Oxford Book of Literary Anecdotes* about an Archbishop who at the opening of the Dublin Exhibition seemed to devote all his attention to the interior of his hat which at first made him look very devout listening to the speeches, but on closer inspection it appeared that he was reading something, and so intently that the man next to him was prompted to look into the hat and he found that the Archbishop had *Middlemarch* laid open inside it – a much better way of listening to "opening speeches".

24 March

My thoughts are very often with my children. They and Alan mean everything to me. Perhaps it was good for them that I came to England. We were too close. They had no chance to be emotionally independent. Alan spoke about death. For him it does not mean anything. As he said, he may be physically uncomfortable, but it will be a release. What a release! Like a prisoner coming out of prison. He would not like another chance to live. I would take any chance. Alan does not mind leaving. When he is about to die, he will say to me: "Goodbye". We spoke tonight about John Grigg and about his father. The father was a full time busy-body. A good phrase. But I said that to be a full time busy-body, one must have money.

25 March

Better not to say anything about Alan's birthday today. Nothing went right.

29 March

I am going to Manchester with Alan, who is going to give his TV talks on the Liverpool-Manchester railway's 150th Anniversary.

Yesterday we visited Disley, the little village where Alan lived happily with his first wife and eldest son for some years. He tells the story of Disley and Manchester in his autobiography and we have already visited Disley once. Now that I have got to know Alan and his family so much better, all the years in Manchester and in Disley get more realistic to me. We had our lunch in The Ploughboy, Alan's local when he lived here. A very nice pub – modernised though – where Dylan Thomas also had evenings with Socialists when he was staying with Alan and Margaret. Dylan was recommended to them by Cameron as a poor friend, a talented, but penniless poet with the request that they put him up for a week and he stayed there for a month. Dylan usually went to The Ploughboy each evening and "sang for his supper" as Alan said. He was usually given a drink by his audience with whom he discussed socialism. Margaret said to him, dinner is at 7.30, but he came back at 10.30; then Margaret got out of bed and gave him something to eat. Dylan rightly called himself "Swinburne de nos jours"; he also had a way with women. He held them under his spell.

Alan bought his farmhouse at Disley from a man called Moodie in Manchester for £500 and sold out later for £800. The farmhouse was called Three Gates House. It is still there, as it was before, with the grocer's shop in the corner. In the grocer's shop there lived a man who never went anywhere outside the village, not even to the sea: he was born in that house and that is where he died. It was to this man Alan went and said with pride when Giles was born: "I have a son."

The view is splendid from Three Gates House. You can see the little town where Alan spoke at the time of Munich. On the other side is the Peak District, where Alan used to go for long walks. Alan did not become emotional about the whole visit, he simply said: "I shall never come back here again." Simply because he thinks he is getting too old. We drove from Manchester to Disley on the road that he usually took in the winter, sometimes driving in heavy snow. It was a chilly day. Life in Disley does not seem very pleasant to an outsider, but for Alan it was marvellous. He loved going for walks; sometimes he had guests here. He was happy here with Margaret and Giles. Before then they lived in a house in Manchester (The Limes) with the Muggeridges for eighteen months.

3 April

Writing about history is a therapy in a way for me and for Alan. Alan again remembered The Limes, their home in Didsbury. Once a neighbour dropped in and said: "Mrs. Taylor these arches are nice in your flat; my servants used to live here. I never saw these rooms." The firm which delivered the milk is still around. Alan came back here with his second wife as well. She was bored. When I am bored I think it is my fault. We both feel when we are depressed that something is wrong with ourselves and we do not blame each other.

4 April

I am often depressed because everybody here is better than me in that they can express themselves more clearly than I. I feel like an English working man. Can't express myself well. I am a creative person. Creating in writing means seeing the past as a period which has come to an end; then I can see how it was. I refuse to accept that my Hungarian past is the past. So I live in the past and in the present at the same time.

13 April, Rome.

I am not really very good at sight-seeing in company. I like to be alone when absorbing things. Alan was like a little boy this evening; he said I was a middle-aged woman with a girlish inside. He also said he never realises how much he knows about human beings. Nor do I.

15 April

I am happier helping than being helped. I do not like the rich and yet I like to live artistically and wear beautiful dresses. On the whole to be rich is an occupation in itself, which would be a boring, nerve-wracking occupation for me. The only thing which I really like is emotional and financial independence. I like solitude but I do not like living alone.

Yesterday we visited Lucia's mother. Very attractive, charming old lady of about eighty. Her name is Clotilde Maghieri and she wrote a book which is called *La Educande* (Vallachi, ed. Firenze, 1972). This book is about a girls' school and about their teachers, who were priests. The girls adored one of the priests, who was a highly educated and good looking man who kissed one of the girls passionately and asked her not to mention the episode to anyone because only their souls had met. Having met the author and been impressed by her intelligence, I would like to read the book, although the story seems rather sentimental.

Yesterday we looked at the narrow streets around the Pantheon, the ghetto and the house where Mussolini and the Pope made their famous agreement in 1923. There we drank *Grappa Giulia* and later a couple sang for money.

17 April

We visited Keats' last home. He could have looked at the Spanish Steps from his windows. Poor him: dying at the age of twenty-five from consumption. Before he died – he was dying from 4.30 until 11 – he said to his friend: "Hold me and don't be afraid of my dying, it will be peaceful." So it was. He had hardly any lungs left.

2 May

We had a very good conversation about Trevelyan and Namier. Trevelyan[1] was not as good as Plumb makes out and Namier was not as bad.

Alan thinks there is nothing wrong with me and I think there

1 George Macaulay Trevelyan (1876–1962) was regius Professor of Modern History at Cambridge from 1927 to 1940. He is the author of several historical works, the best known of which is *English Social History*. He is the subject of a study by J. H. Plumb.

is nothing wrong with him. He is so talented. I told him that he can safely rely on his talents which will last as long as he lives.

4 May

First of all: I got a telegram from my sons for Mother's Day. I shall be happy today. They are wonderful.

As to Alan. The Book Programme tonight was on Nixon's book. Alan was honest, young, extremely sympathetic and clever. Nixon was a bore. The interesting things that I have learnt from this TV show are:

(a) Alan says what he thinks. Of course he says different things to different people, "speaking for effect, saying what is necessary to say in certain circumstances" – as he wrote somewhere.
(b) He underrates himself, he needs encouragement, he needs success.
(c) He needs more contact with people, i.e. more reassurance from everybody.
(d) I must have more self-confidence. I must believe that I am good for him.

Alan looked better than ever on the screen.

Alan said one afternoon he thought I never had grasped how much he loved me. He is the only man to whom I defer. Alan does not understand the part in me which is talented and I always thought it would be worth hiding it; it might come out after my death. I repeat he is the only man, except my sons, for whom I suppress my own needs; but still I must preserve myself.

Tito is dead. Alan does not want to speak about it or see it on the TV.

11 May

We had a wonderful time in Carlyle's house next to Joanna Kilmartin. What a gloomy atmosphere, what a couple they were! Carlyle himself was restless and unhappy after his wife died, and yet they could not live well together.

Churchill's last great plan was to arrange his own funeral. He did it with every little detail. That plan was the so called "Hope

Not" plan. He hoped it would not come. Alan told me about the funeral and about how the Queen was second to Clemmie. Clemmie did not weep like Jovanka at Tito's funeral.

Yesterday we went for dinner to the Seton-Watsons. There was a Professor from Vienna and the Willets. The wife is half French, half English, vivacious and witty. Her father was so disillusioned with British policy during Munich that he wanted to go and live in Russia. But going to the Soviet Embassy in London he had to fill out so many questionnaires that he gave it up. He later became an admiral. We spoke about Arnold Bennett and I recommended her to read his books.

My son, Ferencz, rang me up and cheerfully said he had been accepted to study for a higher degree. I was delighted.

19 May

We were at Norwich. Alan gave a lecture on "Our Finest Hour". He was good, but not at his best. We met the Vice-President of the University. He was a Bootham boy. His wife is American. She told me to read David Lodge's *Changing Places*. When she went back to America, she saw that there were so many things wrong there. Then she made peace with herself. She did not point out to her mother and sisters all that was wrong there as they could not see it. Only those who moved away from that life could understand.

28 May

Grasmere. We saw Wordsworth's tomb. I saw his face in a nearby tea shop. Very moving, clever face, big nose.

Alan told me lots of things about English kings as we walked down from the hills. Robert the Bruce is well known to every schoolboy. After defeat he took refuge in a cave where he watched a spider rebuild his web several times in the course of two days until eventually he succeeded. That taught him never to give up.

I had a discussion with Alan yesterday evening about the monarchy. He felt that the monarch should be a figure above political parties. He pointed out that during the General Strike the King intervened so that the Soviet money could be accepted for the wives and children of the strikers. Another King intervened against Churchill's Normandy project. I said I was strongly against monarchy as it is not fair that someone should live tax-free like that.

6 June

Alan said I believe in the conspiracy theory of history, he believes in the accident theory.

When we came back from the Greenwich Theatre, where we saw Shaw's *John Bull's Other Island*, we saw a Baby Austin. Alan remarked that that was the car which he drove when he came back from Austria. He borrowed it occasionally from his friend.

8 June

We went to the Lancashire coast to make a programme on the Lancashire towns of Southport, Preston, Blackpool and Lytham. Birkdale was the place where Alan was born. Now Birkdale belongs to Southport and it belongs to the Ormskirk area. We came through Ormskirk Alan had never been there before. Ormskirk has a famous church. Southport is a sea port and a fun place to be. We went along Lord Street and tried to find the Japanese Tea Room his mother went to once a week.

Here, somewhere in Birkdale, Alan's mother had a long telephone conversation and he as a little boy said: "Mummy I have to go somewhere". He repeated it several times and no answer. His mother went on and on and on. Then Alan could not hold on and the trousers started to get wet and there was a little pond. His mother then quickly said that they should get away from there, and that nobody should see the little pond. She did not bother about Alan's trousers.

We went along Lord Street, which still has an Edwardian atmosphere with all the verandah-like shops. Victorian ladies could walk along and do their shopping undisturbed by the heavy rain. Alan used to come with his mother to see a man called Blackwell and listened when he and his mother discussed books. Then Alan spoke about *Pilgrim's Progress*, which he had already read at the age of five.

Alan says Southport does not mean anything to him. But I think it does. He showed me the Victorian Bath with sea water, the old temples of money, the great banks of Lord Street and the Grape House. He used to come here with his father and walk along the pier to see the professor who went into the sea with his bicycle.

As we walked along Lord Street Alan's profile was moving. Never in my life have I seen such a beautiful sad profile. I told him. He said he utterly detested the whole of life. He said I was the only good thing left to him.

David Kemp[1] and the whole TV crew discussed Southport with Alan. Alan spoke about his grandfather who used to go to Matlock and to Southport, where he had hydrobaths which cured him. When he was eighty-five he got a cold and wanted to come to Southport, but left it too late. The following day he died of pneumonia. If he had gone one day earlier he might have survived this last cold as well – or so he believed, at least. He said, "I left it too late." He had eleven children and treated his wife abominably; he left her on her own for months. When he was in Preston, before he came back from Manchester, he went to brothels. When one of his sons got syphilis, he said: "Do you know where you caught it? Don't go there again." That was his only comment. One of his sons married a Preston prostitute called Edith whom he picked up on the docks. When he was told that she was not the sort of woman he should marry he just said: "Hm, I think she had her time, but so had I." Alan said: "What a wonderful thing to say." Alan is always entirely fair.

Alan does not think that there is any point in orbiting the earth. When he said this first, he was asked in the presence of the first astronaut, who was so shocked he could hardly speak. His whole life was being made to seem pointless.

I was deeply moved by the Ugandan famine. I can't understand why people do not do anything: thousands of people die day after day and nobody helps them. Unburied bodies everywhere, flies, men and women like living bones, small children dying. Terrible.

9 June

Alan is worried, he thinks this TV show won't do. He does not like to be told what to say. David Kemp, Murray[2] and two pretty girls are with us.

1 David Kemp is the television producer who made the Granada TV series "The Edge of Britain", with A.J.P. Taylor.
2 Murray Grigor directed "The Edge of Britain".

I read today Michael Foot's review on Grigg's *Nancy Astor*, who had a love-hate relationship with Churchill and who said of Churchill that he united "the worst blood of two continents".

12 June

Winckley Square in Preston. Alan has only ever been here twice in his life, though he lived in Preston. One was when his father died and he had to come here to arrange things according to the will, as the lawyers' offices are in this square. The other occasion was when he was invited to speak at a historical meeting here. In Winckley Square there is a statue of Peel, as in all Lancashire towns, expressing the gratitude of the mill owners because of the repeal of the Corn Laws.

14 June

I shall never forget Alan walking along Preston canal, unhappy and elderly, as he explained what a wonderful canal route it had been in his early days and reflected that its present decline mirrored his own. Then he walked sadly along the canal and at the saddest moment he danced. That was very funny and very sad. It was left out of the TV film, though it was a triumph over unhappiness and old age. The triumph of fun.

15 June

At Lytham. Yesterday we had a very good walk along the shore. Here near the mill Alan went for walks with his grandmother's dog, Paddy.

During the Second World War there were sticks on this field to make it impossible for aeroplanes from Germany to land. We saw the life boat list of lives saved during the last seventy years. I saw a life boat out in the estuary. Then we went to see the docks: decay. Later we went to the pub, where Alan spoke about the convoys in the First and Second World Wars and about Dunlop who invented first the gum for bikes.

17 June

Blackpool. A wonderful, clean place. The Old Theatre is now a bingo hall. There are three piers, the North (this was built first), the South and the Central. The illuminations go on for two months from September to October. It was in Blackpool that the first tram service started. The Great Theatre was built in 1894. It must be the prettiest theatre in the country. There were 230 theatres built by the same man (Coliseum, Palladium, Victoria Palace, Hippodrome etc.) and only about eighteen remain. The circus is magnificent. It is the only permanent circus in Britain.

We visited a boarding house (now called a guest house) which cost £5 a day. There are streets and streets of these boarding houses in Blackpool. In June pensioners come, in July and August families do. Usually they come from the same town together, settle down in the same boarding house; sometimes streets are full of the same people from the same villages. They bring with them their own atmosphere. When the illuminations are over, the boarding house people go for their holidays to the Bahamas, Miami, Spain. The boarding houses are full of cheap things, tasteless but clean. No bugs any more. Tea and coffee, though, are poured out from kettles, the milk already mixed in.

We visited a rock factory. There are about ten to twelve rock factories in Blackpool. The one we visited had twenty workers, amongst them sixteen women – a cheap labour force. They export a lot to Saudi Arabia of all places. Blackpool rock is superior rock. Alan quoted Johnson about the factory: "No man is more innocently employed than when making money."

We also visited the illumination factory which is the only one in the country. Approximately one hundred people work here, amongst them one Hungarian and one Pole. In 1956 more than 1,000 Hungarians came to Blackpool. One man, called Mr. Eliot, made the whole factory, he designed everything and said they did not work for profit. The illuminations began before the First World War. They have cost about £800,000 but at least there are eight million people who are drawn to visit Blackpool to see the illuminations and they spend about £50 million. This is a wonderful deal. This year the new showpieces are the saucy postcards as illumination items. In Blackpool everything serves low tastes.

Alan used to come to Blackpool on horse back, riding along the sand from Lytham.

In the old days people used to stay in the Hotel Metropol; we are now in the Imperial Hotel. Labour Party leaders usually stay here for the Conference.

Alan said that in Victorian England the servants used to iron the newspapers before passing them to the owner of the house.

The Blackpool pleasure beach was overrun by fortune tellers, gipsies, old fashioned fairs, but now there are American influences as well.

Blackpool was compared with Paris thus: "By comparison with Blackpool, Paris is sweet and Sodom a Paradise".

20 June

I can't forget the scene when Cedric Robinson, the sand pilot, took Alan through the sands. He was like a father, like Alan's father, good, kind, serene. We stayed at Morecambe Hotel. This was very modern in the 'thirties; it was designed by Hill who did the Hayward Gallery as well. In one of the rooms there is an Eric Gill map.

30 June

Alan said he could not live without me.

I visited a woman in hospital. I saw a couple there. The woman was terminally ill, her husband visited her every day, bought her the daily paper and they read it together. She takes care how she looks and her husband helps her to put a net on her hair so that it looks fine the next day.

I met my old Hungarian colleague in the PRO. He told me that it doesn't matter what I do but how I do it. Very true. Alan and I spoke about Haynau[1] who settled down in Hungary in the end. I never understood why he went to see a brewery in London. In those days it was a great attraction, like the Guinness brewery in Ireland is now: it has organised tours every two hours.

1 F.W.K.E. von Haynau (1786–1853) was an Austrian General involved with the reign of terror which followed the Hungarian war of Independence. He is also known for his cruelty in similar circumstances in Italy.

3 July

Alan spoke at the annual meeting of the British Academy and told them it would be wrong to expel Blunt. It is not the duty of the Academy to probe into the behaviour of Fellows except on the grounds of scholarship. Robert Blake walked out; he did not want to take part in Academy procedures if he was there.

We got the proofs of Alan's new volume of essays.

Alan told me always to put the kettle on when preparing a meal as boiling water will always be used.

Tomorrow we are going for a working lunch with the Davies couple. I do not know what it means. Margaret should write a biography of Akhmatova, I have just read a wonderful essay on her by an eminent Hungarian essayist called Gábor Tolnai[1].

My driving instructor told me that in England it is generally held that nobody can win a debate. If you win your point you loose in that you might cause ill feelings. That is why people never put questions. It is, anyway, so much better to persuade than to debate. That is what education means here, to educate people to accept their situation.

10 July

Comenius said about history: the study of history gives pleasure to the senses, stimulates the imagination, brightens knowledge, enriches language, sharpens one's views of things and situations and, without acknowledging it, develops our wits.

Alan said the essays in his new volume are not as good as the English essays. I do not agree with this.

I read an article about Moscow in the *Observer* which said there are many young workers from all over the country there. One of them said, "Three things are important for me – homeland, work and family." I couldn't agree more.

Money is very important in this society but people are socially aware, in that they know they should give something to the community or be kind to their fellow men or both.

1 Gábor Tolnai is an eminent Hungarian academician and essayist, Emeritus Professor of Literature and expert on the Renaissance and Italian and Hungarian literature.

2 *August*

Margaret died four days before I went to Hungary. She was fortunate in a way because she did not suffer. At the funeral Alan and their eldest son received the people and Alan read this Thomas Hardy poem:

Only a man harrowing clods
In a slow silent walk
With an old horse that stumbles and nods
Half asleep as they stalk.

Only thin smoke without flame
From the heaps of couch-grass;
Yet this will go onward the same
Though Dynasties pass.

Yonder a maid and her wight
Come whispering by:
War's annals will cloud into night
Ere their story die.

When I came back from Hungary, Alan stood at Terminal One, Heathrow, waiting for me. He was very moved. Me too. It was the end of something for him, now that Margaret was dead. When he read the poem, his daughter Amelia wept. They played Bach softly before and after the ceremony and the grandchildren were there.

Coming back from Hungary I understood better how Alan felt. When I visited our small cottage on the Danube with my sons and everything came back to me. My first husband, who died in 1969 aged forty-four, was still there in the cottage with us.

17 *August*

I went to the antique doll sale today at the Hotel Ivanhoe. All the Victorian dolls were way beyond my means. Alan took me down and waited patiently in the car reading the *Observer*.

We had a young Hungarian linguist for tea, Peter Bartha. Alan discussed with him the Dualist regime and the Habsburg Empire. He thinks that it is untrue that the period of the Dualist regime was a more democratic time in Hungary than the previous or following decades. Alan's view is that it was better for the Hungarian gentry and capitalists but it was not good for other nationalities or for the poor.

20 August

The daily papers in London are full of Alan. "A.J.P. Taylor quits Academy", says *The Times*. "A.J.P. Taylor quits Academy over Blunt 'witch hunt' ", says the *Daily Telegraph*. Interviews, letters from all over the country. "Dearest Alan, great to see you on the Front Page. A noble gesture against a bad case" – wrote Elizabeth Longford from Sussex. I collected all the letters; most of them are in favour of Alan, who is very fit. I am ill. Alan discusses everything with me, though he does what he wants.

21 August

Yesterday we dined with Michael and Jill Foot in their home. Jill is an ardent feminist and showed me her room full of posters and books on Feminism, in England mainly. She is a worthy character. Michael is genuine and witty. We have the same views on Arnold Bennett. He told me that Bennett's articles in the 'twenties on politics and on social questions were excellent as well. Mervyn Jones and his wife Jeanne were there too. They often go to Wales; his mother still lives there. Jeanne liked the new biography of Freud. Mervyn said the author's style was not good enough. Mervyn is very critical.

23 August

We sat a bit in the Rose Garden in Regent's Park, then went through it. We settled down at the end again, where there is a little statue of a small boy sitting down. There were lovely scenes. Families, old ladies, lovers. There were posters announcing which band would play in the morning, which in the afternoon. At the children's lake there were small boats. Many, many afternoons Alan came here with Margaret, then with his sons from the second marriage. As we headed back along the road towards Camden, Alan showed me the Zoo from the outside, the lovely wild goats standing still, one bear, two elephants, one elderly and bad tempered.

I had an awful feeling. I had a similar walk with my first husband eleven years ago, before he went to hospital to die. We walked to the Farkasréti cemetery in Buda, and came back through vineyards and meadows. I felt – as he did – that he was saying goodbye to the bushes and trees and views. So did this man of mine now. My first husband always missed his mother, who died in 1960. So does Alan with Margaret. When we went through the rose garden Margaret was there. When Alan explained things to me and showed me 13 St. Mark's Crescent where he lived with Margaret, Margaret was there too. And Alan told me that the train from Euston to Manchester goes under St. Mark's Crescent. In Manchester Alan had the happiest time in his life with Margaret.

Alan is going to review a book about the British Nazi sympathisers. We spoke about the strength and economy of the German National Socialism. Alan said they were no stronger than the French military, but they were prepared for offensive war. Alan regularly gave talks about the situation during the Second World War. Already in 1943, after Kurzk, he knew that the Allies would win; the Soviets had so many reserves, so many tanks. Alan said they won the war with their tanks and with American jeeps.

29 August

My son and his wife, Gabi, are here. They are wonderful, positive, clever people. Ferencz had chosen very well: Gabi is a woman with character, one can rely on her. A rare phenomenon.

We went to the Isle of Wight. Stayed in the old mill, the home of the first Taylor family. Alan bought it. It now belongs to the first family. They have an enormous billiard table on the first floor which was bought from the local British Legion Club for £20 twenty-odd years ago. I was longing for our first little old cottage in Eastern Hungary at Tapolca, where I lived with my parents; later our small place near the Danube looking into the hills.

1 September

We have been married now for four years. The past lives with us all the time.

My son and daughter-in-law went to the Tate. Gabi liked Turner most. He was the greatest English painter, I think. Reynolds was the first to be widely recognized, Constable is the most idyllic and made a great impression on the French. Gainsborough with his portraits is aloof, magnificent, aristocratic.

3 September

Alan was asked by a Canadian journal to give his opinion on C.S. Lewis, which Alan did. Alan knew him well. He was as ardently religious as Alan was atheist. He was the man who told Alan once he had spent a wonderful summer: he had re-read all of Scott. Alan said he had adolescent taste, but a good literary, philosophical, critical mind. Alan wrote a letter to W.R. Fryer to correct his views about Lewis's reasons for leaving Oxford. He loved Magdalen and his colleagues; there were no enemies there, even if they disagreed on politics and religion.

8 September

My son and daughter-in-law left today. We had my colleague from Hungary here for tea. She was in Bucharest at the International Historical Congress and said that the old daco-Roman idea is already dull for everybody. It was a new feature that there were many historians there from the third world and that oral history was well considered. She also said that Michael Thompson is very charming when speaking about his subject. She was going to St. Andrews and Alan told her that the hotels there are awful, full of American golf-widows. Alan said of my colleague that she was very able. Alan is very good at assessing people. It is true that her main characteristic is efficiency. She is a female Len Deighton.

My daughter-in-law said Macaulay reminded her of Alan when she saw a painting of him in the National Portrait Gallery. Alan said Macaulay was very much a politician. He now reads to me every evening Macaulay's *History of England*. Alan enjoys it tremendously.

Alan spoke about Charles Webster. He was a Lancashire boy and loved and esteemed Alan. He wanted Alan to be Regius Professor. He was one of the best referees Alan had when he wanted to be Fellow of the British Academy. I met Webster twice in 1948 when I had a sabbatical year to work on Palmerston. I was happy to know that Alan liked Webster so much because I did too, though I did not know him well. He was very kind to me, very easy going, good humoured and cheerful. It seems to me that Lancashire people are my sort of people in Britain.

11 September

Yesterday we had a very good discussion about Romania. There is no proof of what happened to the Dacians. If we were to research what happened to Prague before it became the capital of Czechoslovakia, we would discover that it was German. Paris would have been Breton, (Bretons are or were of Welsh origin – they still understand Welsh up to a point) and London would have been Celtic.

Alan has a very good reasoning power.

Yesterday we met the second Foot. He is also Michael, but a historian of the SOE. He introduced László Veress[1] to the Hungarian historian, Gyula Juhász[2]. After they met, Juhász rewrote his book on 1943.

13 September

Yesterday was Ferencz's birthday. I sent a telegram and wished him and Gabi, his wife, good health and happiness. In our local post office the wife told me how lovely Gabi was, not a fighter, she added.

A good dinner at the Skidelskys. Gust has changed her hairstyle.

1 Ladislav Veress was a Hungarian diplomat who took part in the Resistance in the Second World War. He lived in Britain after the war.

2 Gyula Juhász is a Hungarian historian, the author of many books on the period 1939–1945, diplomatic and intellectual history. He is head of the Hungarian Széchenyi (National) Library.

Christine and Norman Stone[1] were the other guests. James Joll[2] reviewed Norman's book on Hitler and he liked the review. They agreed with me, that the Soviet Union should not abolish her nuclear power unilaterally.

Robert said Alan was like Keynes. He has written a piece on Alan and over-complicated Alan's character. I said that in Alan there are many Quakerisms which Robert did not know of. Robert could not understand how Alan could be so controversial and in politics – with CND – so one-sided.

Alan has finished the sixteenth chapter of his autobiography. The house is cold, a strong wind blows. We go to Budapest in December.

14 September

I read yesterday Alan's sixteenth chapter, then I read my sixth chapter; we both dealt with nearly the same period. For me it was tragic, for him productive. He dealt with his many works, travels, I dealt with my relationship with people and my feelings. We both dealt much with our children, he mentioned what they saw together, what he learnt from his children, I mentioned their developments, their relationship with their father, with me. The main differences between us show in our autobiographies.

(a) Alan is interested in his experiences and activities.
(b) I am interested in feelings, reactions, relationships. That is why I have to write about my activities and experiences in my diary.
(c) Alan lives in the present. Concentrates firmly on what he is doing.
(d) I am living in the present, in the past and in the future all at the same time. That shows in our work, in our diaries, in our relationships with others.

There is a wonderful phrase in Evelyn Waugh's letters (to his son

1 Norman Stone is Professor of Modern History and Fellow of Worcester College, Oxford. He is an expert on Russian History and Eastern Europe. His book, *The Eastern Front 1914–1917*, won the Wolfson prize for History in 1976.

2 James Joll is Professor Emeritus of International History at the University of London. He has had a distinguished academic career, with appointments on both sides of the Atlantic.

Auberon): "I can only provide opportunities for your achievements."

15 September

Alan read me a longish piece from Macaulay. He observed, quite rightly, that Macaulay had no ears. He could write for instance such things as "William was not willing". Alan spoke about the Wainwright Lectures which he gave in Oxford in 1970 about Beaverbrook. Six lectures. He began as nobody before him had begun: "Ladies and Gentlemen". He also waited outside and when the time came, he opened the door, went straight in and began his performance. He wanted to go in with a clear mind and also, I think he wanted to make an impression.

22 September

We spoke about men and women. Alan said that men do not physically need to be promiscuous, only psychologically. This is the way they are brought up. Men think they should be promiscuous, they think they should need a variety of women to satisfy them. It is not true and we do not know whether women should be promiscuous or not. In old times of course women were more wary of being promiscuous as they became pregnant. Nowadays this is not a threat any more. There are plenty of men who are sexually aroused only by their own wives. As a literary example look at Mr. and Mrs. Shandy. Mr. Shandy used to have sex every week on a Sunday and when he took his watch off, he was aroused because he was so used to the ritual. My whole education was different. We were told to be always charming to men, otherwise they might turn towards other women.

Alan said during the night that the Yugoslavs were called "jugs" and the French "frogs". Alan read to me from Iona and Peter Opie's *The Oxford Book of Nursery Rhymes*. I liked "Birthdays". Alan was born on a Sunday and according to the nursery rhyme:

". . . the child that is born on the Sabbath day
is bonny and blithe and good and gay" – like me – said Alan.

I loved "Worldly Wise"

"A wise old owl sat in an oak,
The more he heard the less he spoke;
The less he spoke the more he heard.
Why aren't we all like that wise old bird?"

Also:

"One thing at a time
And that done well,
Is a very good rule,
As many can tell."

On the TV there was a debate on Nuclear War. E.P. Thompson said he wanted a nuclear free zone in Europe. Lord Chalfont expressed a lot of unpleasant views. Alan said: "The only thing we said was that it was wrong, it was wrong; but we never discussed a solution."

28 September

I am fifty-seven today, Alan will be seventy-five in March. One day he told me: "Eva, I am getting old." He is so sharp, he always knows what is happening to him. His face is sometimes like that of a baby.

He says sometimes: this is my last great involvement (in the Blunt affair), this is my last appearance on the box ("The Edge of Britain"). I wonder, would it be best to end the diary here? Anyhow, it was a nice birthday present for me when Alan said: "I am very glad that you are here with me."

29 September

A man ran after Alan, a heavy working class man and said: "You know the missus and me, we always watch you on the box. I told the missus that I liked what you said." "What was that?" "When you said: 'if people speak about war they will get war.' " Alan said, "That is why I am not often on the box. *They* don't like what I say."

David Kemp was here. He is planning a show on three cities with Alan. One where Alan spent many years – that is York.

Another which is close to his heart – Venice. The third is historic, but forgotten – Alan has visited it: Istanbul.

1 October

The gardener in Peter Rabbit is called Mr. McGregor. This is because the gardeners in England were mainly Scots, just as those in Hungary are mainly Bulgarian.

I went to Kew with Alan. He got his card extended at the Public Record Office. We had a long walk in Kew Gardens, looked in at Cynthia's house, which looks sad now that Robert has left.

We had lunch in the Public Record Office. Elizabeth Barker joined us. She spoke about the funeral of László Veress. There were many who spoke, amongst them a lay priest; there were longish oratorios, and the Hungarian tricolour was placed upon his body. Michael Foot (SOE man) spoke also.

2 October

The Labour Conference voted against the Common Market. The *Evening News*, which Alan hated and never read – has amalgamated with the *Evening Standard*.

I am afraid my autobiography leads me away from Alan. I am less interested in him when I am writing about my past – though it is not completely true. But I have to work on my past in order to live in the present. The problem will be that when I have got my past sorted out and finished the autobiography, Alan might not be alive any more.

7 October

Yesterday Hattie Jacques died. She played in the Players Theatre of which Alan was a member for at least twenty years. He loved it but later, after the war, it was full of foreigners who ate and drank too much. I am sorry that I did not see Hattie more often on TV. Perhaps we shall watch TV more often from now on as today we are going to buy a colour TV.

Yesterday we got copies of Alan's new volume of essays. He

feels he is going downhill and remembered the last volume of essays written by Namier which Alan criticised heavily in the *Manchester Guardian*. Namier said to Carr: "Poor Alan, he has lost his touch."

We spoke about publishers. Samuel Webb and later, on his advice, George Bernard Shaw, published their books themselves.

We spoke about Hitler. Why did he declare war on the USA in 1941? Unsolved and unsolvable questions. Alan thinks perhaps because he felt it did not matter one way or the other.

11 October

We talked about the Blitz, which began in September 1940. One of the worst things about the Blitz was that it hit the publishers square in the city. Many publishers had books in stock, and they were all burnt. There was a firm who had a stock of books from every publisher, at least two million books, and all of them were burnt. In those days bookshops ordered from this firm. The Blitz ruined them and as their books were not insured, the firm never recovered.

The Germans really wanted to hit stations and bridges, but they hardly hit any. They hit many churches instead, which were ruined because the Germans used incendiary bombs and the churches had no guards, so they were burnt down. St. Pauls was hit but was saved because it was guarded.

Isis is an undergraduate Oxford paper. Alan was once interviewed for it. Isis was said to be the Roman name for the Thames (Thameris) and some suggested using Isis instead of Thames to make a distinction between Thames and Thame, the river which goes through the town Thame.

In England children call their father Dad or Daddy. Da is Welsh for Dad.

Rug is a Celtic word. So, probably, is Avon for water. There are many Avons in England: one in Wiltshire, one in Leicestershire, one in Warwickshire.

Alan never has liked milk. He was brought up on Bovril. He did not even like rice pudding when it was made more attractive with banana slices.

Great debate on at the Conservative Conference: why did the London police search demonstrators?

15 October

In *The Times* today somebody suggested that the U.K. should be called the United Queendom. Witty.

Alan once went to the chief Tory dining club in Oxford, the "Canning Club" as a speaker and began by saying "I don't know what I am doing here . . ." and so on. John Sparrow, a member of the Society, Warden of All Souls got up and said, "You spoilt my speech. I wanted to say I don't know what Alan Taylor is doing here." Then Leo Amery, a nice, but boring, man spoke for an hour.

Alan's seminar yesterday. The unscientific approach to the Polish guarantee by Britain: Alan said it was given as a bluff, became serious because of the Polish-Soviet Pact and then became essential because of the popular feeling of honour.

17 October

Yesterday we went to the *Spectator* lunch. These Thursday lunches take place in a relaxed mood, the paper goes to press on Wednesday evening. Alexander Chancellor is the Editor of the *Spectator* and, as we were told, was chosen by the owner as he was the only young journalist whom he knew. Alexander's father and he himself worked for Reuters for years. Chancellor brought the circulation of the *Spectator* up from 12,000 to 18,000 copies within the last two years. Graham Greene always takes part in the Thursday lunch when he is in London. Richard Ingrams was there. He wants to invite us for dinner. Ingrams once called Alan "The Beaverbrook professor of history".

We saw two parts of "The Edge of Britain". It was very good, good music too. As always, I looked awful.

Evening party at Robert Kee's house. Interesting talks with Miriam and John Gross[1]. John was not at all silent as I thought he would be. Miriam, who is an established journalist in her own right, usually has interviews with people at 12 o'clock, because she says, they tend to open up at this time of the day best. Deakin's

1 John Gross was literary editor of the *New Statesman*, and worked on the *TLS* and the *Spectator*. His book, *The Rise and Fall of the Man of Letters*, won the Duff Cooper Memorial Prize.

son was there. He speaks quickly, otherwise he feels he won't get a word in edgeways. This comes of being the third of five sons.

19 October

We went yesterday to Covent Garden Market. It is lovely and colourful, though full of tourists. We gave a dinner party. Robert Kee, family members, friends. We spoke about communism. They don't think it would be a good thing.

I am longing for my sons. Why did I leave them? It seems to me silly, but in reality they were ripe for it. They wanted to be independent.

Robert spoke about his experiences in German prisons. He said they were well treated, but the Russian prisoners were made to serve them: they were really slaves. But the Germans were "nice" to the British.

Kate spoke about the situation in the House of Lords. She is an archivist in the House of Lords Record Office. In the House there are about 2,000 people and the provisions are not good at all. The pamphlets which arrive to be deposited there are not read by anyone.

Giles was very sorry to miss the sex-change programme which was like a soap-opera. Alan said he really agreed with Mary Whitehouse. TV is not for nasty things, but good entertainment and information.

Pink collar job means: hairdressing, cleaning, typing.

Michael Foot has a second article about Beaverbrook in the *Observer*. When the Anglo-Soviet Alliance came into effect on June 22, 1941, he was so happy in Cherkley that "I ran down the stairs and ransacked from the gramophone cupboard the record of the Internationale which I knew was there and turned it on full blast."

What is a genius? Someone who can work hard and find things easy. Nijinsky once said, "Why do people not stay in the air for a minute, why do they come down so quickly?" For him this was natural.

27 October

At Oxford with the Morgans. Lovely family, lovely children. The little boy is called David after Lloyd George. They try to adapt to village life after college life.

Lord Carrington is in Budapest. Boldizsár[1] is amongst the hosts.

Michael Foot and Stewart Innes sent in their works in answer to Alan's essays. Stewart liked his last one best. He said in his letter that he was getting old. Alan said this morning that he is not getting old – we agreed that he is just elderly.

31 October

Alan's review of Isaiah Berlin's *Personal Impressions* did not meet with Terry Kilmartin's approval. He thought it was a bit unfriendly towards Isaiah. Alan did not mean that at all. I am keeping the original review.

When we went to the lunch-time concert at the Bishopsgate Institute to hear musical families play Brahms, Chopin and Ravel, we went from Gospel Oak to Broad Street by the North London Line. It was not a warm day, but the sun shone. Alan sat opposite me. I watched his face in the window. It was a lovely face, fading slowly. How long will he last?

We got the *English Historical Review* for October 1980. A very unkind review of my *Chartism*. Thank God I do not crave praise. I don't know whether I am a talented and a good person or not. I think I am talented and good, but somehow for a woman it is more difficult.

1 November

Yesterday we saw Sean O'Casey's *Juno and the Peacock* at the Aldwych Theatre. A good production; Robert Kee wrote the Introduction to the programme and that was quite good too. Two ladies joined us to say how much they admired Alan's books.

Going home by tube I saw a young man lying on the platform in Leicester Square station. He vomitted and then when the train arrived he got in. He looked very unwell and pale. I was very worried. Alan said: "It is no good worrying, you can't help."

1 Ivan Boldizsár is a Hungarian author and journalist. He is also editor of the *New Hungarian Quarterly*.

It was interesting to hear from Alan that once upon a time *Juno* was regarded as a comedy. How could it have been? It is so Gorkyish.

4 November

Alan told me tonight that he visited his mother for five years during her illness. She came to her senses only occasionally. When Alan visited her, she just smiled and Alan smiled back. Alan said: "When you have a mother who is not with you and a wife who has fallen for somebody else, you don't bother about humankind, you just work. That's what I did" – for thirty-odd years from 1939 to 1976. Disley was good because there were good companions and many things to share with Margaret. They did not discuss love, they just lived. There was no romance in that. Alan was always practical when Giles was born and when he began to walk, Alan walked with him because he needed it. When from the second family Crispin and Daniel wanted to go for a walk, Alan would prefer to go with them than to stay with his second wife. Children ruined his relationships with his wives. It seemed he preferred his children to them. Alan was always very practical with his children.

I heard on the radio that a woman was advertising a Guy Fawkes day firework display and that she thought that the children should go to this rather than have their own displays. The interviewer said that they like to be individually entertained, they don't like discipline. The woman said they would be much better entertained by organized fireworks; the fireworks would be more satisfactory and much safer. Each year fireworks cause terrible casualties among children. It's no good, they want free choice and democracy.

Thatcher's biography has been sent all over the country, free of charge. Mrs. Margaret Hogan, wrote this letter to *The Times:* "Sir, Free copies of *Margaret Thatcher: A Profile* by Patricia Murray are being distributed to libraries, presumably to ensure maximum circulation. I quote from the letter which accompanies the book, signed by Sir John Howard: 'I enclose herewith with my compliments a profile of Margaret Thatcher by Patricia Murray which has recently been issued and in view of the great interest which so many people are now taking in Margaret Thatcher, our first woman Prime Minister, I do hope that your library will be interested in the circulation of this book. I would be glad if you would acknowledge safe receipt of this and your comments on the likely interest in this book would be very welcome.' It would be preferable if unsolicited political propaganda were not foisted on the public in this manner."

It is wonderful how cheerfully the English radio reporters make their remarks about the worst hours of London traffic. They sing, they recite poems about the North Circular Road, where commuters have to wait long stretches.

5 November

We went to Rugby. Alan spoke about himself and about writing history. He said historians always read. In the school the deputy headmaster earns about £3,000 a year and gets a house to live in. At Rugby there are 700 students, amongst them seventy girls. It is an independent school taking children from twelve to eighteen. Two of Alan's children are teachers. They would not teach in independent schools.

Alan does not like it when I work after dinner. Reading – yes, but working – no. You have to keep your mind clear before going to bed.

7 November

Alan went to Russia in the early 'twenties and saw looms in a factory. Four people worked on them, they were called Betty machines. Now forty people work on automatic looms. The automatic loom killed the Lancashire cotton mills. The old machines were outdated and it was cheaper to replace them with Japanese ones or other imported goods. In the old days the Germans always imported yarns from England.

Alan has finished the review of Harold Nicolson's biography (1st. volume). I said that *Some People* was not Harold's masterpiece. Alan entirely agreed.

10 November

One has to look upon life from above. Poor Alan is getting older and he makes the best of it. We had Alan Sked[1] with us for tea. He is such a charmer. Over tea we talked about Beneš, Ripka and Osusky. Alan said the Czechs always stick together. Ripka was warned by a Communist to leave the country in 1948. Osusky was a Slovak.

Each morning we discuss which tie Alan should put on. He usually wears a tie given to him by whoever he is going to meet that day.

Alan gave his review of Michael Foot's book to Valerie Grove who is the literary editor of the *Standard*. Alan told the story about Beaverbrook saying that Michael would one day be PM and Valerie asked Alan to include this little episode in his review, which he declined to do. He has never allowed people to shape his work and never will.

17 November

Yesterday there was a good article on Orwell in the *Observer*. Alan knew him well and he did not give a favourable impression of him. I said to Alan that it was a misfortune that *Animal Farm* came out in 1945. It helped to develop anti-Soviet feeling in this country and elsewhere. I said to Alan that "all animals are equal but some animals are more equal than others" is a very apt description of some Western democracies as well, in as much as those who have great wealth do not always stop to consider the needs of those who don't.

We went to see the Goldfingers. Ursula is a member of the Blackwell family. She showed me a book about her ancestors which was compiled by a racing gentleman, one of her relatives. We spoke about her life. She said it would be the same as Russell's if she were to wipe out "he" and write "she" throughout. I said that in the opinion of my sons she had wasted her life, because her talents were as great as Ernö's, and yet she never developed them; she sacrificed her talent for his. Ursula just said simply, "It

1 Alan Sked is a lecturer in International history in the LSE. He specialises in the history of the Habsburg Empire and Modern Britain.

happens sometimes." How much I love her. Then she showed me her garden and basement flat where her younger son and his family used to live. Ernö and Ursula agreed that young grandchildren are horrible. They are interested only when you speak about their parents. Alan's two granddaughters came with their mother, Sophia. Sophia is an enlightened teacher. The daughters are charming, intelligent and articulate. Six-year-old Rosa, named after Rosa Luxemburg, can tell the time as she has just been given a watch. When they don't eat, Alan takes their meal away and eats it himself.

21 November

Alan said that as he has to write the Langham Diary for the *Listener* we should go and see porno shops and films. It would be a good excuse to see them, otherwise he would be bored by them and also people would be shocked to see him, the famous and old historian, in such places.

We went to the Hungarian Embassy for a folk music evening. Alan would have preferred a nice Mozart or Bartók evening. The Ringroses, Thomas Balogh and George Mikes[1] were there as well. Funny being a famous resident in London entertained by the Ambassador and his wife like that.

The other evening we were invited to dinner by John and Patsy Grigg. Patsy is Irish by origin; she wanted to come to England because she thought it would be a land of milk and honey. Later she realised that it was not. There were Hugh and Vanessa Thomas[2] and Julia and William Camp[3]. Hugh Thomas, the son of a Welsh shopkeeper, is now Thatcher's adviser. He changed his allegiance from left to right. His wife Vanessa said she did not like the idea that somebody like Vanessa Redgrave should have the same name as her, particularly as she does not like Vanessa Redgrave's political outlook. Julia Camp is forty-six and looks

1 George Mikes is a Hungarian émigré author who is perhaps best known for his amusing "handbooks" which include *How to be an Alien* and *English Humour for Beginners.*

2 Hugh Thomas is a historian whose book, *The Spanish Civil War* won the Somerset Maugham Prize. He has been Chairman of the Centre for Policy Studies since 1979.

3 William Camp is the author of several novels and a biography of F.E. Smith. He has been active in Labour Party politics since 1949.

thirty. Very clever woman, daughter of a German and, as she said, an upper class Irish lady. She married Camp, who is half Arab, half American, a freelance journalist and writer. He arranged the election of Michael Foot. He is strongly in favour of Peter Shore, who with the help of the Hungarian Twins (Balogh and Káldor) will help Michael Foot to make a sound economic policy.

This was one fragment of English intellectual life. All those wives expressed views on the misery of being a wife in England. What makes it worse is that with inflation one cannot go out for intellectual pleasure as much as one did before; Patsy asked if I would like to be invited to dinner with the Koestlers. I said no.

26 November

We went to Birmingham and Alan gave a lecture on Churchill. After the lecture the questions were very good. One question referred to the relationship between Beaverbrook and Churchill. Alan said amongst other things that Beaverbrook wanted to cheer Churchill up, as Churchill was ill and dying for a long time. One evening Beaverbrook came back triumphantly and said he had won the evening: Churchill spoke. Alan's lecture was so full of human insight. There he stood, a fragile old man, but so strong in mind and character. He does not want to dominate the audience, he just explains things from many angles with great charm. We met the President of the Historical Association, Ralph Davies, a medievalist and academician. He discussed the 75th Anniversary proceedings of the Historical Association with Alan.

29 November

I met the author of Orwell's biography, Bernard Crick, at the *Guardian* Lunch in Drury Lane. I think it is a good book; the author looks strong willed. I think he achieved what he set out to do: reject the British tradition of introspective, interpretative biography. According to Crick, for Orwell work was more important than any personal relationship and he cared for himself only in his capacity as a writer. We also met Barbara Wootton, who is now eighty-three and corrected someone who said she was eighty-five. We met the writer William Golding. He said I was a strong woman. And of course we met Bill Webb and the two women in his life. Both are the same honest intellectual type; the difference is that one is dark-haired and sexy, the other is blonde and fair and a bit of a schoolmarm.

In Sebastian's house we met his friends, a couple who now live in Hong Kong. I asked the wife what she was doing there as a wife. She said she looked after her garden and read Dickens. I expect she would do that anywhere in the world. Sebastian went for a lunch the other day where everybody was betting. They have bets over the wine, over the waiter's weight and so on. Everybody puts £1 in the pool and whoever wins, wins the lot. How very funny.

Alan, sitting in his bath tonight, said that when we married it was not part of the bargain that he would grow old.

2 December

Orwell's last days made me feel ill when I read about them. Alan laughed at me. Sometimes we hardly speak. There is no need to. We are like that lovely old couple whom we usually see when going to concerts at the Elizabeth Hall. They always sit at the front row, and never speak to each other, because they understand each other so completely.

6 December

The Times reviewed Alan's and Rowse's volumes of essays. One is witty, the other is dull and vain. We spoke about Rowse today. There was once a superb scene in the college between Rowse and Cole when Rowse told him he had not many friends left. Cole answered that he had had one but that friendship was dead. Rowse went pale and left the room. Rowse likes to move in aristocratic circles. All Souls College had Dawson[1], Simon[2] and Halifax as appeasers, but also had many anti-appeasers.

1 Geoffrey Dawson was editor of *The Times* in the 'thirties and a great appeaser of Hitler.
2 Sir John Simon was a Cabinet Minister in the 'thirties. As Foreign Secretary, he took part in negotiating the Anglo-German Naval Agreement in 1935.

8 December

Daniel was right. Alan has no small talk. He can speak about his works, about historical events in the past and in the present. He is re-reading his *Habsburg Monarchy* and thinks how clever he was in those days. He thinks this is the best book he has ever written but he always thought that.

12 December

We came back from Manchester. Alan had to do a lot of work with Murray Grigor and David Kemp on the Lancashire TV show. The first episode will be shown on January 21, 1981. Southport is quite a smart place. I got to know more about it this time. We lived lavishly there in the Prince of Wales Hotel. At one of our dinner parties a friend spoke about Southport's inhabitants. The wealthy bourgeoisie live in beautiful houses, wives are patrons of Arts centres and work there part-time. They sometimes have villas in the South of France or in the Bahamas and they go there in their private planes. One of the TV crew girls, Lizzie, has bought a house in Manchester, a "two up, two down". Murray spoke about the hobbies of English people. Some are so fond of engines that they collect recordings of the sounds of their beloved engines.

I read with great delight a book of Arnold Bennett's collected articles. I love Bennett. He wrote about Zola who had no time to read. A great comfort to me. Also Bennett wrote about an author who wrote a book about how to read. Superficial reading is a waste of time. Very true. Better to read less and well.

14 December

Writing my autobiography shows that it is not possible to carry on with research and write an autobiography. Next year I shall have to decide what to do. It is too much to write, to read and to carry on research. It is also difficult to be independent from Alan and maintain our love for each other.

17 December

Alan and I had a good meal with a Swedish TV man in Wheeler's. The man was nice but very dull. Next day he came and got out of Alan a good deal of wisdom about the political events of 1980. Alan felt that "Fin de siècle" feeling is coming back; perhaps it came with the inflation which brought brutality, racism, anti-semitism and all sorts of things besides.

Then we went to see a film called *Being There* – the last film of Peter Sellers. He was very good; he probably knew he was dying. Melvyn Douglas was also excellent. The music was unendurable. Poor Alan, he did not want this. I promised not to take him to a cinema again. He was exhausted. We had a rest in the National Gallery. There was carol singing in Trafalgar Square.

The Christmas tree from Norway is much smaller than usual. Black, rainy day.

Tomorrow morning we are off to enjoyable, lovely Budapest. Hurrah!

18 – 30 December

A lovely holiday in Budapest. The country is poorer than England, but the people are warm hearted and intelligent, their kindness is obvious. My family received Alan with warmth and love. It was evident that all my academic friends were happy to meet us, and there was not the slightest trace of estrangement between me and my sons. A TV show was made about Alan on Hungarian TV and it was a great success. I was very happy that it was made; it was worth the effort of arranging it. Wodehouse, in his old age, once said that he did not know whether his literary merits were worthwhile but at least, he said, everybody could see he took the trouble. I take trouble and sometimes succeed. My aims for 1981: to do two historical works about Blackwell and Kossuth, go on with my diary, write *The English Husband*, save money, make my children and Alan happy and buy cassettes and books.

I have read an article in a Hungarian paper which claims that the people are not polite enough to each other. Alan said he could remember how rude Lindemann was. Lindemann always gave money to Churchill, hence partly the great friendship. Alan recalled the mistletoe in the Mill at Yarmouth. It was always hung there for Christmas and under it Alan got many kisses from the girlfriends of his daughters. Alan loves to be loved but would not confess it.

In another Hungarian paper I read an article by a leading economist. He said whoever we have taught to swim, let him swim. So it is with my children, though I would like to watch how they swim from a distance.

1981

8 January

A talk in Alan's seminar on Churchill. The lecturer stressed the friendship between Balfour and Churchill. Churchill had liberal inclinations but in the 'thirties there was no opportunity to fight for India. Alan said at the end that Churchill's son said to him that his father was never Conservative. In 1940 he felt that this was "his revenge". Winston was unreliable as a party man.

A conversation with Henry Pelling.[1] He said it was worth while seeing the dispatches of the British Ambassador from Washington. After 1945 the Ambassador was still Halifax. Pelling knows that I am working on *Britain and Hungary 1945–55*.

9 January

Alan said that relations with children are like one-way traffic. They grow up and like to see their parents well looked after but do not necessarily stay by them. That is true, but I think when they are in their late thirties they come closer to their parents emotionally and are like good friends who share their problems.

1 Henry Mathison Pelling has held various academic posts since 1949 and is now a fellow of St John's College, Cambridge. He has written a great many books on the history of the Labour Party and Socialism in Britain and a book about Britain and the Second World War.

10 January

Charles Ringrose, the Secretary of the British Hungarian Friendship Society, asked Alan to be the President of this Society. Alan accepted.

Alan recently wrote a piece on the Romans in Britain. In his view the Romans behaved very badly in Britain, nearly as badly as Hitler behaved. Alan's mind is brilliant. He only wants to live as long as he is bright. He does not like his body any more.

Alan immediately began to think about what he would say as President of the BHFS. He would say – he told me – that he thought he had married one Hungarian and now it turned out that he married the whole of the Hungarian nation.

We got the *New Hungarian Quarterly* today. I read some of the articles. One written by Gy. Juhász is about the negotiations carried on between Hungarians and Foreign Office representatives in 1943 about the possibility of Hungary turning against Hitler. Alan said anyhow it could not succeed because the British forces were stuck in Southern Italy and could not come to liberate Hungary. There was not enough resistance in Hungary either. Tito showed signs of wanting to help, though they were not successful against the Germans; there was, however, a strong resistance movement. The British sent them supplies by ship and by air. Hungary seemed too far away and so even if there had been a stronger resistance, it is not certain that the British would have sent supplies.

I am having great difficulty in writing my *English Husband*. Perhaps I do not know my husband well enough – not that I do not trust him.

11 January

The British do not speak about themselves: see the interview with the Duke of Edinburgh when Mavis Nicholson asked about the lack of confidence he suffered in his early boyhood. The way he evaded the issue in answering this question was very characteristic.

Sebastian, Alan's journalist son, said that in this country the aim of every journalist is to give a summary in the first paragraph of every article in case it has to be abbreviated.

13 January

I am reading Colette: *The Pure and the Impure*. A woman is always alone with a man.

I am not happy with my autobiography. Perhaps it would be better to go back to history. This life of mine gives me satisfaction but not enough change. I am more interested in human beings and in reading than in sight seeing, music and nature. At least I know this at the age of fifty-eight.

25 January

I received lovely long letters from my sons. I preserve them. We went to Liverpool to give interviews with Shelley Rhode. It seemed from the flowers and praise that I was quite good but Alan said we should go separately; he does not like to share his performances. Quite right.

I criticise Alan when he speaks about the Third World War. He should not speak about it, even if he feels it is imminent. The more we speak about it, the worse we feel.

We saw Ralph Richardson in *Early Days*. I thought it was superb. Alan thought it was sloppy: confrontation with success and death. Richardson is a strong man with wonderful, artistic fingers.

26 January

I saw *Une Semaine de Vacances* with Ursula at the Curzon. It was interesting, what she said about it – but then she never says worthless things. She appreciated the characters and said that the French could not be deemed to be better or worse than the English – they are simply different. Ursula would have liked to stay in France when she married Ernö, but he wanted to settle here. She thinks it is unfair to look after an old member of the family. She will put in her will before she gets senile, that she wants to be put in a home. Now she looks after her husband's 97-year-old mother.

We went to see Verdi's *Un Ballo in Maschera* at Covent Garden as guests of Aline and Isaiah Berlin. In the intervals we had dinner with them and with another couple. Isaiah is lively, charming, entertaining. Aline is clever and simple.

The typewriter which I am using now belonged to Alan and he wrote most of his books on it (*The Struggle for Mastery of Europe, Bismarck, The History of England*). He switched over to an electric typewriter when he wrote *Beaverbrook*.

Alan was sent to Bootham because his mother did not want him to be in the Officer Training Corps. This meant that from the age of sixteen, boys in all public schools were trained as officers. Thus in the First World War all officers came from public schools. I asked Alan what he learned at Bootham, he said: "To appreciate Gothic architecture."

3 February

Alan spoke about Zilliacus who was a Finn and was so pleased to know that Alan had written about him in *The Troublemakers* that from that time on he signed himself "Zilliacus, The Troublemaker". He wrote in the *New Statesman* under pseudonyms like Vigilantes and Covenanter. He was a left wing politician, secretary to Henderson at the Disarmament Conference. He believed ardently in the League of Nations and in socialism.

I have picked up a very good expression: "to blow one's own trumpet".

5 February

I think Alan's friend Theodore was right. For Alan one person is not enough. Like an actor he needs attention from many sides.

8 February

We spoke about the Second World War. I said to Alan that in Miskolc, where I lived in East Hungary in the summer of 1941, we did not feel the effects of war at all and not even in 1942. In the summer of 1943 it was different. Each night bombers came from Italy.

In May 1940 peace negotiations went on in Italy. Sumner

Welles was sent by Roosevelt to Mussolini. Historians thought it was just a show to please the electors. This was not so. Roosevelt genuinely believed that it might have been a possibility. Hitler, after the collapse of France, thought he could dictate the peace conditions. Churchill was not in the mood for negotiations.

Yesterday evening I spoke to Pisti on the telephone. He had just come back from Lower Tatra. He had a wonderful week skiing, feeling healthy. Now he realises what health means. He said he would go back once a year at least. I said, "Twice." He laughed. We were in tune. Then he said: "I took your book with me – *The Appeasers* – and could not put it down. If history were taught like that, I would have liked it." I told Pisti that his saying that made it all worthwhile.

I was so happy then that I kissed Alan. We had a long and good conversation about the Crimean War. How John Bright hated it. When he was an old man, his grandson pointed to a column erected for those who had fallen in the Crimea and asked Bright what it was. Bright said, "A crime."

Then Alan jumped up and looked at his *The Trouble Makers*, found the passage on Bright's speech in 1858 in Birmingham, where he said that the balance of power is the creation of the English aristocracy. As he read this to me, he remembered that once at the BBC he read Bright's speech in a Lancashire accent. Bright's family was furious. Alan admitted that he had exaggerated it a bit.

We saw Priestley's *Dangerous Corners* at the Ambassador. An elderly woman helped Alan to put his coat on. He felt insulted. Priestley looked, in a photo, like my first husband, William; they were born on the same day. We spoke about wives, about Priestley's wife Jacquetta and Robert Kee's wife Janetta. Are we not like the couples in Bennett's *Riceyman Steps*? Individually happy, together in marriages slightly ruinous. My love is my profession as well.

15 February

When Alan was in Vienna, Eric Phipps was the British Ambassador there. Living in the huge ambassadorial Palace inherited from the great days of the Habsburg Monarchy, Phipps asked Alan how he liked "this little state". Alan said it would not last very long. Whereupon Phipps said, "I do not think so. There are plenty of nice people here."

Rosa, Alan's grand-daughter, spent the night with us. She tried to teach me how to pronounce "naughty". She is a very sensitive, nice little girl. We played "beggar your neighbour" with her in the evening.

17 February

We discussed the Chamberlains. They were an unlucky lot. Joseph, the radical Gladstonian, never became Prime Minister. Nor did Austen who was the brightest. Neville Chamberlain, who was regarded by his father as the stupid one and sent to South Africa, did it instead. Alan told me a story about Austen. He was once invited as a guest to Mrs. Greville's house. At dinner she used to comment on the butler and once she noticed he was drunk. She wrote to him on a little piece of paper "Go out, you are drunk" but the butler misunderstood and took it to Austen Chamberlain. Austen rose and left the table and when the hostess enquired why he was leaving, he said, "I am not drunk, but I leave."

We went to the Bishopsgate Institute for a lunch-time concert. The Mayoress gave a reception. I spoke to two women sheriffs. They said that the Bishopsgate Institute was established in the middle of the last century as a charitable institute for working men and women. Such institutes were established in Birmingham and in many places throughout the country. The first chairman of the Bishopsgate Institute was Mr. Hall, who was the British representative in the Second Internationale and who left his papers to the Institute.

It is almost Alan's birthday. A good portrait was painted in the *Observer*. The writer rightly said that his lectures were effective, slightly "sexy". In 1934 he wrote his first article for the *Manchester Guardian* and he has written for the *Observer* since 1953.

Alan said about Garvin, then the editor of the *Observer*, that the week before Munich he changed his views on Chamberlain and turned against appeasement.

18 February

Speaking about the Bruce Lockhart Papers, Alan said that under the Commission of the Beaverbrook Foundation they are not to be opened until the end of the century. They are full of malicious gossip and inter-departmental business, mainly confidential.

22 February

We were at a party with Ursula Owen[1] and Bill Webb.[2] Michael Foot was there and told us a story which I already knew from Robert Skidelsky. Robert wrote a letter to Michael urging him to do something to ensure that Alan should get the OM. Michael himself wanted it very much but the answer was: the list is already full: Lawrence Olivier, Peter Medawar[3] and the famous pilot of the Second World War were on the list. Alan said he knew how the Establishment worked. They filled it up so that he should not get it, knowing that he was approaching the age of seventy-five.

23 February

Alan gave a talk to a BBC man and said, "I am a simple man. I think in the past the English caused troubles in Ireland; they are better clear of there today."

Alan said that Mrs. Churchill was so conformist that when Beaverbrook brought down Jean Norton for the weekend, Mrs. Churchill left the house. Sir John Colville wrote a book about the Churchills. Alan said Colville wanted to have the Beaverbrook Papers put in Churchill College, Cambridge. But it was agreed that those papers would not go to Churchill College.

25 February

Ernö invited me to the Royal Academy dinner. It was great fun; painters, architects stood up and told stories about themselves

1 Ursula Owen is one of the directors of Virago.
2 Bill Webb is literary editor of the *Guardian*.
3 Peter Medawar, a medical scientist, has been President of the Royal Postgraduate Medical School since 1981 and was, until 1984, a member of the scientific staff of the Medical Research Council. He is a Fellow of the British Academy. He won the Nobel Prize for Medicine in 1960.

and about others. Afterwards we saw the Daumier exhibition. I spoke to a lovely octogenarian sculptress called Gertrude Hermes who said she did not do anything any more, but relax and feel happy that she has had a nice life.

26 February

I love to pick up unknown words: Brum is another word for Birmingham.

Yesterday Hugh and Mirabel Cecil and Sue and Martin Gilbert came for dinner. Alan finished a review of a new book about Joseph Chamberlain. We discussed at the dinner table why Gladstone lasted so long as Prime Minister. He was still Prime Minister at the age of eighty-four. Why? Alan said: To keep Chamberlain out. Gladstone was the oldest Prime Minister in England, next came Palmerston, then Churchill.

27 February

Pisti wrote a very good letter; he is getting better and better at letter-writing. Alan's son Sebastian wanted to come for dinner. He said he was a religious youngster and wanted to be confirmed. He asked Alan how to go about it. Alan said he could not, it cost £5 and he was not going to give it to him. Then Sebastian changed his mind, it was too much so he gave up being religious.

Sebastian also found out how to cheat with the breathalyzer when drunk. First take many long breaths to empty and fill your lungs, then slowly blow into the breathalyzer.

28 February

We had a lovely conversation about the London men's lavatories. Actually there is a guide about them. Alan spoke with a great knowledge and understanding on the subject and about the attendants.

We had a good evening with the Elliotts. Elza Elliott said there was no way of comparing English and Continental ways of thinking. Gizella Ringrose said she had a guest from Romania who, seeing that the standard of living is so much higher here than in Romania said, "Oh, but you haven't got such a wonderful maid as I have."

Edmund Gosse's *Father and Son* is very good. How splendid when the lonely son taught himself unconsciously how to amuse himself looking out of the window. I used to do this when young and lonely.

Alan gave a very good lecture on British-Russian Connections during the nineteenth century. It occurred to him when he spoke that Ireland for England was the same as Poland to Russia. Alan said that the Polish-Russian frontiers originally were good as they were drawn up according to the churches, Catholic or orthodox. Alan said of Afghanistan that the British invaded her three times; the Russians still have two runs left. Alan said about Salvador, Cuba, Guatemala and Chile that these countries were all run by CIA men. When these men were crossed, they told everything.

March is coming like a lion.

1 March

Alan said I was his constant source of happiness.

A woman not only marries a man but a way of life.

In England for many the war was the great opportunity for reading long novels. Proust was the answer. Now again, Proust, recently translated by Terry Kilmartin, is the answer, as Angus Wilson writes in the *Observer:* "It comes out in times of domestic depression and military threat."

2 March

If I make mistakes, I try hard not to feel guilty, but try instead not to make the same mistakes again.

Alan said I was worth all the difficulties he has. Anthony Storr has written about public school boys and this is a key to Alan as well. They tend to remain emotionally childish, immature in their personal relations. One person at home, another at school. To learn to see a mother as a real person is difficult. Alan's main fault is that he conceals his unhappiness.

7 March

Alan became the President of the British-Hungarian Society. He gave a good presidential talk at Caxton Hall he spoke about his friendship with Michael Károlyi, about the Hungarian Parliament Square where the great historical figures stand and about his commitments to the Hungarian people. It was very moving.

11 March

Yesterday I got a very sweet letter from Robert Kee answering my thank-you letter in which I said that everybody makes a mess of his or her life, only some admit to it and some do not. He belongs to the second category. And he should forget about his mania for making himself and others happy. Some good days, good hours in life is quite enough to expect. He wrote that I was charming. I like him very much.

Alan is worried about himself; he thinks he is going steadily downhill. We went to Chichester and Alan gave a very good lecture on writing history. When asked what he has learned from history he answered: scepticism. Alan feels he cannot walk steadily any more.

13 March

Alan says old age is upon him. He went to the London Library and came home exhausted. It is very touching to see how realistic he is about his condition. He does not like to look in the mirror, he does not like his appearance any more. I said to him it did not make the slightest difference to me and he should not look in the mirror.

Maurice Oldfield died the other day. He was Alan's pupil in Manchester with Betty Kemp. He would have made a brilliant medievalist. War came and he was an excellent Secret Service man and he became the Chief of MI6 in 1973. When he retired he wanted to spend a year in All Souls' College but was recalled to serve in Ireland; then he became fatally ill. Alan was asked to chat about him on the radio. But he did not know much about Maurice as chief, he knew him only as a brilliant student. When they met after the war, Alan never asked him anything about himself. He once said to Alan that he was a cold warrior; Alan said he was against the cold war. Maurice, however, still had a good Communist friend from his early days. He was a shy man and could never make close ties with people. Alan was the only one who was close to him, but, alas, he could not speak of anything personal and Alan hardly knew him.

Alan is reading Malcolm Muggeridge's *Diaries*. He knew him and Kitty very well. Alan used to stay with them near us at 19 Grove Terrace. We saw one of Malcolm's series on the TV. De Gaulle was on the show talking about his retarded mongol daughter. He was unusually soft and kind to her and spent much of his time with her. When she died at the age of twenty, de Gaulle said that, now she had become just like everybody else.

Robinson, the free-lance interviewer, came to our home and conducted a very good interview with Alan, one of the best I have ever heard. I told him so. He extracted from Alan some quite unknown details such as the fact that Alan only lectures on things in which he is interested or is very familiar with.

Today we went to Harrods where Alan signed, in an hour, at least eighty copies of his book.

16 March

We came to Oxford this morning. Alan is the guest of Merton College. We had lunch at Magdalen and met Karl Leser and John Stoyle, old colleagues of Alan's. Then we went to the guest room in the Chapel. Alan was very tired. During lunch Alan's scout said he was going to retire. Later Alan said that he was the last real tie he had in Magdalen. I stayed with Jane and Ken Morgan. They have a son and a daughter. Ken always comes home from Queen's before 6 o'clock to bath the children and read to his son for half an hour. Jane reads to the daughter. After having read to his son, Ken listens to music and relaxes. He does not accept anything in academic life which happens after 5.30. He wants to spend the evenings with his children.

Yesterday we went to Bush House. There was a nice cameraman who kissed me and said many things about East-West relations as he saw them. He had visited Czechoslovakia and found the theatrical life there as it used to be here in the nineteenth century. He has a Czechoslovak friend in Bristol who has a love-hate relationship with England.

Alan is going to be seventy-five on March 25 and there was a talk on TV about him. Ludovic Kennedy was the interviewer and Robert Skidelsky and Asa Briggs took part in the discussion. Alan was very wise and looked fresh.

I have begun to read Bennett's *Pretty Lady*. Alan said it is a bad book. I do not share his views.

18 March

I sometimes forget how undemonstrative men are in their emotions. When I do not get letters from my sons I feel we might have grown apart which is absolutely untrue, when I go back I feel the opposite. Still when I feel unloved I go to the PRO to recover. The archives and libraries are emotionless areas. All the same I think that equality in love is very rare. One partner always loves more than the other.

I think also that living abroad is a bit like being an amateur: everybody at least knows the language better than you do.

19 March

Yesterday we went to a party at Hatchards. We met Harold and Mary Wilson, Callaghan, Roskill[1], Arthur Bryant, Elizabeth Longford and others. I spoke to Mary Wilson, who said that she did not feel the same emotional ties with her grandchildren as she did with her children; they are just good friends. Elizabeth Longford spoke about her friendship with Alan which has lasted for a long time. In her view nothing is more pleasant for a man than to have a woman friend.

Roskill is now safe. Arthur Marder[2] has died. The two naval

1 Captain Stephen Roskill (1903–1982) was a Fellow of Churchill College, Cambridge, from 1961 to his death. He commanded *HMS Warspite* in 1939 and *HMNZS Leander* from 1941 to 1944. A distinguished naval historian, his works include *The War at Sea* (official history in 3 vols.) and *Churchill and the Admirals* (1977).

2 Arthur Marder was made Professor of History at the University of California at Irvine in 1964 and in 1977 he became Emeritus Professor. He held a great many academic posts, most of them in the United States. His works include *The Anatomy of British Sea Power* which won the G. L. Beer Prize in 1941 and several books about the Dreadnoughts.

historians had conflicting opinions throughout their mature academic life.

22 March

England is not only a class society, but a society divided between men and women. They are not equal. For this reason women like to please men so much and men like to please women if they want to be loved. Alan needs male society as well, hence, partly, his drive for his sons and grandsons.

We spoke about hatred the other day in Waterlow Park. He can't hate human beings. "Human beings should not be the target of hate," Alan said. "What else then?" I asked – "What else can you hate? Trees, animals, houses?" "No," Alan said, "one can hate cruelty."

We saw the Hopper exhibition at the Hayward Gallery. Alan was tired. Hopper is a great painter but very barren. No communication between the figures in his pictures. His best for me was "Stairway". Stairs leading up to an open door and through it one can see the trees, grass.

25 March

Alan's seventy-fifth birthday. He is sad and depressed, he feels he does not do enough. I must inspire him to write more and have more self-confidence, which he is losing as he does not feel fit enough physically. Alan's main interest is what comes next, not only as a historian but as a private person.

27 March

I am going on with my *English Husband*. It will be interesting though a bit disconnected. I have always so many things to do, as Bartók said: "Idökoldus" – "beggar of time". There was a review of my *Chartism* in the *TLS* by Harrison – quite all right.

We had dinner at Rules. We met Christopher Faulkus who is now at Methuen. I asked Alan what Methuen is like as a publisher because I was thinking of having my *English Husband* published by them. He said, "Very respectable." Before the war Alan used the small Methuen guide books when he went to see parish churches or went to France.

We got a big cake for Alan's birthday from Rules; we had to leave before eating it. This was a great disappointment for everybody as they all wanted to sing with us. Alan wrote an apologetic letter.

Later we spoke a lot about the Social Democrats. I asked where they got the money from. Alan said that presumably from big industrialists who in this way split the Labour Party so that the Tories should get in.

One of Alan's colleagues in Magdalen, Professor Cyril Darlington[1], has just died. He was not as good in the second half of his career as he had been in the first. When they were deciding whether or not to make him an honorary fellow, Alan proposed making him a half year honorary fellow. The president got very cross at this frivolous remark.

29 March

I have a woman historian friend in Budapest. She is also called Éva. She wrote to me that I was the only one she missed very much. Her father is nearly 100 years old, a charming writer and teacher of classics. He went blind and my friend Éva now spends three hours every day with him in hospital.

31 March

We went to a concert at the Bishopsgate Institute. A Cuban pianist, Jorge Bolet, played Liszt's Hungarian Rhapsody very well though a bit slowly at the beginning.

After the concert we went to see Spitalfields Market and the little houses around it. These houses used to belong to the silk workers of Spitalfields at the end of the eighteenth century. I was sorry that I did not take my camera with me. It is a very interesting

1 Cyril Dean Darlington was Sherardian Professor of Botany at the University of Oxford from 1953 to 1971 and Professor Emeritus until his death. He was made an Honorary Fellow of Magdalen in 1971, having been a Fellow since 1953.

area, very poor. I saw in the basement of a derelict house, workers working by artificial light in the day-time. Poor Bangladeshis live here; everything is cheap and poor here. And not far away in the neighbourhood, is a wonderful, clean modern garage for the cars of the business people. Before we left the area I saw a great big building, like a prison, for down and outs. Three very scruffy, elderly women were sitting outside the building. It was Dickens's London. Then we went to Foster Lane. Saw a little church; inside there was a choir practising. It was so nice, one could have listened to them for hours. That was London too. In the little garden there was a portrait by Epstein. Coming back to Cheapside, I felt I must come back to this area with my architect son, Pisti, to see the Guildhall, which is architecturally very interesting. Our number 4 bus went through the Angel and brought us back to our little home.

3 April

We saw the abbreviated version of Alan's film "The Edge of Britain" at Granada. I met a man there who told me that it is probably advantageous that my English is limited, I try to express myself more precisely because of my limitations. We spoke about Tony Benn, whom I rate very highly. Quite a lot of people around Alan have doubts about him, but then they do not read or listen to him.

We had a wonderful conversation about cockfights. I don't think it was completely right to make cockfights illegal when they let the hunting go on. I wrote about this to my sons. We had a Hungarian couple here for tea, the husband is a journalist, the wife a teacher. They both love Hungary but they want to live here. I do not feel like this, I love the English people, but I prefer our system and our people. I am a Hungarian, they are emigrés.

4 April

Alan told me that when Betjeman visited Blenheim where Churchill was born and where the Duke of Marlborough now lives, he saw at the top of the grand house, forty hidden bedrooms for the servants. At the end of the corridor there was one lavatory and one basin. The little bedrooms had only one little window which could not be opened and which was so high that if the servants wanted to see the sky they had to climb up to look out. Betjeman demonstrated: he took a chair and said that if a servant was dying, he would have to get something to stand on and look out in order to see the sky for the last time.

6 April

It takes only two days to get the daily papers from Budapest. In one of them there was a very good article about the ambassadors of culture in our country. Nobody was mentioned in London. One has to do something.

Yesterday there was a terrible programme on Hungary – like a soap opera. It was refreshing to listen to Naomi Mitchison after the programme. She spoke about real friendship. I am for real friendship amongst nations which means that there should be an exchange of real values and real democratic traditions. There are so few people who work on this without prejudice. Alan and I do, but people often do not understand us.

Esther Rantzen said a funny thing about a funny English man. This man catches fish by playing them music and has observed that they like tangos and Tchaikovsky best.

11 April

I am very upset sometimes, then I try not to think about myself. I tell myself to read Epiktetos again and again. I am happy when I am working. I saw a wonderful film about ordinary people. The wife became selfish because when something went wrong, she only wanted to defend herself. The husband lost his love for her because of her selfishness and was worried about living without his love for her.

In St. Martin-in-the-Fields, there is a rescue plan for homeless men. The church is lovely and is the work of Gibbs, who made the Holborn one, St. Mary-le-Strand as well. The former became an example for churches throughout the States.

12 April

Last night there were riots in Britain. People said it was like the Blitz, the worst outbreak since the Second World War.

I read Epiktetos. Each day I have to read it. Yesterday evening I drove to Wigmore Hall to listen to Berg: Lyric Suite – it was interesting. We came back after the concert, much relaxed.

In the *Observer* there was an excellent article about the Klu Klux Klan. The top man "is a guy who's worked all his life and struggled all his life to be something and here is the moment to be something . . ."

We are beginning to see the first signs that the unemployed from this country would go to Eastern Europe if they got a job there. Levin is furious and so are the Tories. Britain will be again "a gigantic system of outdoor relief for the British aristocracy". Prince Philip preaches "grow old with dignity" – but at sixty is he more dignified, more patient than before?

13 April

I have been in London for three years now. I should not forget how happy I was when I married Alan. I should not forget how much I worked and how much I still want to work. I shall never forget to be human and think about others. It does not matter how you look, but how you feel. One can live a full life anywhere. My next book after the *Anglo-Hungarian Relations* might be *Portraits of Cold Warriors*.

14 April

I enjoyed the conversation with Kate, who is a committed left-winger and said how ridiculous it is that people think that the *Morning Star* gets money from Moscow. Why would they struggle for survival and collect money from people each month if they got money from Moscow? She has got fed up with an acquaintance of ours, a very superficial girl, who, when she comes to London, sees in the shops such a variety of things that she always wants to go shopping and thinks life is much better here. Kate said it was different when you came as a tourist. Kate is very good with her little daughter as she does not fuss about her.

15 April

Foyles lunch today. Alan presided and gave a good, reasoned speech. Malcolm and Kitty Muggeridge, Elizabeth and Frank Pakenham, Max Beloff and Mary and Richard Ingrams were there. Kitty was very nice, always spoke about Malcolm as the old man and accepted faithfully his every extravagance. So did Elizabeth. I sat between Max Beloff and Frank Pakenham (the Earl of Longford). I made Max Beloff furious by declaring that there is nothing wrong with the Kádár regime in Hungary. The country has economic difficulties and many other problems but so have many Western European states. He said there was no difference between the Nazis and the Red Army. I said he was speaking rubbish. So he never spoke to me again during the whole lunch, which was a great piece of luck for me. Frank Pakenham on the other side, being an ardent Catholic, wanted to convert me. I said he would not succeed. He asked about Hungary. I said everybody could exert his or her religious feelings. It is just a personal characteristic of mine that I could not believe in after-life. When he asked what life is like behind the Iron Curtain, I told him not to use this expression, everybody would be hurt by this in Eastern Europe. He asked about my work and later he said I fed his diary. And he, mine.

16 April

June Mendoza came to see us and brought Alan's picture with her, now that she has put the nose right.

22 April

We are off to Autun. At 3.50 we arrived at Charles de Gaulle airport. Paris brought back many memories as I spent three months here when I was working on my book about the Rhine-land Crisis. I remembered my little room in the Rue Francs Bourgeois and how Alan came from London once a month. This time we went to the Mont Blanc Hotel and later looked at the monument for those who were killed by the Nazis. In the afternoon we took the train through Burgundy, through great agricultural areas where one saw hardly any people or houses and eventually arrived at Autun. The train was nearly empty and looking out of the windows I thought how much more colourful the Hungarian countryside is. But Autun is beautiful; we stayed in the Hotel St. Louis where Napoleon stayed when returning from Elba. Autun is lovely in the morning and during the evening.

Every day we went to see the Cathedral St. Lazare and its amazing tympanum carved in the twelfth century by Gislebert. This was the first known Romanesque statue composition of the Last Judgement. In the cathedral museum there were even more beautiful things to see: the statue of Eve, the statue of Ann and the sacred man on the monument of St. Lazare. We did not speak much, just relaxed the whole time. The French people at Autun were not well dressed, very provincial, not very kind, but very polite. The streets were empty after 6 o'clock. There were cars about but no people. They were not as kind to children as in England as far as I could judge and they do not bring them up to be independent enough. They do not fuss about peeing. In the public lavatories the ladies go and they can see all the peeing, standing men. Teenage girls are kind to each other, kiss each other. I found Autun and France like Hungary, just slightly more mellow.

25 April

My son Ferencz rang me up: his first child was born today. Mother and son, Gergö, are fine, healthy and the delivery was smooth. Perhaps instead of writing a diary I should begin *My Letters from England* to my grandson. I am reading Jane Austen's *Emma*. Without Jane Austen, one can't understand England.

27 April

Again in Paris. In the Hotel Mont Blanc at the Rue de la Hachette my whole life passed before my eyes. In 1973 I was very happy here with Alan for a whole week. Everything seemed bright and wonderful. Did I change or is it the hotel which now seems dark and cold? I was loved without any conditions by my first and second husbands and a friend of mine, the historian Éva. Compared with my original situation, I have twice sunk lower: after the Second World War when I lost my parents and after the death of my first husband. My children and my friends, Éva and Alan helped me. They were realistic, clever historians and I shall never forget the love they showed me.

30 April

The holiday at Autun and Paris gave both of us great pleasure. On reflection I thought the French people react to each other more than the English and in a more personal way. What I will always remember about Autun is the relaxed atmosphere and complete happiness between us. We have reached the point where we just want to be together and nothing else matters, neither impending ill-health, or sentimental, emotional worries.

Alan will receive today his Honorary Degree from North London Polytechnic. He is rather a collector of honorary degrees. Next comes Warwick.

15 May

I was ill for a fortnight. Bronchitis.

We spoke about the Scots professors. Professors on the whole are very highly esteemed in Scotland due to the fact that in the eighteenth century Edinburgh University was regarded as a better university than Cambridge. Lord "Little John" Russell went there, Palmerston finished his last undergraduate year there. David Hume, one of the greatest empirist philosophers was a Scot, so was Adam Smith. When Boswell visited Hume on his deathbed and asked him what he expected: "Out," he said, "Nothing is waiting for us."

17 May

Alan is going to review a book on Monty. I asked him what it was he liked about Monty. He said, "He was a professional."

Once he met Churchill. Churchill offered him a drink. Monty said, "I do not smoke, I do not drink. I am one hundred percent fit." Churchill answered: "I drink, I smoke and I am two hundred percent fit." Alan said that with social graces you can show that you are good at what you do in the army, but later, in war, you are really put to the test.

We had what Alan bought in the market for dinner. He likes to eat what he bought. It is usually very good. Our house in Twisden Road is called "The Pink House".

20 May

Alan knew Clapham and Hammond the historians from their Manchester days. Hammond was the Vice-Editor of the *Manchester Guardian* when Scott was not there. Muggeridge warned Alan that Hammond was like weak tea, and so he was.

A man wrote to Alan asking what Dylan Thomas was like. Alan wrote back that he did not want to give any information about him. Dylan despised and mocked people, he did not speak Welsh at all, he wanted to get money out of people, he was a nasty man and Alan did not rate him very highly as a poet, but Betjeman and Spender did. Norman Cameron[1] would not have him in his house, but said he was a great poet.

John Grigg wrote an article about Lloyd George. Lloyd George got from Guggenheim, the American businessman, the sum of £20,000, now worth £220,000, for the benefit of needy people. Lloyd George gave £5–6,000 to charity and never admitted how he spent the rest. He was rather messy about money affairs.

23 May

Peter Sutcliffe, the mass murderer, has been sentenced to thirty years. The mother of one whom he killed said, "I hope he dies in prison. He is an animal."

Terrible Scots fans arrived in London to watch the football match and the Wembley area is closed to traffic.

1 Norman Cameron was a poet and journalist and a very close friend of Alan Taylor.

It is characteristic of the English that there is a correspondence going on in *The Times* about the "patio" and what it should be called. Tea square or quart or what? Alan's mind is also on it.

26 May

We are at Church Stretton, Shropshire, in the Longmynd Hotel. Alan and his parents went to Church Stretton in 1916. Alan's father took a pony and led Alan about on it. I was surprised to hear that during the war some people had good holidays. Alan took a holiday in 1942 near Exmoor with Margaret and Nico Henderson. They had a good time. Alan thought everybody was very well off during the war, only the flower trains from Penzance to London were stopped with the early daffodils. There was such an outcry about this that Churchill ordered that the train should be allowed to go on, so that everybody could buy daffodils. On the day when the train was stopped people who wanted to make money went down to Penzance with suitcases and packed them with daffodils which they then sold in Covent Garden Market at good prices.

29 May

During the night Alan said that in the old days the aristocracy paid young peasant boys to beat the marshes to stop the frogs croaking, so that they could sleep. They slept while the young boys beat the marshes from eight in the evening until four in the morning.

5 June

Alan spoke about Károlyi because when I came back from the PRO, I told him what a wonderful memorandum Károlyi wrote about the Smallholders before he returned to Budapest. Alan said that Károlyi always imagined that he could influence the Foreign Office. He tried to do it with MacDonald through Charles

Trevelyan,[1] then again with Bevin. Alan told him in 1940 and in 1945 that it wouldn't work.

July

Though I decided to give up writing my diary, I found that I miss it, so I am going back to it. Second half of June was very interesting. Pisti and Kriszti were here, when Kriszti left earlier I had long conversations with Pisti. He understands well the cultural and other differences between Britain and Hungary. We went to Yarmouth, which I like very much. Though I do not like the atmosphere of the Mill, the family centre of the Taylors, I really feel at home at Yarmouth, at Norton Bay, Freshwater Bay, with the smell of the sea, the birds, the meadows. I can breathe very well there.

Later in the month we went to Warwick where Alan got his D. Lit. There were three who got it: Sheila Brown, Tom Stoppard and Alan. The previous night Alan sat next to Tom and Tom asked whether a man like Alan in his seventy-sixth year still had his sexual drive.

We spent the night in the house of the Vice-Chancellor, Jack Butterworth and his wife Doris. A lovely couple.

19 August

I have been in Hungary, where I caught bronchitis, for a fortnight. The GP here does not like to give me as many medicines as they gave me in Budapest. After sunny Hungary our Twisden Road house smelt of mildew.

We were invited by Robert Kee for dinner. I like him; I have had many friends like him.

1 Charles Trevelyan (1870–1958) entered Parliament in 1899 as a member of the Liberal Party but, in 1922, he joined the Labour Party. He was president of the Board of Education (1924 and 1929–31) but resigned when his School Attendance Bill was rejected.

20 August

We had Karl Samuelson, the young man from Newfoundland, for tea. He turns up faithfully every year to discuss Hitler with Alan. Alan said firmly that the rumour that Hitler had epileptic fits is not true. It was said that when Hitler got angry he chewed the carpet, "*teppich fessen*" which is a German phrase for being angry. This was translated into English and spread the news – Chamberlain himself believed it – that Hitler was epileptic. All the statesmen who visited Hitler found him very polite.

30 August

I went to the Brompton Hospital to find out what is wrong with my lungs. In the last few years I have often had bronchitis and pneumonia. The Brompton Hospital is more than 100 years old, the most famous Hospital in Britain for heart and lung diseases. I was put in the Victoria Gallery (instead of wards they have galleries). We were in a gallery where there were eight beds. The bed opposite mine was given to the hospital by Mrs. Neale. Every patient shows herself to be strong and brave. It is not done to complain. One of the nurses is a Danish girl and a patient calls her Danish pastry. This patient is a teacher and says very practical things like "one can learn at any age; the most important thing is the attitude of the mind". The nights are terrible, noisy, lights shine in from the corridor. The hospital is very well equipped from a technical point of view. The most wonderful machine is the vitalograph which shows how drugs affect breathing. It must have been a fairly new machine as it was shown to an Australian nurse. One can hardly see a doctor. Humour is everywhere. One patient said that English humour is the consequence of English weather.

There is a whole gallery in this hospital which is full of beds given by people. One bed, for instance, was provided in the will of a young person who died of cancer and because that was her last wish the whole village gave money to establish a bed in the hospital. There are many empty galleries in the hospital. Also many oil magnates or their relatives are here; they pay very well – £200 for a night – and every extra examination is expensive.

One of the patients remembered the war years. At that time she helped in a shop. She said the tea coupons were like soap coupons. Many people bought more tea than soap; they used the soap coupons to buy tea instead. She remembered those years fondly; she said that then, everybody helped each other.

I was told I would have an examination which was called bronchoscopy. I asked one of the patients what it was like because she had had one. She said it made her feel uncomfortable around the nose so she wrote to the firm who produced it to ask them to alter it. When they made one for me, I did not feel much discomfort though it took a long time and two doctors and a nurse looked into my lungs. At the end they praised me and said no women ever behaved as well as I did. I told them it was easy for me to behave well, because it did not hurt. I was, though, very much afraid of what would happen to me before it took place, but I did not want to show my panic. At the end it turned out that my lungs were O.K. It was just a bug and I had to take antibiotics for a whole week.

While I was in the Brompton Hospital the Korean aeroplane was shot down over the Soviet Union. It was interesting to note that in the ward nobody got hysterical or anti-Soviet as they do in the States; they just said they did not understand how it happened that the plane had gone so deep into Soviet territory.

One evening, in the hospital, I watched a film in which Bette Davis played an old woman who did not want to live with her relatives and did not want to go to an old people's home either. Quite right, I said to myself.

1 September

Alan had two telephone calls from the BBC. They wanted him to talk about Speer who has just died. Speer had arrived in London the day before to speak on Hitler's art collection. They wanted to do a film and Speer was invited to contribute. He went to the studio and spoke and then at midday he went out for lunch. He collapsed in his hotel and was taken to St. Mary's Hospital where he died.

We went to White City by taxi. Arrived for "News Night" on BBC. Alan spoke about Speer for a couple of minutes in the studio. I was able to watch him from another room. Alan said that Speer was unique amongst the Nazis: he was an artist. Hitler and he spoke to each other like two artists. Alan was not convinced that Speer wanted to kill Hitler as well, and thought that Speer probably made that story up later. The interviewer asked why. Alan said, "Because it was a good story." And then Alan described Speer's atrocities during the war. Alan also said that Speer's memoirs had not convinced him that he did not know what went on in the concentration camps. Speer's guilty feelings came much later.

2 September

Today we arrived in Dieppe from Newhaven. Dieppe is so different, so Continental. A young sailor said to Alan how much he liked Alan's programme on Lancashire. He also observed: "Look at Dieppe—what a change from Newhaven." Dieppe has an atmosphere all its own and one immediately feels it. The first thing we did was to buy soap, as French hotels don't provide it. I am reading David Thomson's *Woodbrook*. He says on pages 10–11: "When two people meet and take to each other, they start generally to uncover one another's past, and the slower the process the deeper the friendship becomes . . . You see the whole of him and he sees you, the present surface always near and the layers of the past melted into one." No wonder I immediately felt, when I met David through his most enchanting wife, that I loved him.

3 September

Today we went to Dieppe castle. The castle has a room of Saint-Saëns where, astonishingly, I saw the death mask of Beethoven. We also saw the memorial to the Canadians who fell so tragically at Dieppe. Mountbatten let them raid Dieppe in 1942, though he should have been sceptical about any hope of their being successful. Beaverbrook criticised Mountbatten most heavily for permitting this military failure and causing unnecessary mass slaughter.

In the afternoon we lay on the beach, on the pebbles, relaxed and thoughtful.

4 September

We strolled along the new shopping area. I bought a French doll. We were simply happy. We sat in the middle of the street in a coffee house where we had lunch and a chaplain introduced himself by saying he was here for one week and if we wanted to take part in the service on Sunday we were welcome. Alan said we wouldn't, "Why, are you Catholics?" he asked. "No," said Alan, "we are nothing." He was surprised but said that we were welcome all the same. A two-year-old toddler was dressed up like a little Victorian doll and strolled with her father and mother. I smiled at her, Alan smiled at her and we got back from her such a wonderful smile that I shall never forget it.

15 October

We were invited for lunch by the manager of our branch of the National Westminster Bank, Kentish Town. He explained that they preferred to have a Socialist Government in Britain because then they know better how much money will be spent and how it will be spent.

One of the guests was close to a Cabinet Minister who had said to him that it was untrue that Margaret Thatcher knew what she was doing. He had watched her and worked closely with her and he knew that her views and plans were often changed on the spot.

The Taylors had a wonderful family reunion in a hotel at Ross-on-Wye. Alan was the oldest and he was able to tell the others what his grandfather was like. It was such a lovely thing to tell and let them feel the continuity of the family. Alan was the only living person in the family who could recall the image of his grandfather. There were approximately fifty-six Taylors there.

21 October

I have had no success with my *English Husband*. I can't find a publisher for it.

We went to see the church of St. Martin-in-the-Fields from inside. It was early afternoon and in the little pews poor, elderly people slept. It looked like a Kafka story. The people looked like great black beetles in a Kafka-esque vision. Then we went to Soho to see a blue film. It was terrible, porno with hi-fi lesbian horror. I wanted to stay until the end but Alan was such a misfit there, so far from his usual tastes and habits, I thought we had better leave and not leave in a situation which was humiliating for him. Though, in England there are so many unusual things happening and nobody makes the slightest remark. It was so astonishing for instance when Alan told me that Frank Pakenham used to wear pyjamas under his suit and so did Professor Alexander[1] in Manchester.

22 October

We are at Keele University. Alan lectured in the Hall of the University about the origins of the Second World War. It was fascinating to watch how he brought together in his lecture everything that he had read lately. There was the biggest audience, approximately 750 people, I have seen during my three years with him. The ovation was great and hearty. Alan said later: "I have come to the height of my career and prestige at a time when my body is not strong enough." After the lecture he immediately came and asked with his eyes: "Was I any good?" Like Churchill looking up at Clemmie.

3 November

We had Frank and Elizabeth Pakenham and Hugh and Mary Seton-Watson here for dinner. It was a good evening. I told the men that after dinner they should wash up. Frank did not want to. I insisted. I gave him a spoon and a fork to dry because Alan washed up. Frank looked pale; perhaps he was angry inside. Elizabeth rescued him. Elizabeth did the drying up very well. Frank said he would note it in his diary.

Hugh Seton-Watson told me that he had a list of what he should read in his remaining years. Actually he has two lists, the second list is about places which he wanted to visit again.

1 Professor Alexander was a friend and colleague of Alan Taylor in Manchester.

27 November

The seventy-fifth anniversary of the Historical Association was on the 25th. Alan delivered a good speech but he was not content with the delivery, though it was good enough. We were introduced to the Queen. I did not curtsey. The Queen asked Alan what the subject of his lecture would be.

I was very happy to meet a young historian called Bernard Porter who wrote an excellent book about the refugee question in Victorian England. As I was working on *Kossuth as an English Journalist in 1855*, I mentioned to him what wonderful articles Kossuth wrote in the *Atlas* and in the *Sunday Times*. He was very eager to know more about this and we had a happy time together.

6 December

I met Andrew Rothstein[1], who is eighty-three years old, but very lucid and alert: he remembered the time when Maisky represented the Soviet Union in Britain. He said that Maisky wrote a very good book about Mongolia, which I did not know. He also met Ràkosi in 1923. I also met a young woman who works at *Marxism Today* and said that the review now sells better than the *Spectator*.

We were invited to dinner by Jill and Michael Foot and the Morgans were there too. I like Jane Morgan very much. The most interesting thing that Michael said was that if he were to write the last years of Bevan now, he would do it differently. He himself recognizes now that a cabinet minister must make concessions; when he wrote the book he did not realise this. Jill said that Bevan was a brilliant orator but Gaitskell was like a school master. In Michael's view one should read Williams's book on Gaitskell. Then they showed us their libraries. Jill has a wonderful collection of feminist and women writers. I envied her her copy of Harriet Martineau's autobiography. Michael showed me his room, which is full of classics and modern left-wing stuff and Marxist literature. He wanted to show me a leaflet by Béla Kun in English but he could not find it. I pulled out a volume by Thomas Hodgkin and said how fine a writer he was, a forerunner of Marxist economic

1 Andrew Rothstein is a Marxist historian, expert on Chartism, Trade Unionism and the Labour Movement.

writing. When Michael told me this writer is hardly known in England, I said he was hardly known in Hungary either. The room has wonderful photos of his father and mother. I think when he withdraws here he feels at home again in the company of his parents. Their dog is called after Disraeli. Jane Morgan spoke about Wales, how poor the people are and how the shops are sometimes empty. Whoever has a good brain can escape from there, but the manual workers cannot escape; they have very little money, can't afford to travel to find jobs elsewhere. She thought one should speak more in Britain about Wales than about the hardships in Poland or in the USSR.

13 December

I saw a film with Judy Holliday, Alan's favourite actress. Alan was so fond of this girl that he invited her for lunch in Magdalen. She could not come, fell ill and soon died. I understand so well why Alan loved this girl and the film.

Alan loves to teach only by conversation. Then he reveals a lot of his great knowledge, about his experiences and about his thoughts. Alan is also a great worrier but a fun man as well.

Our ceiling is wet, the rain is dripping through. Alan thinks it is charming. The first drop is the best, the second comes slowly and has a deep voice and so on. I am too serious for Alan.

1982

2 January

We came back from Budapest two days ago. What an intellectually inspiring life it has. Here everything is still at a standstill. I shall work hard in 1982.

A good article in the *Observer* about diarists and therapists. Somebody went so far as to declare that "the diary can take control of your life", you accept invitations because it will be fun to "describe it in the diary".

Yesterday at Wigmore Hall we met Sarah Roberts, the funny little widow of that wonderful painter Bobby Roberts[1], who was once Alan's neighbour. Alan was thrilled; I felt close to Sarah immediately.

How many dreadful examples of ways of life there are. Barbara Woodhouse visited Beverly Hills, which is full of famous people who keep pets. The madness of riches. People pay for their dogs to stay in luxury hotels, to watch colour TV. Problems for middle aged women: which is best – group masturbation or playing bridge together or eating sweets?

I must keep to my historical studies. Firmly.

12 January

New Year. A party at the Kilmartins. Terry is sixty. All the society women of literary London were there, or nearly all. Natasha

1 William Roberts was a Cubist painter. Some of his works are on permanent display in the Tate Gallery.

Spender, aloof; her husband, as usual, is in California. Miriam Gross, kind and quick in mind, responsive, enlightened in matters of life and literature. Joanna the tender wife of Terry; she wears the trousers really in this kind household. Their daughter Olivia is too passive to be successful in partnerships, in life. Freddie Ayer's wife, Vanessa, is possessive, clever, responsive and I think, too sexy. Freddie looks a good-hearted man. Cynthia Kee is clever, knows a lot about psychology and alternative treatments. Tony Howard has no small talk, but his wife has. Kingsley Amis is utterly useless in such a party, or seems so. For this reason he is very sympathetic to me. He is like a kind family doctor. How he lives at such an unsuitable place as Leighton Road I don't know. There are often burglaries in that area. I would love to see his home, if he had one. Sara, Robert Kee's daughter, blew the trumpet and Alan gave a little but clever speech with well chosen words for the creative literary critics. I felt I was in a society which was already out of date. A small circle of people who really did not sense how outdated they were. Except us of course.

15 January

Yesterday we gave an evening party in our little home. Ursula Owen and Bill Webb and Jane and Karl Miller came. Enlightened talks. At the end Jane and Karl disappeared into the mist like Turgenev figures. They both smoke wonderful Dutch tobacco. Ursula found out when she went to East Germany how many things were German in her. Everyone was against the bomb there, but there was no agreement on how to make the new CND work.

I might one day see Virago publishing the excellent Hungarian women writers from the first half of this century like Margit Kaffka and Sophie Török.

22 January

A very nice afternoon with Sarah Roberts and John Roberts, her son. A funny couple. John is realistic, Sarah is intelligent, rambling, clever, vivacious. John corrects Sarah when she says something which is not right about her husband. John said: "My father put me in his bad book! and always added things to it." Bob was not very talkative. Sarah is. John listens to what Sarah says and not only corrects but adds to what she says. A complete relationship: they are dependent on each other. Sarah does not like posh things, she does not like the USA, she likes Morocco because there are wide open spaces and poverty. She likes also Virago books and feminism.

28 January

Yesterday we gave a dinner party here; Freddie Ayer, his wife Vanessa, and Cynthia and David Kemp came. Fred was in the SOE during the war in Southern France, where the Vlassovites took charge in the name of the Germans. Alan also spoke about the Cossacks who fell in an Austrian valley and did not want to give themselves up as they belonged to the German army. They killed themselves and their children as well. Alan heard this story from James Cameron.[1]

David has made an eight hour long film about the Spanish Civil War.

Today I heard on TV the "Afternoon Plus" programme about retirement. The same problems as the ones I face, living abroad. Do they lose their identity after having lost their jobs and colleagues?

9 February

Alan gave the Romanes Lecture at the Sheldonian Theatre, Oxford. They organize concerts, university meetings, celebrations, old Greek tragedies here. Romanes was a very good scientist of the mid-nineteenth century, who wrote brilliant articles. He was, apparently, much liked. The first Romanes Lecture was given by Gladstone in 1892. Alan spoke about the wars in our century (first, second and cold wars). He ended cleverly and wisely by talking about the coming nuclear catastrophe. It was not only charming and clever but a serious and responsible warning to all, from a first-rate historian and a wise man. That was his swan song and it was a great success. He was very tense, even ill before it; for days, his hands were trembling, he felt ill and shaky.

1 James Cameron was a radical journalist.

Afterwards he was composed, next day strong and youngish and he drove back to London with great courage.

We were staying with the Vice-Chancellor of the University of Oxford, who is always a scholar whereas the Chancellor is usually an aristocrat. Now it is Macmillan, before him Halifax. The Vice-Chancellor's name is Geoffrey Warnock, a charming Ulsterman, and he was a Fellow of Magdalen. They gave a dinner party for us. Mary's brother, Duncan Wilson, the former Ambassador to the Soviet Union and Yugoslavia, sat next to me and spoke about his wife. He lives now with his sister, Mary, in the Vice-Chancellor's house and works, as he is retired, on Murray Gilbert. His wife is the co-editor of the English-Russian Dictionary and not long ago the co-editor from the Soviet side stayed with them in Scotland. She had not much conversation so Duncan used to read to them after the meal, mainly the texts of Churchill and Jane Austen which (the latter) the Soviet co-editor liked very much. Duncan was very fond of the Russian people and also the Georgians with their great hospitality. He did not like the people at the Foreign and Trade Ministry as much. He served in the Soviet Union in the 'sixties.

At this dinner party there were also Professor Robert Blake and his charming wife and Raymond Carr, the Warden of St. Antony's. Raymond Carr said he liked the Hungarian scholars at St. Antony's very much because they were as bright as the Portuguese. Raymond Carr called himself a mercenary and said he would do anything for money.

14 February

Alan said when he received the invitation to deliver the Romanes Lecture he was speculating on what on earth he could talk about. First he thought, as usual, when in doubt talk about himself.

It came as a great shock to me to hear that my best girl friend, Mary Ujházy, had committed suicide. She had cancer and did not want to suffer and make her son and husband suffer. She was a professor of English and American Literature in Budapest University and wrote an excellent book on *Moby Dick*. She was a brave woman.

25 February

Mary's funeral is today, in Budapest. What a cruel and honest death. She loved London, she was very fond of many English people. In memory of her I recall what Alan said about St. James's Park which she loved so much. He told me that Charles II loved the park and used to go there with his dogs. Painters often painted him with them in St. James's Park. Chamberlain was a keen birdwatcher, and he often slipped out through the back garden of Downing Street, to see the birds. Walking across the park I saw the pelicans in St James's Park for the first time and looked at number 10 Downing Street: I was amazed at how tiny the place was.

Alan also said (which I did not know) that the Cabinet sitting-room is the private room of the Prime Minister. Thus when a cabinet meeting is taking place, the Prime Minister opens his or her sitting room door and says: "Come in gentlemen."

26 February

We went to see Sarah and her son John in St. Mark's Crescent. They showed us the little exhibition of Bob Roberts's work. Bob had a fantastic sense of humour and a good sense of movement. His self-portrait is very revealing. I also liked his beach paintings and those depicting his small family. He liked to paint dogs, though he would never have kept one. He liked to watch them. Also he liked to watch the Camden Canal life and the life under the canal bridge, mainly the activities of the old Irish drunks. The exhibition was arranged in his little room. I asked John whether the room got the sun in the morning. Yes, it did. It was moving to watch Alan as he looked out of the window. Boats were chugging along quietly. The captains used to say to the sightseers on board: "Now we are passing the famous historian's house." Alan used to watch the ducks as they moved about in the water. Sarah used to look after the garden, John after the boat. When we came home in the dark, and in the rain, Alan looked very old; I felt that only now are we properly married: Margaret's shadow has disappeared for ever.

11 March

We had a working tea-party with Kriszti Mikó, a visiting Hungarian lecturer, George Cushing a professor at SSEES, with Ursula Owen and Alan. Alan soon went off for a concert. Cushing washed up. He is a very nice man. He told Ursula everything that she should know about Margit Kaffka's *Anthill* which is the Hungarian *Frost in May*. Cushing said that the short stories of Dezsö Kosztolányi[1] are the best in world literature. I asked him to write his reminiscences about Hungarian literary life. He translated Gyula Illyés's[2] *Puszták Népe*. He lives near Canterbury in a 200-year-old house and plays the organ in the church on Sundays.

28 March

Alan is no longer the independent man he was. He is now dependent on me. He does not hide this fact; he writes about me with warmth and tenderness. I must take care to give him much happiness in his new position.

An interesting article appeared about death. Many people think that when one meets death, the soul goes out of the body. Also, many people think that when somebody is brought back from death, the soul, which waits for a while at the ceiling, comes back into the body. The author tried to write about this rubbish in an academic style. I thought how this idea could be applied to me as, in England, my soul goes out of my body and watches what happens to it. When I go back to Hungary, my soul goes back into my body. And how much better it is to live in a body than outside it.

30 March

Mary and Richard Ingrams came for dinner with the Kees. Richard was so surprised that I have joined the Cobbett Society

1 Dezsö Kosztolányi was a Hungarian poet and writer of the first part of the twentieth century. He belonged to the Nyugat (West) circle. His short stories were held by many to be equal to Maupassant's.

2 Gyula Illyés (1902–1983), also a Hungarian poet and writer, is known for his works, *Petőfi* and *The People of the Puszta*, which have been translated into several languages.

that he sent Alan and me his new book called *Cobbett's Country Book*, edited and introduced by him. Cobbett was one of my favourites when I wrote my book, *Chartism*. And Alan often said that his style came from Cobbett and Shaw.

Today we saw the film *On Golden Pond*. It was lovely, but for us it was a most unsuitable thing to see because we are not young any more and it reminded us of the inevitability of death. We came back through Dean Street where I saw at Quo Vadis a plaque which said that Marx lived there between 1851–56. We went to a pub called Cockney Pride; a man played old songs at the piano and asked me where I came from. At Rathbone Street we passed the Duke of York pub, which was a strong gay men's pub in the inter-war period, but the owner did not know about it.

4 April

I can now follow England's behaviour at the possibility of a war: a war over the Falklands. The whole atmosphere is patriotic, full of bravery inspired by Thatcher who wants to save British prestige. It does not matter what the price will be. The people go with it. Can't be helped.

Alan spoke about his father. He was always generous with money. He felt he ought to pay for everyone. That's how Alan feels as well. The example was set in his early youth.

Richard Ingrams wrote to me that he could really hardly believe that a foreigner had joined the Cobbett Society. He had already told me that, but my answer was that he did not know the foreigners. I sent him my *Chartism*.

10 April

Tony Benn gave a good speech. He said that we do not fight Thatcherism, we fight capitalism. He also said that it was hypocrisy to stand up against Argentina now when until the Falklands crisis Britain had been sending guns and helicopters to that same "disgraceful Argentine dictatorship".

12 April

Alan read my book about the Rhineland. He said, "English historians express their views more, you recite the events." I think he is right, but I did it this way purposely. I must think about it and decide which is the better way to bring history alive.

28 April

We went to Venice for a week with four of Alan's grandchildren and we met my younger son and his wife there. We all stayed at the Hotel Calcina. The manageress of the hotel was born in Fiume; she spoke Hungarian, English, French, Italian and German. The grandchildren were very independent. Pisti my son liked St. Michele very much and took many photos.

Italian tombs are so different. Families who were wealthy enough had wonderful little chalets made for their deceased relatives, into which they put the characteristic or beloved possessions of the dead person and also his photo. Architecturally these chalets are very interesting; some are classical, some modern.

We went out for dinner to a family restaurant where Alan was kissed by the three daughters and their brother. Peggy Guggenheim used to come to this restaurant in the last years of her life in Venice.

When we returned from Venice, we went to Lancaster where they were holding a literary week and Alan gave a lecture. Though Alan is a declining lion, he is still a lion none the less. His level of tolerance and understanding is very high. He gave a very good lecture, but his voice was a bit low.

We often discuss one of the characteristics he probably inherited from his father: evasiveness. Alan said himself that his father was evasive. For instance: his father usually took his little girlfriend to the swimming pool at Lytham on Sunday mornings. Once he came back late and his wife, Alan's mother, asked: Why did you come home so late? Alan's father told her that he had been teaching a little girl to swim. This happened to be true but, as Alan said, his father forgot to mention that he took this girl to the swimming pool every Sunday and he liked to be with her.

In Lancaster we were invited for tea by a queer old lady, who sat out in front of her small and very neglected house. She was sweet and told us that she was quite famous in Manchester as an enlightened educationalist who had adopted five children. Once Namier visited her and saw two of her adopted sons quarrelling with each other. He asked his hostess: "Are your sons twins?" "They are not related to each other at all," she answered. The father of this woman saw a public hanging in England.

I bought a little Victorian doll at Lytham which was nearly £100. I felt ashamed to spend as much as that on a doll. But I love dolls and love Victorian things.

5 May

I feel ashamed for Margaret Thatcher. Until now they sent munitions to the Argentinian Junta. Now jingoism and hypocrisy have taken over with the Falklands war, the papers are manipulated. The most patriotic are those who won't be called upon to die for their homeland.

28 May

I understand now that many émigrés' activities are connected with muck-raking. Alan said quite rightly: émigrés have to prove they are right and the country that they have left is wrong, otherwise the essence of their living abroad is reduced only to their choice of an easier way of life.

I am convinced I was right to persuade Alan to publish his autobiography (which he dedicated to me) in his lifetime. Otherwise some people might have doubted its authenticity.

3 June

Yesterday I heard in the interview with Margaret Thatcher that "we have wonderful cemeteries everywhere, wonderfully looked after".

I saw a film too on TV about the Norland Nursery Training College in Berkshire. There, for £6,000, they train nannies for mainly upper-class families. The film was not about people at all; many things were said about their uniforms, about the methods of their training. Sometimes these nurses look after children whose mothers care more for their dogs and cars and engagements than their children's emotional development.

6 – 12 June

Day by day heated debates with Alan over the Falklands question. Alan spoke to a German TV about jingoism. He even sang a song to them which dated from 1878. During the night we sang the national anthems of many countries.

I am very lucky with my sons and with their families. Kind and good-looking people. My daughter-in-law Gabi is a born teacher and understands my views on bringing up children. She listens to what I say and applies what she thinks fit to her child with her own methods which are better than mine were.

I have read Jane Miller's clever article in the *London Review of Books* which showed what terrible problems British schools have to face today.

12 June

Many retired admirals and civil servants live in Yarmouth; their wives speak about their gardens, they invite each other to lunch. They dress up for their lunches, I saw one of them very smartly dressed buying potatoes and carrots. A retired admiral came to the same shop that day and paid his weekly account. He had his things brought to his house during the week. "Here is your money," he said abruptly to the greengrocer. The whole amount was £5.

26 July

On the Heath we had a little conversation about colleges in Oxford. Then Alan remembered his friend Joyce Cary, the writer. Cary and his wife used to live in Oxford near to Holywell Ford. They were friendly with the Taylors; they met sometimes at dinners. Cary's wife had cancer and she died before Christmas. She arranged everything for Christmas. When she died, things still arrived and kept coming as she had ordered. On Christmas Day, people came to see them and Cary told visitors that she was upstairs. So she was – dead. When Alan remembered this story, tears ran down his cheeks.

The Heath was autumnal and empty. We saw an elderly lady with her dog. The dog wanted to pick up an orange peel, she said: "Oh, no!" She explained to us that her dog had already eaten a banana peel that afternoon. We saw a tired jogger. From the top of the hill we could see people like little ants. There was one man swimming in the pond, the rest were ducks. There was a dog swimming in the other pond, and a child feeding the ducks. It was like a picture of happiness, apart from the world. I suddenly felt very sad.

John Gross would like Stephen Koss to write Alan's biography. We discussed this. Alan would prefer John Vincent[1] or Robert Skidelsky. I think he is right.

Alan said wittily about a woman who reached the age of ninety-nine that she was weary of life. I said how funny that those who are worn out by life don't commit suicide. He said: those who get to such high ages are those who want to live; the suicides are those who have not enough life in them. For this reason the former group lives to the last minute. Alan had his prostate operation today. He was bathed and given an injection. When he was put on a trolley and taken to the lift he was already becoming unconscious. Next thing he saw was me. He opened his eyes and said, "I love you." Then he tried to remember and said here were many aggressive nurses who told him to behave himself whereupon Alan said "Heil Hitler", meaning that they were aggressive. Alan was once more witty and clever, could speak coherently and said how sorry he was that I had to experience all this and how ashamed he was that he had come to be in this state. I said he was silly and that I loved him as he was and showed him in the mirror how well he looked.

Alan, to show how well he remembered everything, said: "William the Conqueror 1066" and showed me his face so that I could see how nicely he had shaved. The nurse said that when somebody has been awoken from anaesthetics, he may dream, for instance, that everybody is aggressive.

Before Alan went to the operating theatre, he ordered his lunch for the next day.

1 John Russell Vincent has been Professor of Modern History at Bristol University since 1970. His books are mostly concerned with political history and the workings of Government in Britain.

5 September

My Hungarian girl friend, the historian Éva H. Balázs[1] interviewed Braudel[2], the famous French historian and I translated the text of this interview to Alan. We discussed what Braudel said. We both agreed that he was a historian who gave static views and not moving ones. His approach is broad minded, but like a painter, he paints a moment in the universe, and there is everything in it. Braudel always said that Lucien Fébre stood behind him. Alan once met Lucien Fébre[3] in Strasbourg. He wrote a very exciting book called *Combats des Historiens*. He was much older than Alan and at that time (just after the Second World War) he was not yet liked and recognised by French historians. Alan also recalled that Austin Gill[4] invited Fébre to Oxford as his friend. It happened when Gill was a representative of the British Council in Paris after the Second World War. The British were eager to make good contacts with the French, and so Gill, who later became a Fellow of Magdalen and an expert on French literature, arranged that when Fébre was in Oxford, he should meet Oxford historians. Somerville College invited him to give an after-dinner talk to English historians in their room. Austin Gill and other French experts were there and about twenty English historians sat around. After Gill introduced Fébre, he jumped up and began his talk: *Qu'est-ce que c'est que les faits?* And he tried to explain that the facts were made up by historians who could choose them according to what the archives offered them. These English historians were quite amazed; none of them discussed anything. They found Fébre quite funny which was more than the French academics did.

The first great French personality who came through Gill was André Gide who gave an entertaining talk (in Somerville again) saying how much he would have liked to stay amongst them and how sorry he was that he could not do so. That was regarded by

1 Éva H. Balázs is a Hungarian Professor of History. She is an expert on late eighteenth century Habsburg history and Freemasonry.

2 Fernand Braudel was an eminent French historian whose influence spread all over Europe.

3 Lucien Fébre (1878–1956) was an eminent French historian who headed the editorial board of the *Encyclopédie Française*. He was also editor of the Unesco sponsored *Journal of World History*.

4 Austin Gill was Marshal Professor of French at the University of Glasgow from 1966 until he retired in 1971. He was tutor in Modern Languages at Magdalen College, Oxford, from 1945 to 1950.

the English academics as very shallow and affected. When he was invited to Magdalen College, only one professor, a mathematician called Dixon, would entertain him. After dinner, going to the Common room, Gide was offered port, he said, "Oh, I will take *un peu de syrop*". That was the end of contacts with French personalities in Oxford.

23 September

I met Elizabeth Barker the other day at the PRO. We spoke about Attlee, whom she saw only once and heard him speak. She found him middle-class, which is how Elizabeth would describe herself. I could not explain to her that Attlee understood the working class people better probably than any other Labour politician, living and working in the East End. Elizabeth said: "Oh, I know what it means. I hated going to the East End when I was a school girl (at St. Pauls), I hated the smell when I arrived each week to do a good job in the East End and I could not say anything to them." On the other hand she is very understanding with Indian women. Perhaps it is characteristic that middle-class liberal intellectuals are far away from their own kind, but are interested in more exotic people.

June Mendoza and a young Hungarian mathematician, János Pach, son of the Professor of Economic History, were here for tea. Interesting mixture. They both asked Alan about the massacre in the Lebanon. János said that his father telephoned from Rome and said he had spoken in Latin to the Pope. June Mendoza is a natural, nice girl; her portrait of Alan is good, mainly because of the colours. She is going to paint Solti, Heath and Thatcher.

The great health service strike is over. One of the finest slogans was "Maggie had her veins done, now she needs her brains done". I have a feeling sometimes that lots of people here are good at smiling and answering letters, but do not bother about people's human needs. Alan is not interested in human beings, I'm sorry to say. I asked him how, if that were the case, could he write so well about human beings and about their activities. He said cleverly: "I am like a critic of dramas. I watch how they play, what the acting is like, what the dialogue is like and so on. And then I write about it."

30 September

We went to Shrewsbury. Alan's lecture about the "Great Allies" was a tremendous success. He was in very good form; the lecture was very enlightened and very witty. I did not know many of the details which Alan gave, such as the fact that the Americans and the English did not give much help to the Russians and that what they did give was mainly in the form of American jeeps which helped them occupy Germany quickly. The audience was with Alan the whole time.

I met a professor of philosophy from Birmingham who had lived with the Taylors in Oxford at Holywell Ford for a term when he was a student in 1948. He said that Alan's and Margaret's lives ran along different lines. Everything he said about her proved me right. I felt after this conversation that I understood Alan even better.

10 November

Alan is looking fine. Though he has Parkinson's disease and has to take pills for the rest of his life, he looks very well indeed. Carr and Roskill have just died and he is wondering when and how he is going to die. He gives himself another year. I think he still has many hidden resources.

We came back from his seminar. The young bright ones always excel. I have so many things to say and don't dare to open my mouth. A terrible feeling. Alan said about Churchill that he accepted money from Indian princes. There were about six hundred princes; some of them ran countries the size of France, others, countries as big as Kentish Town. Churchill did not want to give up India and the princes used him for their own political ends.

When I told Alan that Joan Thirsk[1] had shown one of my former colleagues a great many medieval towns around Oxford, he said, that he had heard that in medieval times when a Fellow of Magdalen lived in one of these little towns (of course in those days they were members of holy orders) the birth rate went up.

1 Joan Thirsk was Reader in Economic History in the University of Oxford from 1965 to 1983. She has written several books on agrarian history.

Alan is going to read Beatrice Potter for Channel Four. He said in his Introduction that he has read Beatrice Potter for more than seventy years. First for himself, then for his children, then for his grand children, and now for everybody who is interested in her. We owe this programme to Cynthia Kee who is a great and enlightened friend to both of us.

My sons work very hard. Life here is very easy for me, but it gives me great pain in that I can't be near them and can't be more helpful to them. How shall I make them benefit from my experiences? When life is fair in one way, it is terribly unfair in others.

25 November

Yesterday we went to the *Guardian* Lunch. I had a good conversation with Richard Gott[1]. He was in the Soviet Union in Georgia before Brezhnev died. He liked it very much. Whenever he asked anyone about his successor, he always got the same answer: Andropov. Charles Townshend[2] and Richard Gott are the closest to us intellectually, and they are good characters as well. During the lunch we conversed with Glyn Hughes[3] who had won this year's *Guardian* Fiction Prize. He told me that the funny Irish Professor, R.B. McDowell, had said that when he was in London he longed for Dublin and when in Dublin he longed for London. I am against rootlessness. Look at the example of Geraldine Chaplin for instance. She spent seven years in California, twenty years in Switzerland, fifteen years in Spain and she longed for London where her father lived. Glyn Hughes spent four years in Athens where he wrote one of his best works, and it was about Yorkshire.

1 Richard Gott is a writer and features editor of the *Guardian*.
2 Charles Townshend is Senior Lecturer in History at the University of Keele and has written several outstanding books on Irish history. He contributed to the volume of essays published in honour of A. J. P. Taylor in 1986.
3 Glyn Hughes has been Warden of Glegynog, University of Wales, since 1964. He was chairman of the Broadcasting Council for Wales from 1971 to 1979. He has always been heavily involved with the Arts in Wales.

8 December

There was a very good talk in Alan's seminar on CND by Martin Keegan. Alan introduced it very well but he did not look well. He said, amongst other things, that in the 'sixties many new universities were created and these opened their doors to radicals, agitators for CND. They found cultural or other activities to put in the place of their anger.

14 December

Another Foyles Lunch at the Dorchester in honour of Richard Ingrams's book, *History of Private Eye*. Malcolm Muggeridge, Richard's great friend, was the chairman. We sat at the top table. Alan was happy next to Kitty Muggeridge and I sat next to John Mortimer whom I like very much. There were many photos taken, many friendly talks and fond embraces. I talked to Kitty about Stalin's daughter who had visited them. Kitty found her very strange. We spoke about Kitty and Malcolm's Catholicism. Kitty said they received many letters about this and only one percent were unfriendly. We saw Susan Crosland, who looked sunny and Auberon Waugh who looked shy.

I asked John Mortimer straight away if he was the hero of his estranged wife's book *The Pumpkin Eater*. He asked whether Alan was the hero of my *English Husband*. I said it was different. He did not speak to me any more, but not because he was being unfriendly, but because his neighbour was a more interesting person than me. A man of course; I think that when men are together they prefer to speak to each other. André Deutsch came over to see us; he has got very thin; he left early to go off on his skiing holiday in Switzerland. The Ingrams would like to come with us to Venice; we look forward to it. At the end of the lunch I saw the Muggeridges trying to find the way out; they had great difficulty finding it and it struck me that this is also how they have tried to find their true faith, first one way, then another, always close together. Mary Ingrams took Richard back to Berkshire in her own car. We at last went too. It was raining. Hyde Park looked empty, deserted, but the Christmas lights in Oxford Street invited the shoppers in. When we left the Dorchester behind, I could still picture the eyes of the nice eager young journalists; Christine Foyle's somehow sad face as if she knew she was not much liked by radical and socialist people, and Alan's agent, Bruce Hunter, happy foxy smiles – the merry literary world of London.

1983

6 January

We spent two weeks in Budapest at Németvölgyi Street. My son and daughter-in-law made us very welcome. They said that the two systems – them and us – operate perfectly well side by side, which is true. My first grandson, Gergö, is splendid, the parents are liberal, treat him emotionally and otherwise as part of the adult world; as a result the child has a wonderful appetite, feels secure and friendly with everyone. My son played backgammon with Alan in the evenings. I developed a high temperature on the last day, but I felt comfortable and read Alan's autobiography which I still found charming.

We had a good talk with Alan about Alfred F. Pribram who took his name from a small Bohemian town where his father was a stationmaster. Pribram was born in Brighton as his father was there for a couple of years. After the Anschluss, Pribram went to Budapest on a local train and then fled to London where he lived with one of his sons in Kew, up until the end of the Second World War. Alan visited him once in those war years. Pribram still wanted Germany to win, get rid of Hitler and build up a liberal state. Alan said that the Soviet Union would build up its influence amongst the surrounding small states of Eastern Europe which Pribram did not want to believe, not trusting Russia's strength.

24 January

E.H. Carr and Alan often marked examinations together and often came to the same conclusion. They did not stand behind the silly and lazy candidates. Carr was very appreciative when he found a smart and intelligent student. In Oxford the examinations were much more formal than in Cambridge, where often the students carried on the examinations in their own room, in their ordinary clothes, whereas in Oxford they have to dress up. Carr and Alan once executed together a student of Max Beloff.

Carr's book on Bakunin is a masterpiece. Alan reviewed it in the *Manchester Guardian* and Malcolm Muggeridge in the *Daily Telegraph*. They both found the book frightfully funny.

At Colindale I was working on the *New Statesman*'s articles on Hungary. As it was handy I collected some of Alan's articles and letters there as well. When Kingsley Martin wrote about the Wroclaw Congress in 1948, he wrote about Alan and noted the little wart on his forehead. Cromwell also had two of these, and when an artist wanted to paint a portrait of him, he said: "It must be life-like, those warts must be there too."

26 January

When we were in Hungary, my son gave a party, where we met Mr. Fisher, the Cultural Attaché of the British Embassy in Budapest. He told me he was preparing a biography of Tom Jones. Alan knew Tom Jones slightly. He was a Welshman of humble origin, who began as a Labour man. Lloyd George made him a Deputy Secretary, next to Hankey. He was important during Baldwin's leadership, then became the chief advisor of the Astors. His son became the financial editor of the *Observer* as long as the Astors lasted. Tom Jones's daughter was a Labour woman. She wanted to publish all Jones's diary because what was published was not the whole story. The spicier bits remained unpublished and everyone was hoping to read the whole diary one day, but Jones's sons did not want to let it be published. Alan met Jones at the Athenaeum; he had become a rather chatty old man, keen to let one know how important he was.

15 March

Today a journalist, Mr. Shakespeare, came to see Alan. He had an interview with Otto Habsburg, whom he called Otto von Habsburg. Alan insisted, that he was not "von", but Dr. Habsburg. Shakespeare said no, because Otto did not resign from everything. He kept his right to the Hungarian Crown. He also told me that Otto was present when Admiral Horthy died. As he was dying, Horthy apologised to Otto and said he should not have kept for himself the regency and the right to govern Hungary, he should have resigned in favour of Otto. I found this extremely interesting from the point of view of the history of my country.

17 March

It is astonishing that we are still alive, me after having pneumonia and pleurisy and Alan with his Parkinson's disease.

13 April

Adrian Liddell Hart, the son of Basil Liddell Hart, came to see us and the three of us had tea together. He had two main points to make about his father. He thinks his father was a great military thinker, but he also thinks that his father was not always right. He told us stories about his father and about Major-General J.F. C. Fuller. When Liddell Hart lived in the Lake District he often visited the prisoner of war camp where the German Generals were kept. When they complained he often gave them rugs or other things which they seemed to need. Adrian's godfather was General Fuller, whose wife was a German from Hamburg. Fuller was a Fascist and wrote full of praise for the Dachau camp. When he finished his visit to Dachau, Fuller asked Hitler if he should have given the man who showed him round a tip. Hitler said no, because there were so many scoundrels amongst them. Fuller and Liddell Hart had a correspondence for a long time. They agreed on many military questions; for instance they both thought (as did Churchill) that the creation of a second front was absolutely unnecessary, because they thought it was against British tradition and that it would cause great casualties. They all thought that the British Army was only able to fight in small battlefields and it was a fatal mistake to fight the way they did during the First World War. The Americans and Beaverbrook did want the second front, the Americans, because they thought that the enemy would be confronted with greater effect and strength. Liddell Hart told Maisky that he was in favour of the second front just because he wanted to show that the British were not against it. He himself, however, was against it because he wanted a strong Germany after the Second World War to keep the balance against the Soviet Union. Liddell Hart and Lloyd George saw eye to eye on most things. If things had turned out differently, Lloyd George would have been the British Pétain. Fuller and Liddell Hart were also counted upon in the event of a separate peace with Germany or if the Germans invaded the island. But the Battle of Britain ended all this speculation.

Michael Foot knew that Fuller had praised the Dachau camp but he thought there were not many outstanding British Generals and preferred to dwell on that side of him. Fuller's widow has burnt all the compromising material which Fuller left behind.

10 June

Isle of Wight. Would we be happier here or, for instance, near Oxford at Chastleton, where Penelope Mortimer[1] lives? Alan goes up the stairs at the Mill but is not as lively as he used to be and prefers the Scots method of emptying the pot: garden loo.

I have changed a lot. I am not such a workaholic as I used to be; I like to meditate, I like sightseeing, I like fun, I like to listen to classical music and watch the birds. Perhaps I am not as strong for work as I used to be. Perhaps this is the result of the many bouts of pneumonia I have had, or of ageing. Anyhow, I am not afraid of death any more and I used to be so afraid of it that I shivered.

23 September

We are at Dickens's house, Doughty Street. Alan is shaky. He has to sit down often. It was a wonderful day. The last day of summer, sunny and warm. We came back through St. George's Place, one of our favourite gardens. Dickens should be re-read. This house of his is only one of the many houses he lived in. I wrote about his American tours to Ferencz but perhaps he has not got much time to read in Philadelphia where he is carrying out research on

1 Penelope Mortimer is a writer. She was married to John Mortimer (see page 184).

cancer. We saw Dickens's reading table which he designed himself. He really killed himself with his reading tour in America. Later in the afternoon Alan gave a full account of Dickens's novels according to their merits as he saw them.

When we came back from Dickens's house, we went to a pub, ate a pork-pie and drank beer and pineapple juice. We sat next to an old, fat man who drank beer with whisky. He complained about his age. He said: "My dear, the whole thing is not worth it any more. I sit in my empty flat and think to myself: 'If you had known before what you know now, you would have done everything differently.' I think what a fool I was to have led my life the way I did. Too late now."

The problem of our lives nowadays is that Alan is declining physically. He naturally dislikes this very much. He has no interests other than history. He has lost the enthusiasm to write another book. He does not lecture any more. He is not interested in people. He would like to stop the whole show. Though, when there are good days, he gets up with the hope that he has regained his old self, which is a nonsense. He soon gets tired and disillusioned. Parkinson's disease works this way: one day is hopeful, the next is dreadful. The problem is that he would like to give me a more interesting life. He can't and he knows this. I do not require a more interesting life, but he won't believe me.

28 September

Alan begins his last TV lecture series with the title "How Wars End". A lovely young woman called Stacy Marking is the producer. She is of Irish stock. Before the show started we sat together. She told me that her ancestors went to Ireland at the time of Cromwell. We spoke about the present day-conditions in the South of England. In one of the Panorama programmes there was a whole documentary on British agriculture and there was not one word about the agricultural labourers. It has happened, even in this century (around the time of the First World War) that an agricultural worker was convicted because he did not take off his cap when the landlord drove past him. Her next show will be about the Tolpuddle Martyrs.

We were invited to dinner by Cynthia and James Joll and Brian Foster was there too. The latter is a young historian, one of the editors of *History*. He has many interests. The other day he visited Diana Mosley, who is over eighty, but still an attractive lady. She spoke about Churchill and Hitler. She only hated Churchill because Churchill sent them to prison. As everybody knows, at Holloway the conditions were not rosy and her daughter was only four months old. But she still feels close to Churchill; they belonged to the same clan. Mosley's son Nicholas wrote a good book about his father. He thought his father was nasty and wicked, but Nicholas loved him all the same. He is an excellent writer. His novel called *Accident* (the film based on this novel was also called *Accident*) has a hero who is a well known Warden in Oxford: Raymond Carr. In another novel of his, a woman is raped by her own dog. Disgusting – but a very good novel all the same. Brian praised Beryl Bainbridge and Elizabeth Bowen, but he was sceptical about Margaret Forster whom I rate very highly.

Brian and James both said they would help to find a publisher for my *Kossuth as an English Journalist* and *Attlee and Hungary*.

I got a wonderful letter from my daughter-in-law, Gabi. Her letters about the child should be published.

29 September

Sixty years. Not very much. I hope I live a long time. I like life. I think every moment is interesting. I would love to live as long as possible and near to those whom I love.

My son telephoned from Philadelphia. I was touched. His son Gergö misses him very much. When I stayed with them, little Gergö went to him each morning. I will never forget his thin, kind voice saying: "Papa, Papa".

I got a letter for my birthday from my second son and daughter-in-law, Kriszti. Pisti is so thoughtful, he wears his "second sonness" with kindness and tolerance. Just as my second grandson, little Andris, probably will also. Second sons have an even more difficult time when the first is so bright.

Alan took me, for my birthday, to the Gay Hussar in Soho. Alan's son Sebastian and his wife Mary were the other guests. Victor, the owner, waited on us; he is sixty-nine years old now, speaks very good Hungarian and Lancashire English. He has just come back from Hungary where he visited his Hungarian mother-in-law. During his stay there he discussed Hungarian cooking with his mother-in-law the whole time. She is also an excellent cook. Victor does not like those guests who come to his restaurant with their hands in their pockets. But he likes Alan very much. Victor lives in Kentish Town in a small house. He is not very rich.

We were invited to the Hungarian Ambassador's for lunch. One of the guests returns to Budapest after spending four years in Britain. His ten-year-old son, who is fluent in English and already settled in his school, will be sad to leave behind two things in England: his school and the toy department at Harrods.

11 November

My second son and his wife move to their new home. They are expecting their first baby. I spoke to them on the phone, about nothing really, but it is the voice, the emotion behind it which is important. Since we speak on the phone regularly we don't feel the distance. My two-year-old grandson speaks well. He says to himself, being brave: "It is not really dark in the loo." Nine-month-old Andris kindly speaks some easy words to everyone. We are going to Budapest for Christmas again. I asked whether it would not be too much having us for a fortnight. No, no, they all love us and there will be no estrangement in our family between generations, they said.

1984

15 January

When we came home after our Hungarian holiday, Alan was hit by a car on January 6, in Old Compton Street. Since then life is painful and grey, especially for Alan. He fights well; his accident was in a way lucky, because his pelvis was not broken but only hurt and he had to spend three weeks in the Middlesex Hospital. When he came home we made the necessary arrangements in the house and though Alan feels the end is not far away, he tries hard to get back his ability to walk properly. His fight is very brave because he has to fight so many things at the same time.

25 January

I gave my seminar talk in the Institute for Historical Research at the Seminar of Alice Prohaska,[1] Ben Pimlott[2] and others. Alice introduced me well and Ben was very kind too. The talk was mainly on British policy towards Hungary. Coming home Alan looked tired and small. Cynthia, dear, sweet Cynthia, looked after him. Terry has sent me today Dorothy Thompson's[3] book on Chartism for review in the *Observer*.

Alan said last night, "I won't last long you know. And you

1 Alice Prohaska is now the Secretary of the Institute for Historical Research, London University, and a good historian in her own right.
2 Ben Pimlott is a historian of the British Labour Movement. His latest book is a biography of Hugh Dalton.
3 Dorothy Thompson is an expert on Chartism and Social History. She is married to E.P. Thompson.

must always remember how much I loved you." After his accident he felt he had become an invalid and had no strength left to fight. He wanted to fight, but had no physical strength to do so. I do not see why he could not last a little bit longer – his heart and lungs are good. But somehow I am afraid to go into our common bedroom (I have been sleeping in my study lately) to see if he is still breathing. Our friend the Baroness Hatvani told me that she begged her seriously ill husband to keep on living and as long as she heard his breathing she felt all right. My grandsons and daughter-in-law fly to the States on Saturday. I hope everything will go well.

29 February

Ivor Montagu came for tea. He was with Alan at Wroclaw in 1948, and wanted to win Alan over to his side. Ivor is a good man: straight character, smart, intelligent, Marxist with a broad outlook. He is going to be eighty soon. He spoke about his friendship with Chaplin and Einstein and remembered the plays they did together. He spoke about the plays which English people put on during the nineteenth century. For instance there was a play which revolved around the following question: You will get £1,000 if you push a button. This will, however, cause a Chinaman to die. Would you push that button? The way each person answered showed his character.

Ernö Goldfinger rang us up. He said now he was all right if we wanted to visit them. He has got six years to live. He has cancer.

At the moment I am reading A. J. Blackwell, who was a British agent in Hungary and wanted a strong, independent Hungary and hoped to be the first British Consul in Buda. He could not convince Palmerston about this because Palmerston believed in maintaining the balance of power and thought a strong Habsburg Monarchy a necessity. Blackwell liked many Magyars but on the whole he thought that the Hungarians were not practical enough; many were self-satisfied and vain and could not get on with each other, but were able to speak up or just speak and speak and speak.

1 March

I saw a middle-aged man taking his dog for a walk in Twisden Road and they seemed to me to suit each other perfectly; they even looked alike. The dog held a leather glove in his mouth. That is what he likes when he goes for a walk.

The picture of Alan painted by June Mendoza will be hung in the private dining room of Magdalen College, Oxford. On March 17, there will be festivities, the President has invited many people and June herself will be there as well. A fund has made it possible for the portrait to be bought for Magdalen. Chris Cook established a fund, called the Taylor Picture Fund and more than £2,000 was collected. An unknown person gave me £1,000 to pay in to this. Chris asked if the person who gave it was a foreigner. "Yes," I said.

3 March

I miss my children and grandchildren very much at the weekends. My eldest (three-year-old) grandson, Gergö, told me that he was a cry baby. I felt very close to him. I would have said this about myself when I was a child. His little brother, who will soon be one year old, marches about his home happily although he plays second fiddle. I must re-read Russell's book about the wisdom of how to be happy. I do not know this well. The publisher has sent me back my manuscript of *The English Husband*, as he is worried that the reviewers might cause Alan much pain. That is true. But I am not entirely convinced any more that I was right. Perhaps I am hypersensitive.

5 March

Keith Kyle and his wife, Sue, came for tea. He liked my book on the Rhineland question. I was amazed that Keith had read it. Then he explained that he was very much interested in the Rhineland question because this problem was his first interest in international relations; when he was nine or ten years old he began to read papers and there was a great deal about the problem of the demilitarised zone of the Rhineland and the German troops marching in. Keith and Sue like Alan very much. They both worked under or with him, Keith as an undergraduate, Sue as a TV producer.

Alan is writing a review; he says he is going downhill.

10 March

I spoke to my son Pisti on the phone. His first child, Andrea, is very organized, plays alone, serene and happy. Her mother Kriszti is a worrying parent but my son is not. He says for him Andrea is not the first child; his brother's sons, who were born earlier, were first. I learn a lot from my sons, wisdom and firmness.

15 March

A middle aged woman rang up Alan today. Mrs. Thatcher wanted to invite Alan to dinner with the West German President, von Weizsäcker. Alan politely said he was not able to go as he is still suffering from the effects of his accident.

I got a letter from my son in Philadelphia. My grandson, Gergö, calls a skyscraper a "moon reaching house". I thought that was rather nice.

15 April

Alan has problems with his bladder. This is partly as a result of the Parkinson's disease. There was a test made which made him ill. He developed a very high temperature and our GP, Michael Modell, called for an ambulance which took us to University College Hospital. I made a detailed account of Alan's stay in the hospital. I spoke to the nurses a lot; they were very enlightened; I was shocked at how badly they are paid for all their hard work. They were always very nice and tolerant with Alan, even in his delirious state of mind. They were perfectly straightforward with him and asked me whether they can coerce him against his will to take a bath. The staff nurse, who was a young man, said to me that one has to try to persuade the patients and let them preserve their dignity in whatever state of mind they are in.

16 April

Alan is confused. He has septicaemia. He has got a very strong new antibiotic called, I think, ceftazidime. He did not recognize me when I visited him. Our GP who visited him as well said we have to wait and see what happens.

17 April

When I came to the hospital Alan was standing outside his room like a lost child and did not recognize me. The whole morning was a terrible struggle; he did not want to stay in his bed, in his room; he strolled along the corridor and did not want to obey the nurses and doctors at all. The nurse asked me by telephone to come in earlier in order to appease him. Alan thought I was Margaret. He said to me as if I were Margaret: "You must be nice to Eva, she is lonely and sad." The whole day was awful. I thought he would never be the same again. But when Dr. Spiro came and asked him to go back to his bed, he did so. Amazing how authority influences even mentally disturbed people. Dr. Spiro and the other doctors said that the powerful antibiotics would cure Alan.

18 April

The new drug began to work well today. Alan was nearly normal, but he still thinks I am Margaret and we are in India, not in London in a hospital. It was heartbreaking how we carried on our conversation. He revealed, unconsciously; much about his relationship with Margaret since we got married and since I came to London to live with him. It became obvious I was right: he shared a lot with Margaret and discussed everything with her, did as she advised, but Alan always loved me and said to Margaret that we had a very good life together.

19 April

Alan spoke a lot about his father. He felt guilty that he did not spend more time with him. Alan said he had wanted to show human beings respect all his life.

Michael Foot visited Alan twice. It was disturbing to see how far Alan was from realities, but Michael said it was great fun to be with Alan, as always. Michael also talked about the miners – he was worried about how long they could go on; the Government was too skilful in treating them and the government could wait; it had resources for a long time.

I spoke to my son and daughter-in-law by telephone. The little ones spoke to me too. It cheered me up. The children have a sense of humour which is so necessary in life. I never had enough.

6 May

For Mothers' Day I received a huge and colourful bouquet from my family. They (all seven) signed it – what lovely people they are. In the evening we went to dinner with Ursula and Ernö. Ursula only buys dresses once a year. She is a very practical woman. Ernö pours out all sorts of reminiscences. They had many famous guests during the decades. Ernö thought well of Maisky. He is a lion like Alan, but an undisciplined one.

17 May

Alan is feeble and disorientated again. I kept him in bed for two days. Cynthia was here, she has just come back from France where she did an excellent interview with Simone Weil for the *Observer*. Cynthia was enchanted by Simone Weil. Cynthia then went to the South of France, visited the Káldors who took her to Katus Károlyi. Katus is ninety-one years old, her face is still beautiful and she asked Cynthia to tell Alan to send a copy of his autobiography to her. Her house in Vence is charming. Cynthia also went to Brussels and described it as a madhouse. The European Parliament is over-organized, a bureaucratic nightmare, the whole thing.

Cynthia looked at our patio and she liked it very much. I have painted many parts of the walls and pavement red, blue and yellow to cheer up my often-depressed man. Cynthia said it was done in a pop style. I also told her about what I have seen in the garden, the activities of the birds, the cats and the sex life of the snails, which I watched and photographed. When Cynthia came back from the patio, she found Alan on the floor on his back. He often does this nowadays, it relaxes him. Alan told Cynthia what he experienced in his delirious state of mind. Cynthia just did not know what to say: snail sexuality in the garden, delirious dreams – and from outside, the house looked like a very ordinary semi-detached late Victorian house. Twisden Road. Every house is nearly the same in this little road and who knows what goes on inside them, innocent as they look.

20 May

Alan said, "I am not good enough to accept my defeats, am I?" John Betjeman died at the age of seventy-seven; he had Parkinson's disease for more than a decade. But there are many sorts of Parkinson's disease. It is not always a killer.

22 May

The tragedy of Alan is that he can't work properly. Before this he felt he could not keep on at his old level. On the other hand, without his historical works and articles to journals his life is not worth living. That is what he says. I don't agree. He still has things to offer. He writes less and much shorter pieces than he used to, but still the value in his thoughts and the style are there. I said to him also, that it is a great thing in life if somebody is a good, fair man, like him. He said that in his whole life his principle was that it is not the fairness and niceness of a man that is the most important thing, but his brain. With me the problem is different. I am happy with my intellectual work but sometimes if I am in emotional trouble, I can't concentrate well. On the other hand, intellectual work pulls me out of emotional distress.

26 May

We spoke to Alan's consultant Dr. Gerard Stern. He said that the septicaemia left practically nothing behind and Alan's Parkinson's disease is mild and stagnant. A great relief. Alan was very amusing today. In the evening we spoke about Lutyens whom he called the imperial architect. Also Alan said he will take the place of Betjeman as the nation's Parkinsonist.

I had a good talk with Alan, who said that in retrospect it was wonderful that we could discuss everything together. Now that the end is coming he sees clearly that his mind will go on, but his body is not good enough any more. I wept as he said that nobody would love me as much as he did; he also added that he was happy to see me strong and standing on my own two feet. This evening Alan wrote a consoling letter to Penelope Betjeman.

4 June

Alan is in hospital. He had to go back to the private wing of University College Hospital. When I brought him back for the weekend, he hurried out of the hospital, tried to get quickly into the car; he opened the car door with his own key and felt happy. I told myself when this session in hospital ends, I will keep Alan at home at any price.

11 June

I went to the States for a few days and visited my son and his family in Philadelphia, saw Washington, Boston and visited my sister and her family in Wellfleet. This was the first time I had been to America and I felt extremely relaxed. I made separate notes about this journey which I gave to my son, who made me very welcome with his wife and children.

When I came back from the airport I went straight to the hospital. I saw Alan immediately as he was going towards the bathroom. I saw his back and when he saw me and went back to his room my heart sank. He seemed to me very pale and neglected, his face was very drawn. Cynthia visited him daily, sent us beautiful red roses for my return and told me Alan had a good time. The family visited him, even took him out for a nice sunny afternoon and he felt happy amongst his children. Alan's appetite was fine, and the nurses were kind; still, he became anaemic and was very happy to leave the hospital. Now he is at home, having peaceful sleeps and dreams on our sunny patio and seems content. We go out sometimes to the local pub. But there are bad days, mainly when it is rainy or windy, when Alan complains of aches and pains everywhere. The physiotherapist comes twice a week.

19 June

We were invited to the Langton Gallery. Alan gave an interview about David Low[1] who was of Scottish stock on his father's side, Irish on his mother's. Beaverbrook employed him as he recognized his outstanding talent. Low was given carte blanche by Max and the association was to last for twenty-three years. Alan added his own personal views on Low and we both enjoyed seeing the exhibition, which included some of the very best of Low's work.

22 June

I have been thinking a lot about men in general. I think for them life is more difficult as the desire for success and the feeling of responsibility weighs heavily on them. I think they can face life, on the whole, because they are less emotional than women. Alan was safe up to the age of seventy-eight. Now that he is feeble he naturally does not like it. Yesterday he told me I was appalling because I had persuaded him to accept the invitation from the *Sunday Times* to take part in their "Gardening Hat" photos. Alan did not want to take part because, as he said, he was not a gardener. But the *Sunday Times* people promised that they would give the picture a caption like: "Only the hat is for gardening– the bearer is not". They also promised to tell the story of the hat, which was bought by Alan's two daughters in Italy some fifty years ago and I mended it. Actually this picture happened to be one of the best pictures taken of Alan in the last few years.

I think about my sons a lot, partly because I think about men a lot. They belong to the middle generation, they are at a difficult age: when they work on their careers, they have to build up their own family life and finances and they feel responsible for me as well. I think about this a lot because my first husband died at the age of forty-four and I had the opportunity to watch how men cope, looking at these four men, close to me, in three different age groups. (William died at forty-four, Alan is seventy-eight, Ferencz is thirty-three, Pisti thirty-one). Myself, I have always wanted independence throughout my whole adult life. Only now

1 David Low (1891–1963) was an outstanding cartoonist on the *Daily Express*.

that I am getting on do I reflect more often on how my parents acted, how I solved the question of responsibility and dependence.

24 June

We visited today the cemetery at Abney Park where, among others, two famous Chartist leaders lie: Bronterre O'Brien and Henry Vincent. Alan was asked to give a memorial speech at the tomb of O'Brien, who died 120 years ago and whose tomb was recently discovered. This Abney Park cemetery is beautiful. It was described thus by the landscape gardener John Claudius London in 1843: "The most highly ornamented cemetery in the neighbourhood of London". The cemetery had close ties with Isaac Watts and other famous non-conformists. A small, but enthusiastic group of people consisting of several Irish people, left wingers, middle-aged and young people gathered at the tomb. On the stone there is a mistake: it says that Bronterre O'Brien lived sixty-seven years, but in fact he only lived sixty. Everybody was happy to see Alan, who said in his little speech what a great democrat O'Brien was and that he was going to join him soon. There were music and singing at the tomb and I felt happy. It would be worthwhile to publish the works, articles, speeches and letters of Bronterre O'Brien, who was a clear political and economic thinker and a good scholar of the French Revolution.

25 June

Chris Maguire the electrician, who really organised the memorial gathering at O'Brien's tomb rang us up and said they were touched that Alan went and spoke. He offered to see to any electrical faults in our house, should any arise. Also, he had read in my *Chartism* book the chapter on O'Brien and liked it very much. I felt so happy that what I wrote on O'Brien in Hungary reached English readers at the right time, in the right place.

5 August

My architect son Pisti, his wife Kriszti and their daughter Andrea spent their holiday with us. Alan made them welcome and I was very happy to see them happy. I was thrilled when Pisti told me that I am his best friend apart from his brother and that we make him strong and full of confidence. Kriszti is a nice character and a good mother; she has a harmony and beauty. Andrea is in good hands and is a very good humoured and co-operative child. I have learnt a lot from them.

There are two letters in *The Times* which I thought should be known widely. A. Williams from Nottingham wrote about the Dresden air-raid. He was a navigator in one of the Lancaster bombers which devastated Dresden and he thought that this was a black mark on Britain's war record. The other letter came from M. Tolfree, Eastbourne. He reminded the readers of the price that was paid in connection with the settlement with the Church in the 1944 Education Act. That consisted of the imposition of compulsory religious instruction and daily "Act of Worship" for all children in all schools in the country. "The churches did well out of it. For the past forty years their beliefs and doctrines and opinions have been promulgated through the schools. All our schools have been brought (and remain) under the religious umbrella. This law remains on the Statute Book despite its increasing archaism."

Mervyn Jones and his wife were here for a drink. We had a good conversation. Their very good friend, Basil Davidson[1], had such bad experiences in Hungary in 1940–41 that he never wanted to visit the country again. Perhaps he has changed his mind by now; this Hungarian Government is not responsible for what the Horthy police did, and Davidson's book about Africa is translated into Hungarian.

16 August

Alan stayed in the hospital for a couple of days. It was assumed that something was wrong with his stomach or bowels. He was prepared for a colonoscopy. When it was done, it was very, very painful. While the doctor made the test, Alan cried "Stop it, it is agony". The doctor said later: "A tough guy." Nothing was wrong in these parts of his body.

1 Basil Davidson is a writer and a historian. As well as writing numerous novels and many books on Africa and African history, he has been foreign correspondent for, among others, *The Times* and the *New Statesman*.

24 August

Jeanne and Mervyn Jones came for dinner. As a small boy Mervyn knew Freud. Freud smoked a lot and so everybody gave him lighters as gifts. Freud himself always used matches, thinking that if cigarette lighters had been invented first and matches only later, everybody would have thought, how much simpler it was to light cigarettes with matches. Mervyn was thinking aloud: What happened to the lighters in Freud's collection? After some negotiations the Gestapo let Freud take with him to London his valuable treasures but he did not bring his twenty or thirty lighters.

Alan and Mervyn had an interesting conversation about Kingsley Martin and about the English pubs. Mervyn very much loved Kingsley Martin, who had no children and who liked teenagers very much and knew how to converse with them. Martin's wife Dorothy was an expert on China and Burma. She was the heart and soul of the "Save the Chinese" movement in England during the Korean War.

An insane woman kept approaching Kingsley, and she even went to Dorothy and begged her to share him. But Dorothy said with her thick Irish accent: "He is not an apple that he can be halved." According to Mervyn, Kingsley was not a coward, but uncertain; he could not make decisions easily. Norman Mackenzie said about him that he was the "unconsciousness of the British left" – meaning that Kingsley could not make up his mind definitely on one question or another.

Speaking about the English pubs, it turned out that it is only in recent years that one can take a woman to a pub in Scotland. In Ireland the grocer's shop is also the pub, and so a man can go shopping in the morning and return in the evening, drunk.

According to Mervyn the pub as a social institution developed in England as a result of brewing real ales in the villages. Perhaps a family would decide that they would brew the ale for the whole community and invite them all. To go to a pub was first of all a working class habit. The homes of working class families were very poor and cramped, they had not enough glasses, not enough places to sit and very few chairs. But in a pub they could meet friends, neighbours, whom they could not invite home. The French coffee house and the English pub serve the same aim: social life. Mervyn said that people did not even invite their best friends to their homes, only members of their families. When Alan wants family members to be invited to our house, this is also perhaps a tradition.

I have learnt today that our 93-year-old neighbour, who lives in the house she has rented for seventy years, has no bathroom, and only an outside loo.

13 September

This morning, Alan got a letter from a post-graduate who has written his thesis about Alan, i.e. about his historical works. The young man asked if one could judge a historian if one did not know the historian as a person. Before I married Alan I would have said, "Of course." Now, knowing him better, I say: "No."

Let us see Alan as a historian. When he writes about Max Beaverbrook, John Bright, Francis Joseph or Otto von Bismarck, one can see that this historian is a very sensitive person. One can feel that this person is sensitive enough to describe the weak points in his heroes' lives; perhaps he understands them better because he has had unresolved situations in his own life.

An example of how living with a historian leads one to understand his history writing better is this: Alan stroked my hair yesterday evening and said: "We have to accept that things are going worse than we expected." "Why?" I asked, "because we are getting older?" "No," he said, "in youth also there are many things which are worse than one thought. But why get angry when one can't help?" This is his mental hygiene. But this is also valid for his political views. For this reason Cobden is in many respects Alan's hero as Cobden had the idea that because he could not change the foreign policy or the war policy of his government during war time, the best thing to do was to withdraw, not to interfere. Alan's main principle is not to interfere in personal life and in public life. There was one exception: CND. This was the most important political event in Alan's life; he gave great initiative and zest to the campaign and the campaign gave him great excitement and an aim in life. But the campaign did not achieve its ends and did not change anything. Alan came out of it strengthened: it is not worth entering political life.

When he answered the post-graduate's letter about what he thought about the poor and the rich, Alan said that the rich look after their wealth, they are afraid of losing it. The poor have no wealth so they are not selfish in this respect and as they look at each other, they consider each other. I asked. "What do you think — are the poor selfish in other respects?" "I do not know," he said. He stands on the side of the poor. Although Alan does not know the poor, his heart is generous. Alan does not know the poor, not because he has not met them, but because he is not interested in them as people. He is not interested in people and he does not notice their personal needs or problems. He does if he reads about them. For instance I had to persuade him to give weekly donations to the miners. He would have been able to say no to the woman who collected it. Alan does not believe in any sort of charity. This was not charity, I told him, but solidarity.

Now as I am preparing a book on Kossuth as an English journalist (he contributed to both the *Sunday Times* and *The Atlas* in 1855), I am reading a lot on the Crimean War. I read Alan's essay on Bright. This is a good example of the fact that, although there is no question about Alan's genius, he can't analyse the problems which his genius poses, and describes, and which he brings together. He recreates the truth as he sees it or as the protagonists saw it, but it is not always the objective truth. Alan is an anti-establishment man, but he is not a dangerous one in consequence of his own character.

When I am writing, I think, as I collect my data, about the structure of the book. At the end my thoughts and my collected sources give me the key. Throughout my research – that means sometimes years – the problem is there, the sources make or change or add to the problem; they may or may not solve it. But the best method of describing, analysing and solving the problem is to have a good structure. Therefore, before I begin to write, I think about it over and over again. Just as in a building, the steel or wood gives the base, the structure, and as in the human body the bones keep men straight, so my structure keeps the content in order.

Alan is back into the swing of things. Because he is so clever and stores everything in his brain like a computer, and because everything is connected to another thing, his thoughts work from two ends and he knows immediately what he wants to deduce from his theme and manages to present a many-sided picture in one clever, unpretentious lecture. Alan always lets himself be led by his data, whatever it is. For this reason he is a great historian and an honest one. He does not search for motives, because according to him they are simply there.

23 September

I read a very interesting letter in *The Times* from Lord Gladwyn, whose views I became familiar with in the Public Record Office files when I wrote my article on 1948–49. Surprisingly he wrote these lines (surprisingly because I thought he was taken by the Cold War): "Whatever may be thought about the Communist regimes then imposed by the Soviet Government on the 'liberated' Eastern European countries, they are greatly preferable to the appalling fate which would have been in store for them had the Nazis won. That they did not win was very largely the result of the heroic resistance of the Russian people. And there is a rather natural feeling in Russia that in no circumstances must Eastern Europe again be the base for yet another assault by 'the West' on the Russian motherland."

24 September

This morning the man arrived to redecorate our kitchen. He is a very kind man, with tattoos on his arms. He asked: "What does 'historian' mean? What does a historian do?" I don't think such a phenomenon as this man exists in Hungary.

I heard on the radio this morning that in the event of a nuclear attack there is nothing one can do. London is very dangerous as it is full of targets. If the population wanted safe anti-nuclear cellars they would have to be deeper than it is possible to dig. Anyhow London would be closed. There will be no way out. It is well known to the Government. All the same, they don't do anything about it.

Yesterday Len Deighton and his sweet wife, Isabel, visited us. They have two sons and they have had them educated each year in different countries. They will study later in Ireland or in England, but privately. Len hates the class orientated English school system. He is surprised that his sons are so passive. Their father is English, their mother is Dutch, the daughter of Dutch diplomats. They don't have strong roots, perhaps it is not important for them. Isabel has found an emotional rock in Len. I offered them my cottage on the Danube if they happened to go to Hungary.

There are two interesting articles in the *Observer*. One was Graham Greene's interview which ended by Graham saying that he would rather be in the Gulag than in California. The other was about the second son in the family and in the society. As I have two sons and one of my sons also has two sons and both second sons were astonishingly different from the first one, I read this article with great enthusiasm.

30 September

Cynthia drove me to Greenham Common to see the peace camp and the residents there. Children and women sang and played happily near the Green Gate where we left the car. The camp itself is an enormous field surrounded by wire fences. The protests of these women began in 1981, when the missile heads arrived from the States. The protesters did not succeed. Michael Heseltine, the Defence Minister, acted and the devastating nuclear arms were smuggled into the base. The area is guarded partly by British, partly by American soldiers. Outside the fence the women have settled in, they stay here in the summer, in the winter in sleeping bags, in tents. Good, radical people from all over the country bring them food, wood and candles. The women are peaceful, but whenever they begin to move together mounted policemen surround them and force them to withdraw and to disperse. People from all over the country come and go round the camp and say "hello" or "good afternoon" kindly to the soldiers. I did not do it. The women think that with kindness, with smiles, with peaceful talk they can win over these soldiers, policemen or policewomen. I just went along the wires looking taciturn and suddenly a soldier greeted me in a very friendly way from within. Then I greeted him too with a smile. Perhaps there is something in these friendly, patient peace building activities? I discussed with Cynthia and two other young women how to go on with these protests. Should one convince people patiently or form a party? Many women take their children to the mounted policeman and they both speak quietly to the horse and to the man and stroke the horse's head. Many of the policemen and soldiers are simply male chauvinists. They are not moved. A great part of the society in Britain despise the Greenham women; they say that only misfits and lesbians go there. I spoke to a woman who came from Wales: her background was partly Polish. She spent some time in Poland during the summer. In her view the popularity of Solidarity there has gone. I spoke to another woman who led a delegation to the Soviet Union in the name of the Greenham women. They very much enjoyed meeting teachers and other women in the place they visited.

2 October

Jeanne Jones visited us. She said that many miners came from Yorkshire to Camden Town. Two or three people could stay in their house. One of the miners said to her that they had so far lived on their savings, but perhaps they will now sell their few bits of jewellery. Before the strike he had his house redecorated on the outside; now he would willingly scratch the paint off to get his money back. Many people give them money for their cause. Jeanne said that in their bathroom they have a bath every day, wash their hair and use more shampoo for three days than her daughter uses in a month. But she does not mind this at all.

21 October

I told Alan, to cheer him up, that he does not know what it is like to marry an intellectual woman, because when he married me, he was so proud and happy and repeatedly said that this was the best thing he had ever done. Alan said with a twinkle in his eyes, "I just bow to it."

29 October

Stephen Koss is dead. He was only forty-four, as my first husband was when he died. We were both moved, Alan and myself, historians in this country and in Hungary. Alan wrote about him in the *Observer*. My Hungarian historian friend T. Iván Berend[1], who stayed in Cambridge, wrote to me about Stephen's illness. He spoke to him on the telephone in New York, two weeks before his operation and he was very optimistic and spoke about his

1 T. Iván Berend is the President of the Hungarian Academy and an outstanding economic historian.

plans for the future. He was a good historian and a friend of Britain and Hungary.

14 November

John Birch[1] and his wife came for dinner. He represents well his class and his profession: a British Diplomat. He is one of the "two nations of Britain" which were so well described by Disraeli. He was educated in a Quaker school where it was important to develop a hobby. He washed up with Sebastian after dinner and he confessed this was the first time he had ever done this.

They had been in Afghanistan as well; John had a post there probably before he was in Hungary, where I got to know him. They said that it was better if six children out of ten in Afghanistan died because the land is unable to support so many people.

16 November

Alan said today that he did not want anything else, just to survive; he does not want to achieve any more.

22 November

Pamela and Charles Gott came to stay with us for a couple of days. Charles is one of Alan's best friends. We had a very cheerful time together. I learnt two things from them: 1) The best thing to do against rheumatism is to put both elbows into lemons. 2) A party game: two people sit opposite each other and fold *The Times* newspaper. Whoever folds the quickest and best way is the winner.

I took Alan to the dentist. Before we went in, the secretary of the dentist gave us some flowers and a card to greet the dentist as it was his birthday.

Sometimes I visit a little shop where women usually sell old

1 John Birch has been head of the Eastern European Department, Foreign and Commonwealth Office, since 1983. He was Councillor in Budapest from 1980–83. He is now in the USA on a diplomatic posting.

things. It is a church shop and the income goes to the church. They sometimes sell bits of Victorian bric-à-brac from households or modest pieces of jewellery. I had the feeling that they sell the belongings of deceased lonely old people because it is usually the vicar who decides the prices. One morning I went there and the lady told me that she often refuses to buy things for her children because she has to feed the dogs and this costs a lot of money.

23 November

I had a long and sincere conversation with Alan which made me feel happy and reassured. I feel that when he hurt me in the past he did not mean to, whereas my reactions are consciously hurtful. Alan is stronger than me and not as sensitive, or at least, he is sensitive in a different way. He belongs to another generation and our dialogue is thus very enlightening, because it shows that different reactions might come not only from different characters and different degrees of sensitivity, but from different experiences created by a different age or period.

10 December

My son Ferencz spent a few days with us on his way back to Budapest from Philadelphia. He is fine, sees the world situation well and in it, the Hungarian scene. He is positive and scientific, an unbiased husband and father. He explained very well why he did not want to live close to me or to his in-laws. I agreed with what he said.

11 December

Zara Steiner[1] came for tea. She recalled the Oxford days when Alan, a brilliant lecturer, came into the hall. Before him a lecturer

1 Zara Steiner is Director of Studies and Fellow of Modern History at New Hall, University of Cambridge. Her publications include a volume on Foreign Offices throughout the world and one on the Origins of the First World War.

in Oxford would have spoken about everything and done so boringly. Alan was fresh, had chosen his subject well, everybody enjoyed hearing him; the lecture room was always full. Zara said she did not know what sort of character Alan was at that time, because she did not know him well enough, but she knew what a wonderful lecturer he was because she listened to him. Zara comes from America. After the war they got a handbook as young undergraduates on how to behave in England. She got a Fullbright scholarship which they called Halfbright. The handbook stated, among other things, that in England one does not ask for second helpings, and one should not express political views.

Namier was her husband's godfather. Zara disliked Namier's second wife, Julia, very much. Julia was not a good character and also she was very religious. She brought out the worst in Namier, who became very anti-Communist. Once they visited Namier and Zara asked him how he was. Namier's response was, "Why do you ask, are you a physician?"

1985

7 January

Coming back from Hungary I found Twisden Road very quiet, very few people on the street. The postmaster and his family were smiling at me as usual, nice Indian smiles; the advertisements on the TV struck me as coming from an old, long forgotten civilisation, always the same, the comments and jokes on the radio and TV again, always the same. The slogans about dignity and Britishness, about necessary compromises, the upper-middle classes' anti-Scargillism, the lovely rich animal foods, the self-importance, the holidays and new cars and the ever-present self-interest. How cleverly George Orwell wrote about England in the 'thirties and 'forties in *England, my England*. When I read his essays I feel that everything is said about England, there is nothing more to add. When he said in 1940 that the English always felt they were more distinguished than foreigners, the British left-wing tried to alter this view for twenty years. If they had succeeded, perhaps SS soldiers would have marched on the streets of London – remarked Orwell. I think he succeeded in showing the complexity of human behaviour, human history. Somebody told me that Orwell's essays are much better than his other writings. I feel he was right. The essays are excellent. Should be compulsory reading for foreigners.

20 January

I feel lucky that I am staying in England during the miners' strike and during the activities of the Greenham women. Alan's daughter Sophia told me that during the weekend they visited a picket-line somewhere near Nottingham. During the night they went out with the miner's family where they stayed, approximately forty of them together in the great snow and cold and dark. As Sophia understood the situation, many miners go down to the pits to work in order to get their salaries, but they can't begin to work unless the security men arrive. Now the practice is that if the security men arrive and the picket line threatens their safety, they can go home and still get their salary. Thus the forty people went out during the night and cold because they were the picket line; they became the threatening pickets, they shouted in the cold night to the security men: "Men go home, men go home." The whole dark night echoed with their voices and the security men, obeying the "threatening force" went home. Thus the miners in the mines could not work either. But all of them got their wages. The whole thing was a comedy but it served a good cause.

30 January

I visited the Szepsi Csombor Society, which is a Hungarian Society in London. This Society or, as it calls itself, "Circle" is composed of Hungarians living in London and its aim is to cultivate Hungarian language and literature abroad. One of the main members is Lóránt Czigány, who wrote an excellent book on Hungarian literature (called the *Oxford History of Hungarian Literature*) which I read with great pleasure. The society arranges lectures and this was the first time I had been. They gather in the Polish Club and it was a funny feeling to listen to the lecturers, who were under the spotlights while the audience sat in the dark hall listening as though to some sort of nineteenth century secret society's lectures. The audience consisted mainly of Hungarian emigrés who emigrated before and after the Second World War and during 1956. Some – like me – just married Englishmen. The lectures were in honour of the deceased great Hungarian scholar, László Cs. Szabó, who lived – I think – his last twenty to thirty years in Britain and wrote wonderful essays on Shakespeare, Dickens, Constable and others. He had a European or rather Renaissance mind, beautiful, witty style and a lively and polished mind. Cs. Szabó often felt that Britain could be an isolated cell to live in and somehow he was disappointed that his marvellous writings did not really reach the appreciative artistic literary England. He wrote about himself, that he was a political zebra, his radical lanes mixed with his conservative ones, and thus he became an imperfect but open human being. I spoke about him to Alan who had been to a Wigmore Hall concert with his son Sebastian instead.

Before the lecture in the hall I was happy to buy a book written by David Angyal, a good Hungarian historian, and published by this Society. It opened my eyes to new points of view. I found out that I belonged to the Ranke-school, whose research is based on primary archival stuff. Secondly, that Count Stephen Széchenyi, who came to England many times during the first half of the nineteenth century and memorised lots of things and brought them to Hungary was not a Benthamist but a Mme de Staël-ist. He believed in the development of nationalities and felt that the Magyars had a great future. Actually, Széchenyi also smuggled out from England the WC and made it familiar in Magyarland.

31 January

Today an elderly lady helped me to get off the bus. I was astonished and understood what Alan has experienced in the last couple of years.

2 February

Yesterday on the TV they showed English guest workers in Germany. It was wonderful to see the clashes of the two cultures: English cockneys with their legère behaviour during and after working hours and the dogmatic, tidy Germans who were often shocked. The English workers seemed to me more democratic, more individualistic, more charming and though their manners were not sophisticated and shocked the Germans, their feelings were there: as human beings, they were more civilized and more fun. The Germans often felt above the English workers and sometimes, when the English ones made criticisms, they asked "why don't they go home?" The English just said that they got more wages there, and there is more work to do.

9 February

I saw yesterday the English-Czech film about Heydrich. I did not know that those soldiers who killed Heydrich were told to do so by Britain, the Czechs themselves did not want it very much because they were afraid of vengeance which came in the form of the killing and devastation of Lidice. Thus, because of one man, hundreds and hundreds died. I was told that Eduard Beneš was involved in this plan. He wanted to show to the world and mainly to Britain, where he lived during the war, that there was a Czech resistance. The British did not have much to lose; the three soldiers were well trained British people of Czech origin and Czech patriots. Alan knew this story and about Beneš's involvement in it from Ripka.

14 February

Yesterday on the TV I saw a wonderful programme about strippers. It was funny, it was sexy, it was merry. There is a tradition of strip-tease acts in the East End and the male audiences enjoy themselves tremendously; they speak to the girls, make noises, try to touch them and pay for the fun but they don't go further; they don't really get vulgar or aggressive and if they do not want to pay, the girls make them. Such a show could be done only in England. On the Continent it would end in obscenities.

My old girlfriend's son and daughter-in-law went to a ball at St. Paul's school for the parents. I thought it was such a good idea. She also told Alan and me that when she was still living in Hungary – perhaps it was in 1945 – she had good experiences with the Russians. They were hiding in a monastery at Péczel. When the Russians came into Péczel, which is a small Hungarian village, they were staying with families. One of the Russians said to the young woman where he was stationed, "Either you let me bath your son or I will rape you."

8 March

Many of our national heroes or writers knew and learnt a lot about England: István Széchenyi, Lajos Kossuth[1], József Bajza, Mihály Babits. Babits, one of the greatest of the twentieth century Hungarian poets and writers, used many English phrases in his poems such as "to join the majority". I also learnt from his novel *The Sons of Death* that at the turn of the century in small Hungarian towns, patchwork curtains, tablecloths were made and used in modest families.

23 March

Alan's seventy-ninth birthday is coming. We had dinner with his son Sebastian and his family. Mary, his wife has a good sense of humour. She told me that Sebastian often forgets to take back library books. Then the librarian comes to the house, hunting for them.

Alan said: "Love is practical." It means preparing breakfast for your loved one and greeting her warmly when she comes home. Alan said that nobody was more important in his life than me. He says this many times. He feels that he can't surmount his feebleness. It is a terrible feeling for him. Until now he always succeeded in not showing that he was feeble. His mother always told him he was feeble. He never showed it. I thought perhaps he disliked his mother because she told him this. But Alan says this is untrue, but he did not love his mother anyway. He just could not tolerate her. His mother was always interested in something else. Alan was always used as a means to some end.

12 April

I am homesick. The basis of homesickness is that although I love England, it is my second interest. My first interest is Hungary, the

1 Lajos Kossuth (1802–1894) was a Hungarian revolutionary and nationalist who promulgated the Hungarian Declaration of Independence in 1849. After the failure of the revolution, he left Hungary to live in England, America and Italy. Together with Count István Széchenyi he is considered to be one of the greatest Magyars.

Hungarians. But the English, and even Alan, are not interested in Hungary. They are interested of course in England. I can follow their interest, I can take part in it, because I am living here. Most of the English don't understand what my main interest is, most of them have never been to Hungary and never will. This contradiction can never be solved for me, in my lifetime. It will not be as interesting for the coming new generations; music, pop music, cars, computers are common, international interest for them and will be more so.

One of my favourite Hungarian novelists is Ernö Szép, a fine spirit, who died some thirty years ago. He wrote a book called *Human Smell*. In this he speaks about a book called *A Life With My Father* written by Clarence Day. In this book the author describes houses where the telephones had just been installed. In those days the telephones were put in the kitchen; the cook or the maid picked it up and rushed in and out to the Madame ten to twenty times to-ing and fro-ing between the caller and the listener. I asked Alan whether he had read this book. He had, but he did not remember the details. He said in their house in Preston the telephone was in the butler's pantry.

18 April

I think the Meals on Wheels service is wonderful. Mainly young women bring hot meals to the elderly and they merrily sound their horn at midday: "We have arrived." Also it is very agreeable that you can ring the chemist and ask for your prescription and they bring it to your house. I was told there are many elderly women who ring the chemist ten times a day, just for somebody to talk to.

21 April

I think Jessica Mitford's *Hons and Rebels* is a wonderful book in every sense. Her first husband, Esmond Romilly, nephew of Churchill, was a fine man; his views about Churchill are superb. He deserves not to be forgotten and silenced. Jessica wrote many valuable social and political things, here is one phrase from the book: "living materially in one world and spiritually in the other". That is what Jessica did for a while.

3 May

We saw a film, *The Shooting Party*, with Stacy Marking. It was James Mason's last beautiful, simple, clever performance. It is true what Dezsö Kosztolányi the great poet and writer said: however great the artist, the writer will be what he leaves out. It is impossible to tell, to present everything. You are what you choose. In *The Shooting Party* there are wonderful, characteristic details: the aristocratic father, his relationship with his grandson, his views on what is good in writing a diary. (You don't disturb others with your own problems.)

Afterwards we discussed the film with Stacy and her position in society. It gave an immediate impression. When a film makes you speak about yourself I think it reaches its object socially and artistically. She was a child sent back from India, the daughter of an aristocratic family who became a left-wing producer. We spoke about the feeling of insecurity abroad, her travels to Havana, to Burma. The meaning of solitary confinement. She is one of the most splendid examples of women in post-war Britain, i.e. Britain without the Empire.

4 May

There was a party at the Imperial War Museum which we went to. A bearded, neglected, funny man who just dropped in, without an invitation, arrived very late. Everybody was kind and tolerant towards him and explained what the exhibition was about. It showed that, as long as one does not prove the opposite, people are trusting.

5 May

I learnt from a TV programme that approximately ten percent of the population reads in Britain. Doris Lessing's view is, if the teaching of literature were improved, at least twenty to thirty percent would be readers in this country. But first good teachers are needed.

7 May

I heard from an expert on Indian history that the British gave India up so quickly because there was a possibility that if they had not done so, there would have been a twentieth century mutiny. Due to Mountbatten's skill there was not much waste of time.

14 May

My former colleague came for tea. She said they had invited a young English boy from the countryside to stay with her daughter in Budapest. The English boy hardly said anything, he did not like anything, he did not like the food. It was not a success.

24 May

My new grandson Bálint has arrived. His mother was convinced that this time she would deliver a boy because – as she jokingly remarked – she wore all the pregnancy dresses of her sister-in-law who had two sons. I think parents do not realise how much a grandmother can think about her grandchildren.

26 May

Mary Seton-Watson came for tea. She is very brave. She would not like to go to Hungary again because she had bad memories of being there during and immediately after the Second World War. She is a good example of how a widow should behave. She went to Southern Italy which she and her husband wanted to visit before he died. She is now thinking hard how to begin life again. She took a lodger in her house because, she said, it is a good thing to begin a day when a man leaves the house. She did not like Sir Owen O'Malley who was British Minister in Hungary before the war. Mary said to Alan, "He is not one of us." Later I asked Alan what she meant. Nobody ever said anything good about O'Malley. He was called fishface. When he served in Spain and then in Hungary, he was very much in sympathy with Franco and Horthy. He was the man who insisted that the dynamite which the SOE wanted to forward to the Hungarian anti-Nazis and was kept in the Embassy at Budapest, should be thrown into the Danube. He wrote a very controversial report on Katyn in May 1943 to Eden.

Alan's political and scientific fairness is shown in how *he* wrote about Katyn in his book on the Second World War. His opposite is Norman Davies, an expert on Poland, Alan's pupil, a kind, clever man, but he is often unscientific and emotional. Still, we like him and his new Polish wife and sometimes we invite them to our house.

27 May

Pisti's daughter, Andrea, is a very good looking and very intelligent child. She is my only grand-daughter and she is very close to me, whenever we meet. All the others are very close too. What a wonderful thing to be young. I must preserve my love for children and for human beings.

30 May

I want to make Alan happy, give him pleasant hours. He is aware of his decline and of course does not like it. I have just read, in a book about Parkinson's disease, that people who suppress their sentiments, for whom success is very important and who mask their personalities, are most likely to contact the disease.

We went yesterday to Aldworth to see Mary and Richard Ingrams. They look happy and young. They intend to go to Malta for a holiday. I like their house, their two dogs, their garden, which are all like them: kind, aloof, radical, funny, humane. Mary is very happy with her book shop and Richard with Beryl Cook's painting. They are very economical. What they do, they do with style and they are proud of it, but they are also, on the whole, modest people and choosy in their values. It was an interesting but tiring excursion. We travelled sixty miles in six hours to have lunch. Alas, we had no time to look at Mary's shop.

12 June

My Hungarian girl friend who also married an Englishman does not understand that I live in two countries, that I read the daily papers of Hungary and Britain. She and her husband were even more surprised when I said if I had lots of money I would give it to the reconstruction of mines and hospitals in Hungary, for the benefit of the neglected children and for the improvement of the gipsy population in Hungary. They said one should live as one wants and let them live as they want.

13 June

Sonia and David Landes[1] came to lunch. David is an outstanding historian from the States. I have not seen him for twenty years. He was then a very fine pensive looking man; now he is wrinkled, he has a very intelligent face, like Auden's when he was getting old. Sonia is a sweet intelligent wife. They are at All Souls, Oxford, for three months, but David said he did not work much as he has to go often to the Bodleian. He does not like this, he prefers it when every book which he needs is on his desk or in his study. I agreed. He asked for my *Chartism*. Ten years ago he had a terrible accident and he had thirty-five percent burns. He then understood how easy it is to die when you are burnt. The first danger is the loss of the fluid in the body, the next is infection. The present anti-bacterial drugs do not have much effect on this sort of bacteria.

Sonia told me that the outstanding economic historian Simon Kuznets[2] also has Parkinson's disease and she said one should not accept only one physician's opinion. She gave an example of a French woman who was declared to have only a few months to live because of cancer of the liver. Then they heard about a physician in the States who was experimenting with this illness. He gave injections straight into the liver and when necessary he gave complete blood transfusions. The French woman is still alive. Sonia also spoke about the success of Judi Blume,[3] whose fame has spread to Britain as well; she is widely read by English teenagers. I

1 David Landes is an American economic historian.
2 Simon Kuznets was a Russian-born economist, author of many works on economics and economic history.
3 Judi Blume is a writer of children's fiction.

asked how she could explain her success. She simply said Judi Blume treats children as adults and she knows what their problems are. Sonia also told me that the main difference between American and British wives is that the former speak about their cooking, the latter about their gardens.

Meanwhile Alan's youngest son telephoned from Gosport. He told us the news of the birth of his son Carl, who was named after that great man Karl Marx.

In the evening we saw a film about incest. The father was shown and his family—wife and two daughters. The father had had sexual intercourse with his eldest daughter since she was eleven. The film showed the resentment which the wife and daughter felt against the man and also showed how they helped to sort out their feelings and to plan their future with the help of the social workers and with the help of society. After this I watched E.P. Thompson, who interviewed György Konrád the Hungarian writer. They were both fair. Konrád seemed to have a more disciplined mind, they were two writers who felt responsible for the future.

I spoke to a teacher. She told me useful things about teenagers. For instance how to make them form a club if they are bored. She explained that everybody belongs somewhere, but to belong means that you have to accept the rules. When youngsters make up their mind that they are going to form a club, they work out the rules. Amongst these rules is the naming of the club, its activities, its aim and also a rule which is very important. Whatever they do, afterwards they tidy up everything. It never happens that one gives ideas, another carries them out and the rest tidy things up. They have to do everything together.

14 June

Alan's old friend Katherine Bligh came for tea with her daughter. She used to work at the Beaverbrook Library and when it was stupidly dissolved, she got a job at the House of Lords Record Office where many of the Beaverbrook papers were finally kept on Alan's recommendation. Katherine is a very good archivist and a very good single parent. Her daughter is clever and charming. She said there was not much hope of developing the archive at the House of Lords Record Office as there is not enough money.

Her friend visited Leningrad recently. She is an architect. She was refreshed by two facts: there were no advertisements and in the shops the shopkeepers did not press their goods upon you.

23 June

Yesterday two young solicitors and their wives came for dinner. They knew the great Thompson firm which was established by Alan's uncle and which is now run by his two sons, Brian and Robin, Alan's cousins. The Thompsons were and still are on the left; they always were on the side of the trade unions, always defending interests of the trade union members. One of the solicitors said that sometimes even with the best arguments, with the best knowledge and intentions the solicitor's task could be difficult. He gave an example. For instance the members of the Firemen's Trade Union always get enormous sums in compensation, even if they are hurt when playing table-tennis. Even if the enlightened GLC saw this they would try to win the case against them. Also it is well known that the Firemen's Union is the most right wing trade union. I wonder if, in multi-national London, there are any coloured firemen. Also they are very well paid.

24 June

There is such a variety of dogmatism in the world. Somehow the old dogmatism in Hungary, when Rákosi was in power, and the present dogmatism in the States during Reagan's presidency resemble each other a bit. The main thing is to suppress illegalities. Often the answer to one illegality is another one.

25 June

My main aim is to make life easier for Alan and for my sons. Often when I feel unhappy, I dream something which makes me happy. One day I shall describe all my dreams.

26 June

I got a letter from my historian colleague in Hungary. When we were young historians we created the Club of the Merry Historians. I wrote to him suggesting that it might be a good idea to revive it. His answer came in a very witty letter: "No, because there are one or two members whom I only want to see when I can see the middle of my back."

The two women with the best characters I ever saw are my two daughters-in-law, the choices of my sons.

When I first went home from England, everything seemed so different because my life has changed so much. Objectively there is not such a great difference as the individual feels.

28 June

I go home tomorrow. Alan has gone to the Isle of Wight. I went to Camden Lock. What charm is there in these people. I saw a hippy couple who were selling everything for 5p. Their faces were so attractive. But there is so much grief here as well. For instance the women's prison at Holloway is dirty, smelly, with patches of menstrual blood on the beds. And young or old women are here not for serious crimes but for petty theft, breaking windows and are severely punished. Some women punish themselves, hit their heads on the walls, commit suicide.

I do not like signs of nationalism or narrow mindedness. At Wimbledon one of the American girls played tennis in a leopard suit. The whole English press abhorred this. She should not play next day in this costume. The TV commentator said, "Surely these are her underclothes."

The other day I read a document in the Public Record Office about the Germans during the Second World War. I have never read such a horrible story about them, though I know quite a lot of stories. The story is this: During the war a German woman wrote to her soldier husband in Soviet Russia: "Please send me some child's garment if you can, it does not matter if it is full of blood, I will wash it." This was in the report of an Englishman who heard it first hand.

29 June – 12 July, In Hungary

My visit to Hungary was full of interesting details and full of love. The difference between England and Hungary this time did not amount to much. Why? Is it that Hungary is developing and England is not, or simply that I have got used to both? At home the people are very enlightened. They – or those whom I met – don't adore the West any more. Amongst the country people whom I got to know a bit at the Mátrahill were some who were very encouraging. In the post office the young woman did not want to marry; an old peasant woman in the bottom of an old Castle gave very good information about the roads; in the Károlyi Castle the young teachers and the children on a holiday were friendly and interested. Of course there are many shortcomings; many places are neglected, some people are prejudiced. What I liked most was an elderly, thin man who was in a hurry behind me when I was looking around in one nice square in Budapest. I heard a voice from behind me saying, "Are you strolling or walking?"

My sons are very good teachers. My younger son, as he now has his own children, has gone from being a younger son to a paterfamilias; his character shows more and more. What I like in all of them is that they have good characters besides intelligence.

When I came back, Alan was expecting me. I decided not to leave him again even though he was looked after well and his family gathered around him lovingly. He sees himself so well, he needs me, he is dependent on me. He is slightly fragile and he thinks he is going downhill. But his historical mind – as I call it – is still untouched and his style is still with him.

In this period of his life he has found himself again. He has still inner strength and style.

31 July

We went to Sissinghurst. It was very hot and I meant to take my big straw hat with me. I did not and when we got there I was relieved: nearly every woman there was wearing a hat, perhaps imitating the aristocratic way of wearing hats as they imagined it, and of course, imitating Vita.

Perhaps I am too critical. I thought Sissinghurst was a great English aristocratic cheat. The parents, Vita and Harold Nicolson, made it, the sons and the nation, i.e. the National Trust, the big business developed its myth and glory. In the middle of a vast meadow there is the castle-like house and in the tower, the room where Vita, the aristocratic lesbian woman, worked and lived. Alas, I did not go up to her tower room because I did not want to leave Alan behind, and he was tired and bored. To go to Sissinghurst was my idea; I wished to see it so much because I liked the writings of both Vita and Harold and I developed a romantic dream of seeing the place. I saw near the entrance their library, the books on the natural wood shelves, the picture by László Paál of Vita, and so on. I had the feeling that the traditions, the way of life which they held and which was mirrored partly in their library made their life, their everyday life, somehow dry, lacking in comfort and warmth. This dryness was maintained theatrically and shown to the visitors. I experienced the same feeling with other aristocratic, grand houses.

The garden of Sissinghurst, which was described in many books and visited by many, is not a wonder. It is a layman's aristocratic dream, executed by gardeners and now it brings quite a lot of money to the National Trust, which runs a tea room there with lovely creamy scones and with a shop which has a smart lady sales-woman with upper class English manners and pronunciation. I think it is wonderful how appetising the whole show is and how well organised it is. And at the same time it is very practical. Everybody gets good value for money. The house is lovely to look at, it is easy to stay there with the car, one can have a quiet afternoon on the lovely well-kept lawn and a lovely tea when it is tea time. Nothing is forbidden, the names of the various flowers are there in front of the plants. When we had tea, where one gets ice-cream as well, I asked for tea and a scone for Alan and ice-cream for myself and two pots of cream. Everybody laughed: "Two pots of cream for the scone?" "No," I said, "one is for my ice-cream." When we started to go back, we went to a pub where Alan was immediately recognised and advised the best way home. Alan looked serene and happy. It was a good feeling for him that he was recognised near Sissinghurst, otherwise he would have thought that he is completely forgotten.

9 *August*

The members of CND painted white bodies all over London streets to commemorate Hiroshima and the living human bodies which became shadows. I don't know who in London would have noticed these white shadows. The CND-ers probably worked all night.

Michael Howard tried to explain in the *TLS* that the war would have been so much bigger and so much more devastating for the Americans and for the Japanese if the bombs had not been dropped. Another English author, William Carr, tried to demystify the legend which Churchill created: how much Britain did throughout the Second World War. He says in his *Poland to Pearl Harbour* that the war from 1941 on was essentially a war between the USA, the USSR, Germany and Japan.

At the time of Hiroshima and Nagasaki everybody spoke about the yellow peril. Even now, veteran British soldiers maintain the view that there was no possibility of coercing Japan into giving up without Hiroshima and Nagasaki.

11 August

I have finished my autobiography. Perhaps it is not really literature, but for me it is essential to write. While I wrote it, I followed my life, I lived it again visually and then verbally. Now Alan is listening to Mozart in the sitting room; I am writing on the first floor in my study and I feel at home, mainly because I am writing my life.

20 August

I have so many good friends. Gizella is so clever, understanding. She is furious when our mutual Hungarian friend speaks about his girl friend as an old piece of furniture. Another English friend of hers said to her that women cannot be attractive over fifty. And men?

Cynthia is also very clever. She thinks that in every human relationship one has to draw the boundaries.

I saw a wonderful film on TV about hooliganism. The name "hooliganism" comes from an Irish family name. In the 1890s there were many problems and violence at football matches. Hooliganism flourished under Victoria as well.

There is a tradition in Britain: middle or upper-class parents send their children to public schools, working-class boys have fun playing association football. Nobody knows Britain well unless they go to a football match. Nobody would then speak about English cold-bloodedness.

My eldest son and family are spending a week at a small island near Istria. I think a lot of what would happen if Alan left. Alan at least has me. But then I pull myself together and tell myself that there are two alternatives:

(a) I shall die and won't be really old.
(b) I am strong. If one is strong one can face living alone. This is a different thing from loneliness.

Alan Sked was here for dinner. He came last Sunday as well. He is a pleasant boy. I asked about his Scottishness. According to him the Scots do not feel inferior to the English at all. He was invited with his twin brother to Yorkshire when he was a child. They were told how peculiar their accents were. But they thought that the people in Yorkshire had a funny way of speaking. He said that in his opinion a foreigner could be closer to the English than a Scot or a Welshman.

21 August

I watched the film of the late Rock Hudson called *The Starmaker* on TV. This film was excellent because it showed the male attitude very well. The story is this: A famous film producer recognizes talent and beauty in young women and makes them famous. In the process, he falls in love with them and regards them as his own creatures. The women also fall in love with this wonderful, creative man who, with his strength and male beauty, gives them his own, deep love. This man is a male who needs the adoration of the females whom he made great. But the tragedy is that the famous females begin to act on their own, they want to create themselves, they do not want only to adore their creator. The man goes from one woman to another and the whole process repeats itself. I liked this film so much because somehow I recognized partly our relationship as well.

22 August

You can be terribly ill mentally or physically, but you always are and remain sensitive to love.

25 August

Without knowing the rules of cricket it is difficult to understand lots of things in Britain. I was told – I could not judge whether it is true or not – that the distinguished Communist who made the rules for the British Communist Party became a Communist for his lifetime, because he was not elected to the Cambridge cricket team against Oxford. I was also told that cricket is in the hands of a gang. Abroad they think cricket is the establishment itself.

I saw the play by Tennessee Williams *Sweet Bird of Youth*. Sour, true play about power and humans becoming monsters. I think this theme is a problem theme for Harold Pinter.

I heard a saying which made me think a lot. When you get old, you give up whatever your interest in life was. If you give it up, you may die. Maybe you should choose something else instead, then you might stay alive.

18 September

Greta Garbo is eighty. I watched her film *Queen Christina*. The first time I saw it was fifty years ago. I understood only now how wonderfully sexy she was. She is Alan's favourite, mainly in *Ninochska*. My favourite is Louise Brooks.

Laura Ashley is dead. I am very, very sorry.

I might rewrite *The English Husband*. Some things had to be said then. But I will leave the original as well. Perhaps I wrote it too soon. As a therapy it was useful.

27 September

Tonight I saw on TV how a secret gun-parts factory, the so called "Guy Fawkes Club", worked under the Houses of Parliament during the Second World War. There were very few skilled labourers, skilled technicians in this field, so they taught women to do the job. In 1940 they had already chosen some for this job amongst the alien foreigners as they needed them. That, I call elasticity. I also became less rigid.

28 September

I am sixty-two years old today. No comment.

30 September

I think what is great in the English is that they are so self-confident. Or if they are not, they don't show it. The whole education develops this. And who dares wins. This goes for their driving as well.

Simone Signoret died of cancer at the age of sixty-four. Her daughter said she was very brave. I am very sorry. The picture of Yves Montand in *The Times* is moving. There is grief in this picture for their whole lives. I feel again as I did after the Second World War, that every day is a gift for me.

4 October

The English are not only self-confident, they also like it if they are left alone or in peace. They are not interested in each other's personal affairs, or if they are, they won't show it. They prefer to speak about sightseeing, about their holidays. Also women do not make remarks about each other's dresses.

Alan's *Bismarck* has come out again after a long time. He wrote it some twenty years ago. His last chapter is very revealing about himself as well. He says that the genius knows when to stop. Alan is now nearly eighty, as was Bismarck in this chapter. Alan said this morning,"I live in a total bewilderment", and laughed heartily.

The English are very sensitive to whether or not they are loved. If not they drop the person for good.

5 October

Hungarian musical life develops great talent. The director of the City Music Society, Ivan Sutton, his secretary Alan Paul and the director of the Wigmore Hall, William Lyme, all know the merits of these Hungarians. They often invite the Takács-Nagy and Eder Quartets, the pianists Dezsö Ránki, András Schiff, Ferenc Rados. Except for the members of the Takács-Nagy Quartet, most of them cannot display their great talent light-heartedly. One feels they suffer or they feel too intensely as they play; they take themselves or rather their art too seriously. The English do the same but the delivery is done with ease; they smile when they thank the audience.

Alan Paul and Ivan Sutton promised to speak about their lunch time concerts to the Hungarians. It is such a wonderful break at midday, it would be good for many Hungarians, as they tend to die at an early age because of tension, too much coffee-drinking and smoking.

12 – 26 October

My architect son, Pisti and his daughter Andrea stayed with us. Pisti is not hopeful or full of illusions about life, still he does everything that he can for mankind. He can judge without prejudice. Andrea is very discerning and I think this is the aim of education or one of the aims. She has certain sympathies and antipathies, also she won't go in certain houses where she does not like the smell. She played well with a little English girl of her own age, how they had talked to each other goodness knows, but they seemed in complete unison. Alan is very welcoming, my son understands and appreciates Alan very much.

30 October

In South Wales there is a hospital financed by donations which deals with the elderly. They look after the elderly so well that I do not think there is another institution quite like it. Each elderly person is looked after according to his or her own needs and character.

I saw a film about a father who looked after his blind and terminally ill son. He said his main aim was that his son should get as much happiness as possible during his short life. He dealt with his son realistically, explaining everything, trying to ensure that the son should do certain things and look after himself as much as possible.

2 November

I ought not to send so many presents to my grandchildren.

I saw a small, very thin prostitute when I came back from Camden Lock; she can't have been more than twelve.

Sometimes I feel it will be quite interesting to die. There are not many surprises anyhow in life after sixty. With humour, life is so much easier. I never had enough sense of humour, but I have found out lately that one can develop it.

8 November

When my little two-year-old grand-daughter returned to Budapest, she explained to her mother that we massaged Alanke's knees (Alanke means little Alan).

Alanke – Alanke is not well. Yesterday we went for dinner to Max Beaverbrook's godson, the Canadian, Maxwell Bruce, who is now about fifty-eight years old, an eminent international lawyer; looks after the Pugwash Conferences in this capacity. His second wife Nina, Russian by origin, is a very talented artist. She is very puritan looking, has a great sense of humour; she is like a teenager. Maxwell told me he was going to meet Thomas Mann's daughter, Elizabeth, for breakfast the next morning. She is very lively and bird-like. It was a very interesting evening because there were two other couples, who had something to do with the Russians. One was a Belgian diplomat whose grandfather came from Russia and when he got a diplomatic post in Moscow, he felt at home. His wife liked living there because she really enjoyed it when she got what she wanted in the shops. The Canadian young social scientist was also second generation Russian, probably aristocratic. He was very sober and radical and disliked a Hungarian colleague of mine, whom I disliked as well and with whom he worked at Cambridge. This man told me that the young Hungarian dissident historian was very clever but paranoid: he saw conspiracy everywhere.

10 November

On BBC 1 there is a French woman who reads the news about France in English, but at the same time she repeats it in French.

It would be a good idea to do the same on Hungarian TV – let's say a Czech woman, in Czech-Hungarian co-operation.

Today is Remembrance Sunday. At 11 a.m. the whole city is quiet for two minutes remembering the dead in the two wars. There is a great parade. In front of the Cenotaph, the Queen, the Prime Minister, the leaders of the political parties, veterans, Field Marshals, Chiefs of Staff, members of the Commonwealth countries and many more important people lay wreaths in the great, great silence of the nation. It helps to maintain the national self-confidence. Some people think that in England, in this country of traditions, there are no real problems with the national conscience. But I doubt this. Somehow this nation is more and more the land of the two nations which Disraeli described in his famous *Sybil*. And I think not only two nations, the rich and poor, but also multi-national and multi-economic.

11 November

This morning Alan said, "I am a wretched man." Physically, he meant. I said we should go on as usual.

14 November

Dinner party at Ursula and Ernö's. Ernö is also unwell. Both are clever enough to feel sorry about leaving life and us. Perhaps Ursula and I will go first, but we can't think about death, we have to look after our men and cheer them up. And there are our children and grandchildren. No, we can't go yet. But how awful; nobody knows how my back aches and I can hardly speak, my voice is so hoarse.

15 November

Yesterday we were invited to our charming neighbour, Jean Byers, for a drink. She invites her five neighbours in Twisden Road every year. There was my Malaysian girl friend, my favourite little mother with her daughter Henrietta, an English friend's son from India. My neighbour at the party came from Wales. She told me that the Welsh people are self-confident, bureaucratic and gossipy; they love to sing, very similar characteristics to the Hungarians. I asked why there is no more wish to be independent. She said perhaps because they feel or they are afraid that they can't manage their own affairs efficiently. The Anglo-Indian son of the English woman has lived in England for three years and wishes to spend fifteen years here. He said that in England everything is well organized, you can feel it as soon as you arrive at Heathrow. But he is longing to go back to the chaos in India, to the anarchical state of affairs, where an individual could probably be happier.

I saw with Alan a film called *Letter to Brezhnev*. It was made cheaply but well, mainly by Liverpudlians. It is about youngsters living in Kirkby, a suburb of Liverpool, when two Soviet sailors arrive. It is a very moving and true film.

17 November

I drove myself to the film museum and saw a wonderful Hungarian film called *Resolution* made by two talented Hungarian producers. Coming back, Alan felt he was dying. We played the Beethoven sonatas all afternoon. Then he got better and went to dinner with his son Sebastian.

I watched an excellent interview with Marguerite Duras on the TV. She recalled her youth and her relationship with her brothers with great talent and sensitivity. I felt her close to me; my relationship with my two sisters is a separate story which I will tell one day.

Alan came back and said, "I am tasting death already."

18 November

In the Thatcher interview she said that her father always told her that she should make up her mind what she wanted to do, independently of what other people think or do. That means that she should not do things because others do them.

23 November

In a very misty, wet November afternoon we went to the Holme Garden at the edge of Regent's Park. I remembered Alan brought me here in 1976 before we went to see where he lived and he introduced his first wife Margaret to me as a colleague. This is Alan's favourite place in London. One can withdraw and hide here amongst the best roses, the most wonderful roses like the Typhoons. We had one of our best afternoons together here. Behind the rose garden there was a neglected hut from which enormous well-fed pigeons flew. One or two of the rose buds had some potential. I illegally took two – who knows if they will bloom, though?

26 November

I went to see *The Package Tour* with Alan at the Everyman. A film made by my nephew once removed Gyula Gazdag, about elderly Hungarian Jews who visited Auschwitz on a package tour. Alan did not like the film as much as I did. The audience was enthusiastic and after the film put many questions to Gazdag and he answered well. I think he can create atmospheres.

28 November

At Question Time the very stimulating woman economics professor from Bochum said firmly that it was not enough to develop high technology. High technology brings good results only with organised industrial and economic leadership. Look at Japan, Germany, France – they are ahead of Britain in using technology.

1 December

Alan was not asked by Terry Kilmartin from the *Observer* to list the three best books he has read during the year. Each year the *Observer* asks writers, historians, politicians and so on to name their favourite three books. Alan was asked every year until this year, so was Ayer, Spender and Foot – all of whom were asked in previous years. Why not Alan? I did not understand this behaviour. Alan was not hurt at all.

5 December

Frank Pakenham is eighty. We went to his daughter Antonia's house for a big party. There were very many people there; I could not breathe. Frank and Elizabeth are very kind to us. We had a conversation with Harold Pinter, their son-in-law. Harold and Antonia have just come back from the States. Harold said the Americans whom they met were completely apolitical and did not want to hear about radical politics. I said, "Where?" He said in California. But I said America is so huge, certainly there are places where you can discuss politics. He said tell me one place. I said, "Cape Cod." He said I was right. We agreed that in all places, at all times, one should speak against the bomb. There are no two sides of the coin. He is a nice fellow. I would like to get to know him better.

There were Stephen Spender, Harold Wilson, Isaiah Berlin and many other "literary snobs" as Alan called them. I asked, "And you were one?" "I played the role." When we got back, I had trouble with the car. Martin Gilbert saw us struggling and he gave us a very friendly wave and encouragement. I waved back to tell him that he should go, because it was not only us, but him also who was holding the traffic up.

7 December

I think I have learnt how to be alone. I watched the TV programme on Yoko Ono and John Lennon. John was a great artist, a musical artist inspired by love for mankind.

This morning an 87-year-old woman asked for advice on the radio about her fruit trees. She said these trees kept her alive.

8 December

Somebody asked me what were the ten most remarkable things which I could be proud of in my life. My sons and the books I have written – not quite ten.

10 December

An eight-year-old girl nearly blinded an old woman with a spray. The social security woman advised the old lady when she got out of hospital to move to another flat because "the little wilful miss" won't let her live and an eight-year-old girl could not be taken to court.

Alan thinks that everybody should know how to defend him or her self.

13 December

Yesterday the gas man came because there was a leak somewhere. He was a strong young man, an athlete. He said he was a shop steward. He said also that Thatcher wanted to denationalise British Gas in such a way that the workers would buy shares and then they wouldn't go on strike. Strike action and trade unionism would be forbidden.

15 December

If I look back to my diary and to the years between 1978 and 1985 I can say I am not sorry about what I did. I would have been sorry if I had hurt Alan or my sons in any way with my behaviour. I do not think I did, but I do not think that for them it was easier with or without me. I do not think that my character has changed, but my considerations have. I have become a member of a middle-class England where I do not need to fight for money. I have become a freelance historian in England and tried to work well and I have found many attractive sides of my life with tolerant and kind Alan. I have found also many radical, enlightened English people very attractive and modest; I find them tolerant and socially aware. I love those English parents who give their undivided attention to their children. But I know there are many unattractive sides to this life here. Statistics say that in the country three to four children die weekly, because the parents neglect or wound them. All the same I think England is the second best place for me.

18 December

It is amazing. Alan told me tonight that his mind is disorderly. He does not think in a controlled way any more. I asked, "Do you mind?" He said, "Not at all. I still enjoy my life, playing my records; as long as you are with me – and I know you will be – I am happy."

Tonight in the Spanish restaurant, after consuming a litre of the fine Spanish wine, he confessed: his happiest days were when he saw that his youngest son was cured and could look forward to a happy life. "It could have gone completely wrong, you know," he said. I knew.

Alan added: "My children never ask me to go with them any more." I said: "You always told me bringing up children is a one way road." And I added, "It is a nice broad road, you know, it is an avenue. We also can see far ahead of us on this avenue. We can see how they live their own lives. As we did with ours."

* * *

Alan read my whole diary. He said: "The poor old fruit does not get a look in." I answered: "That will make a good ending."

Eva H.T.
3 March 1986

Index